Micro to Mainframe Links

Micro to Mainframe Links

Ronald F. Kopeck

Osborne **McGraw-Hill**
Berkeley, California

Osborne **McGraw-Hill**
2600 Tenth Street
Berkeley, California 94710
U.S.A.

For information on translations and book distributors outside of the
U.S.A., please write to Osborne **McGraw-Hill** at the above address.
A complete list of trademarks appears on page 281.

Micro to Mainframe Links

1234567890 DODO 89876

ISBN 0-07-881228-3

Jon Erickson, Acquisitions Editor
Lyn Cordell, Project Editor
Pamela Webster, Text Design
Yashi Okita, Cover Design

To my wife Ela, whose patience and tolerance during this writing were saintly, and who chose to wait for the movie

Contents

Acknowledgments

I thank all those who supported me and contributed ideas that helped shape the content of this book. I appreciate the time taken by individuals to discuss the audience and the appropriate tone for my work. Special thanks to Stan Miastkowski, who edited the initial manuscript so thoroughly and continually reminded me of my intended readers, and who offered sound advice on illustrations. A genuine thank you to Larry Dietz and The ALEC GROUP in San Jose, California, for reviewing selected portions of the book, particularly those concerned with data security and integrity, where Larry's special expertise was most valuable. And, finally, thank you to Jon Erickson, the chief editor who patiently reminded me of my schedules, audience, and commitment to make this book something special and different.

Introduction

Micro-mainframe links are a hot topic of conversation throughout the information processing and communications industries.
These links allow personal computers to be connected into host
computers, which is critical for meeting end-user computing
needs. With so many personal computers being sold into the
business environment, it is important that you understand how
links can benefit you and what your options are.

◥ WHO THIS BOOK IS FOR

This book is for anyone who is trying to get perspective on the
whole issue of linking personal computers into hosts. It is for
people who want to be a little more well-versed on what is happening out there. At least four types of individuals can benefit
from reading it:

- Managers concerned with data center expansion and strategic
  planning for increased personal computer usage in the organization.

- Managers responsible for developing a plan for linking personal computers into hosts.

- Managers thinking of ways to provide departmental processing with host access.

- Technical individuals and managers responsible for selecting and implementing micro-mainframe links.

You don't need to be a technical wizard to read this book, but it won't bore you if you're a technical person who needs to evaluate and test link products. Anyone involved with the different aspects of link integration problems can quickly find selected chapters that are of special interest or address the needs of a particular job. This book offers you insight into the kinds of problems and issues you must address in integrating personal computers. After you read it, you will understand the opportunities that micro-mainframe linking can give your business.

If you are thinking strategically, then personal computers and workstations must be a part of this thinking. This book gives you an idea of things that your people have to deal with.

If you are responsible for developing a micro-mainframe link plan, you will find this book useful in identifying the steps in building such a plan. It provides a guideline that you can follow in asking the right questions and establishing a sound methodology. If you have to do any planning and thinking, this book will help you construct the framework that lets you build a solid plan.

If you have a department not easily serviced by the computer center or are in an area that is easily isolated, you'll find this book useful in dealing with how you select products for just such situations. It gives you food for thought about how you can proceed and how you can organize yourself to take the process step by step.

Finally, if you have to implement and test selected links and do the piloting, this book helps you quickly identify how to establish a test plan and what to look for in products.

Use this book as a reference. You don't need to read each and every chapter; you can refer to those chapters that are of the most interest to you.

Understanding Your Needs

If you're a manager responsible for information processing, you must deal with user demands every day. You're continually called upon to expand your activities and horizons. Not only do you have to concern yourself with the evolving business needs of your company, but you are also expected to know about the new link products on the market. Your company wants you to understand what the end users need and work it into an overall plan that the corporation can use to deal with personal computers.

These expectations can be overwhelming. What do you do when upper management says that they want a personal computer link integration plan in two weeks and that it must be consistent with the rest of the information processing acquisition and growth plans? Suddenly you are looking for products that can link these personal computers into the host, and you hope that you select the right ones. You often select a few well-known brands and hope that they do the job. You rush to your technical gurus and tell them that you need to have a link plan, complete with product recommendations and evaluations. You need to know why they are recommending specific links, and you need to know as soon as possible.

You've seen hundreds of advertisements in the trade journals for the latest and greatest links with the newest whiz-bang features. Surely your technical person knows which are the best to choose. But your technical person is just that, a technical individual who does not necessarily know what the business needs are or even what your critical factors are.

Maybe this person is as confused as you about where to start. Have you thought of or even considered this? Two weeks later, you are still looking for that plan. You're frustrated that you don't seem to have gotten any further than you were two weeks ago. Your management is anxious, and they want to know what the problem is. They know that it is confusing out there, but that's what they thought they were paying you for.

There are many "maybes" out there, and a lot of "things should evolve if I give it enough time." All of a sudden you don't know where you are, the pressure is building to connect personal computers into hosts, and you are still flailing around wondering what to do.

Questions This Book Answers

How do you know what links are the right ones for your company? How do you know who the reputable vendors are? What about maintenance and warranty? These are some of the questions that you must answer—especially if you anticipate any kind of growth for personal computer installations. Numerous options are available to you, and it is tempting to make plans and selections on an ad hoc basis. But selecting links is a major commitment: you are talking about products that become part of your communications networks, products that you may very well want to expand upon in the future.

Questions, answers, probabilities, and uncertainties are all part of the business world. You try to minimize as many as possible. So why expose yourself to risks in developing networks for linking personal computers into hosts? These hosts can be DEC or Data General minicomputers. They can be Hewlett-Packard systems and they can be IBM or Burroughs mainframes.

◥ WHAT THIS BOOK IS ABOUT

Each chapter is devoted to a segment of personal computer integration. Each walks through a set of descriptive issues and activities you can follow to establish and implement a personal-computer-to-host integration plan.

- Chapter 1 gives you a brief review of what micro-mainframe links are and how they are used. It talks about why links are important.

■ Chapter 2 offers a historical perspective of computing and discusses how we evolved to a stage of needing micro-mainframe links. It provides a framework for establishing how we use computing.

■ Chapter 3 describes the different types of micro-mainframe links. It takes the confusion out of knowing where links fit and builds a foundation for understanding the options available for addressing personal computer integration.

■ Chapter 4 profiles how information flow and end-user computing needs are changing. It describes data-gathering processes and what end users expect to do in retrieving and using information.

■ Chapter 5 describes a methodology for assessing your company's integration needs and requirements. It identifies business and technical issues and discusses how to decide what role workstations will play in your organization. Security and data integrity are discussed for protecting indiscriminate user access with links.

■ Chapter 6 offers approaches for establishing personal-computer-to-host integration plans. It gives examples of how different types of companies have used each approach.

■ Chapter 7 describes how to build a link implementation plan. It analyzes total costs of installing, maintaining, operating, and training users on micro-mainframe links. It offers points on how to schedule and monitor progress.

■ Chapter 8 concentrates on how to go through the link selection process. It focuses on establishing criteria that form the basis for comparing and eliminating links. Sample selection criteria are provided as a start.

■ Chapter 9 deals with issues of developing and implementing link pilots and prototypes. You gain an appreciation of the steps required to focus link testing properly to meet your defined needs.

- Chapter 10 addresses how to review the results of your proto-typing and testing relative to the needs that you defined. It advises on what to look for and how to assess the results.

What This Book Is Not

This book is not a review of different micro-mainframe link products. It is not a quick-and-dirty treatise telling you what products to choose and which ones are best. Your information processing and end-user requirements are unique to you, and it is virtually impossible for anyone to identify a few links that can be useful to all of you. Finally, this book is not a rehash of communications theory that can be found in any number of books already on the market.

This book definitely is a text for reference on each aspect of the personal-computer-to-host integration problem. You can start using it right now by turning to the chapter that is most pertinent to your particular needs.

1 Links and Management

❚ MANAGING LINK INTEGRATION
❚ MANAGEMENT INFLUENCES
❚ THE TRANSITION TO MANAGING LINK INTEGRATION
❚ EXAMPLES OF MANAGEMENT APPROACHES

In today's information processing environment, you are constantly confronted with issues of how to interconnect personal computers, CAD/CAM graphics workstations, word processing systems, or any type of intelligent terminal to a "host" mainframe computer for accessing information. In some cases you must connect a few computers; at other times perhaps several hundred. Micro-mainframe links are products that allow you to do this. The term *micro-mainframe link* is a generic term that can apply to any product whose purpose is to allow this connection.

These link products can be hardware or software, or a combination of the two. Each product option offers different levels of complexity, features, performance, security capability, and expandability. Micro-to-mainframe links interface the desktop device (personal computer) into the host through a user interface that provides some form of simulation or emulation of a particular dumb terminal. These links can be emulators, local area networks (LANs), intermediate processors called *file servers*, or pure software systems. All of these are described in much more detail in Chapter 3.

This book, as we stated in the introduction, deals with the process by which you understand your requirements, select links, establish an implementation plan, and test and evaluate the results of your selection and configuration.

◥ MANAGING LINK INTEGRATION

For now, consider the activity of management and organization to support the proliferation of personal computers that must somehow be integrated into the entire information processing environment. There are applications, user productivity, future end-user computing needs, and resource allocation that need to be considered to meet the demanding and growing needs of a business. These are all significant issues. In addition, as technology continues to change the way we think and perform, you must be able to adjust to the demands of your changing role.

You will have to consider the fact that your organizational structure might have to change to cope with the activities that are arising from user demands. Different companies all have varying requirements, and each company will handle this adjustment in different ways. It is important to consider for a moment that organizational changes might actually be necessary to achieve an efficient operation that deals with personal computer integration.

◥ MANAGEMENT INFLUENCES

Stop and think for a moment. Ask yourself what is changing that makes what you do different—not necessarily more difficult, but simply different.

One change is that in today's information processing environment you no longer can decide what is good for the end user simply because *you* are in control of the system. In the past, the end users didn't always understand what they needed, so *you* provided them with what you perceived they needed. Occasionally you asked for their advice, but more often than not, you gave them what *you* thought was best.

Another change is that you can't keep up with technology changes and products in the industry as fast as you used to. In the past, you only needed to keep track of the latest large mainframe computers and a few large host software manufacturers. This is no longer true, as you will see if you look at the number of vendor catalogs that exist. Entire directories are now available to keep track of where vendors are located and what products they manufacture. It's impossible to know all of these things all of the time.

One big change is that there are more end users than ever before, and they are more knowledgeable. Someone can always show you a product in the link arena that you haven't heard of, much less seen. You can't possibly keep up with so many people unless you are doing it full time as your only responsibility.

You can't keep up with your reading, either. Trade periodicals available to the public have increased dramatically since 1980. Reading all of the material can occupy eight hours a day. When you begin to run out of time, you scan each page for articles that catch your attention. You sometimes read articles unrelated to you, but that you have an interest in—like who is merging with whom. You then clip articles directly related to you, expecting to read them later. You never do. Finally, you simply look at the table of contents. If there are articles that you should read, you do. If not, you either file the publication or throw it away. You probably missed information that wasn't in the table of contents. But your end users caught it, because they haven't gotten to the stage that you did several weeks before.

So what is different is that you are being driven by your end users, who are sometimes better informed than you are about the possibilities. What's worse is that they want to do whatever they want to do *now*, because they know how to do it and don't understand your need to worry about the other aspects of running a data center. Don't get overwhelmed by all of these differences. Learn to cope with them in different ways that make your job easier.

◥ THE TRANSITION TO MANAGING LINK INTEGRATION

To manage link integration systems, you have to address the issues of servicing the applications that end users are demanding. Companies are using many different methods to anticipate and structure the influx of technology. Their goals are to make technology work for them, not to have technology drive them.

Let's talk about some of these approaches to managing link integration that demonstrate a number of different options so that you can see how they might relate to your own situation. Maybe you and your company can't make changes overnight, but you can let the seeds of these ideas germinate into a structure that does fit your needs. Transition is the key because that's what the link industry is all about.

◥ EXAMPLES OF MANAGEMENT APPROACHES

Most companies have evolved around the philosophy that data processing reports to a single executive who is insulated from the end-user population. This can vary from one organization to another, but generally this is true. From time to time this executive solicits user input or has user groups consolidate and input future application needs to the central data processing department. Distributed processing affects such a philosophy because it forces you to be aware of processing needs of individual groups to service them properly. Sometimes it is difficult to consolidate application needs across disparate groups.

Not all of these approaches are appropriate for every company. They are described here simply to provide you with examples of how some companies have begun to manage the emergence of new technology, including links, to address the real problem of end-user computing. Companies of different sizes will favor different approaches, based on their corporate culture and their political situation. Treat these approaches not as givens, but as stimulants to thinking of other arrangements that might best suit your needs. Try to look at the examples from the viewpoint of what's right with them rather than what's wrong with them, or why they wouldn't work in your situation.

Example 1

One company modified its organizational structure to provide for two independent groups: one responsible for the traditional aspects of operating a data processing center and the other responsible for addressing what they called office applications. The former continued to do everything normally associated with efficient and trouble-free operations of a large computing center. This included communications, host computer resource allocation, equipment planning, security, performance planning, database administration, and problem resolution.

The second group, office applications, retained responsibility for fielding end-user application requests and identifying technology to support the requirements. As the end-user community gained confidence in this structure, they generated more application requests. In time, the new department could profile the trend within the company for the type of applications users needed and the way that they were using the host system and working at their personal computers. In addition, this group was able to begin consolidating requests in cases where requests overlapped or where there were very similar needs.

This new group worked with vendors to assess the feasibility, performance, and usage of identified applications. They prototyped or used pilot systems for new technology that supported these applications. Thus, operations became insulated for the initial trial periods until the group had something that they felt would be the right approach. They interfaced with the users and collected the necessary information before passing requirements or demands to the operations team.

The office applications group also interfaced with operations management and reviewed pending technology directions before full installation. Operations management could do their planning and preparation for the introduction of these systems to their hosts. If any inconsistencies or additional resources were required at the host, they could be identified before host connection occurred.

The members of this office applications group have varied individual skill sets. The group includes people familiar with software applications used at personal computers, like spreadsheets and databases. They are well versed in distributed systems concepts and are able to understand the latest technology and how it might be applied. Their personalities lend themselves to instructing others on how to use the system after implementation; hence, they have some teaching ability. They are oriented toward the requirement of applications rather than large host systems. After all, you don't duplicate costly expertise that already exists in your host operations department.

Organizationally, this structure can only be successful if it reports at a sufficiently high level. Effectiveness quickly diminishes if users perceive that the system offers no capability to get anything done. The structure must have management attention as well as visibility if user requirements are going to begin to funnel through it. This type of structure works well, provided that users are comfortable with it, know that they will get results, and know that their requests are listened to and approached with the same reverence as the most complicated system problem. Figure 1-1 shows how such an organizational structure looks.

Example 2

A variation on the structure just described is to establish an advisory group that consists of a key individual representing specific aspects of the computing environment. This is not a permanent group. The structure described previously remains exactly the same. This advisory group consists of an individual representing the applications area (user requirements), a person from data/telecommunications, database management, performance, and operations. It meets once a month or whenever it is called together to review applications and technologies that the office applications department is currently reviewing or piloting. Its purpose is to identify critical requirements or exposures that must be resolved before any implementation of communications link products.

The purpose of such a structure is to maintain consistency among all of the participating parties. After a period of time together, members of this group get to know each other, cover the right questions, and regard each others' responsibilities and needs as their own. In essence, they will begin to appreciate each others' problems even if debates about proper methods and products arise. The point is that there is a forum for discussion.

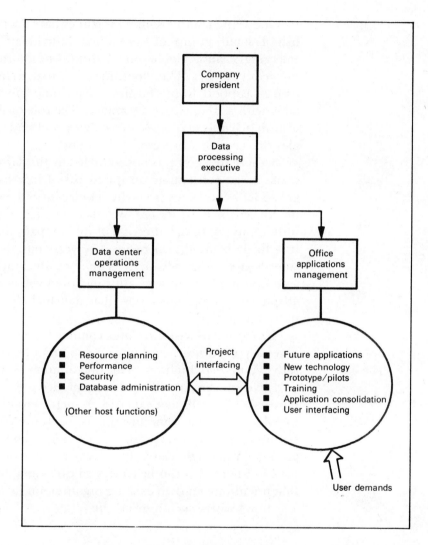

Figure 1-1. ▶

Office applications structure

Example 3

Many companies have come to realize that the micro-mainframe link situation is a subset of the whole technology issue. You can't look at only a piece of technology before you quickly realize that it is affected by, or affects, other technologies as well.

One approach that some companies have adopted is to establish a small group of specialized individuals who evaluate emerging technologies beyond their present information processing requirements. They look for ways that technology can be used to support future business trends and provide their company with a competitive advantage. The role of this group is to identify what technologies are evolving and how these technologies can be used in future applications.

Because this group is not restricted by the day-to-day needs of users, it can concentrate on the merits of new technology. The group looks at things from the standpoint of how the company might benefit from its use. Members of such a group must be fully cognizant of the direction of the company and know where it is likely being driven two to five years out. Although this is considered to be an advanced technology assessment group, such a group can be of great benefit in helping you establish an overall network communications plan that includes personal computer integration.

To ensure its visibility and command the attention that is necessary in projects of this scope and nature, this group typically reports very high up in the organization. Reporting directly to a division president or at the senior vice president level is not unusual. The skills and expertise of such a group are varied, but include voice/data communications, computing systems, workstation technology, software (applications), and business backgrounds. You might think that this assortment of backgrounds is hard to find, but it can be cultivated over time. In fact, you may find it within your own existing organization if you look. Figure 1-2 shows where such a group fits.

Example 4

Our final example involves a different approach. This structure is used by some companies that have several divisions and whose activities and computing needs are highly diversified and distributed. Each division might have responsibility for its own information processing, and little or no overall corporate control

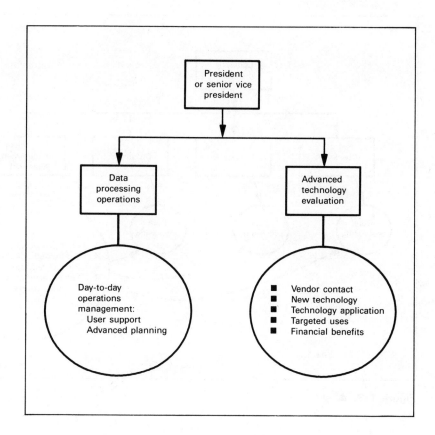

Figure 1-2. ▶

*Advanced
technology
structure*

is imposed. Each division is responsible for its own profit and loss, and computing systems are a part of such financial management.

You have the risk of exposing the corporation to a proliferation of a variety of micro-mainframe link products that do not fit together. Even if the selected products overlap, because each division does its own procurement, you may lose additional discounts that you could get if the orders were all batched together.

Take the illustration in Figure 1-3. Several companies have tried to use a single department to do all product procurement for personal computers for all divisions. This monstrous task often fails because each division contends that it confronts unique

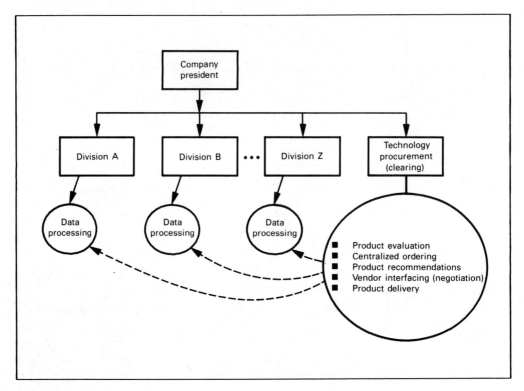

Figure 1-3. ▲

*Centralized
evaluation and
procurement*

requirements only it can understand and satisfy. A central procurement group merely slows this process down—a process that may already be too slow. It is also highly unlikely that such a central group can assess all of the needs of end users in each division. You don't have enough time or people. Finally, each division will eventually find a way around the process, no matter what executive management dictates in an effort to expedite their own purchases.

So some companies have instituted a variation of this process. First, the company does not expect a central group to procure all of the links and other products for all of the divisions. Each division can define its needs, select products, and procure them itself.

Second, a separate group performs a product evaluation function that is used to serve the divisions, not impose products on them. For example, it might evaluate different emulation links on the market or graphics packages and boards for personal computers. When a division indicates a need for an application requiring such products, it asks this group for suggestions based on the group's product evaluations. This group, which performs evaluations independent from end-user requirements, maintains an evaluation notebook that compares products and noteworthy features.

Third, the independent group represents a steering function for product procurement. In this capacity, it must have teeth in order to be effective.

In one instance, a large financial institution maintains its own stocking warehouse for high-volume products (links included) that are often used and requested by the divisions. Both the vendor and the company benefit enormously. What makes this approach effective is that the divisions know they can obtain faster product delivery from this group than they can directly from the vendor. This frees the division personnel from vendor negotiations. The company obtains greater price discounts because the group orders in higher volume than would occur otherwise. The vendor deals with a single corporate interface. In this case, the company authorized even stronger reinforcement for the group and established reasons for the *vendors* to use it. The group pays vendor invoices directly. It can also debit the division accounts automatically for product delivery. Hence, the vendors prefer to work with the group because they are actually paid sooner.

Not all companies want to maintain their own warehousing function, nor do they want to grant a single department the authority to automatically debit another division's budget for products. But in some situations, this system can work well. It maintains order and it provides continuity between evaluating new technology on a methodical and regimented basis.

Remember, this group never tells a division what it can and cannot purchase. The group merely suggests what it feels is relevant—what works and doesn't work. But because the group has "teeth," divisions do not hesitate to pass equipment requirements by it.

◥ SUMMARY

These examples provide you with several ideas to stimulate your thinking. You as managers and executives are concerned about long-term implications of managing the influx of technology as well as the business. We all know that this entails more than technical reviews and configuring products and networks. It means organizing for the business in an efficient and cost-effective manner that works for you, not against you. It requires an approach that embraces the needs of the end users rather than delivers applications that have to be forcibly fit into their everyday role.

The changes that you implement today are the changes that will determine just how well you can function tomorrow. This is particularly true with the requirements being imposed by end-user computing, which is driving the need to link these systems into your host computers and databases. By 1995 the world will change yet again, and technology will have continued to affect how businesses are run and how they compete with one another. But 1995 is not that far away. The structures that are set in place today will play a major role in determining how you will be positioned for entering the next century.

2 Personal Computers And Hosts

Numerous changes have taken place since the early 1960s when computing technology began to emerge. Although there are many arguments for dating its birth much earlier, the early 1960s provide a good base on which to build for our purposes. It was the beginning of communications and its role in today's business.

▼ BEGINNINGS

We have become conditioned now to absorbing technology as a part of our work and daily activities. But at first, computers were something of a mystique to many people, who regarded a computer's very size and capabilities with wonder. Companies fortunate enough to afford a computer treated it with reverence while they used it to automate aspects of their business.

13

System integration, not only an unknown term at the time, did not exist as a concept. The general public rarely saw the effects of computer automation directly, although they feared losing their jobs because of it. Companies benefited from improved record keeping, inventory control, accounts management, and so on. There still prevailed a stratum of individuals that clearly felt (and knew) that they could be more effective and efficient on the job than a computer.

As people became more familiar with computers and the mystique slowly fell away in the late 1960s, requests increased for improving and modifying data keyed into, and spewed out of, these monolithic centralized systems. Entire departments were established to address the growing number of requests from the evolving mass end-user colony for automating and improving tedious business processes. Some end users learned to program and make their own changes and updates as well as, on occasion, to develop their own programs with cards. Many of us wonder how we ever worked this way, but we did.

Terminals Arrive

In the early 1970s, the industry established time-sharing systems that allowed a user to interact with a centralized host computer through a television-like device called a *terminal*. But like those who accepted (or did not accept) computers in the early 1960s, at least two classes of people existed: those who refused to accept this new "instant" terminal updating and those who were jealous of anyone on whose desk the rare terminal sat. A metamorphosis needed to occur to cross over to a new level of computing. It took many forms, including (still around today) terminal rooms for general use. Even then, forecasters projected one terminal at every desk for every worker.

By the mid 1970s, terminal usage continued to climb. Minicomputer vendors evolved to distribute computing away from giant mainframes, and terminal manufacturers enjoyed healthy growth as demand seemed insatiable. More people began to realize that working interactively through terminals connected to host computers was more efficient. System performance and management became a task of balancing the division of resources between mass program execution and interactive users on terminals. People with expertise in this area were much in demand. Their skills were on the leading edge of what every computer data processing installation began to encounter: efficient use and tuning of very expensive computer system hardware and software to minimize investment.

As terminal use increased and more terminals were connected with hosts, resource balancing became critical in mainframe installations. Minicomputer manufacturers grew successfully by offering smaller computers to perform interactive work. These systems proliferated in areas not requiring or able to justify a multimillion-dollar computer investment. At this point, using a terminal became an accepted way of doing work. Networking, although being studied, did not start to occur even though minicomputers were being installed in many companies, and terminals were being accepted as a major production tool.

Personal Computers Appear

With the introduction of the Apple computer, in the late 1970s, a new phase began. Like the mainframe and minicomputers before it, the personal computer met resistance from all but a few visionaries. Those that introduced the Apple into the business environment did so for many reasons; the most important revolved around insulating themselves from the availability (or unavailability) of the host mainframe. Complex software application systems that had been developed for hosts offered poor user interfaces for end users.

Management information systems (MIS) departments traditionally provided the people resources that could understand, design, and deliver the solutions necessary to resolve business programming problems. Such problems could be reduction of data into reports, a system to create new data, or simply a program to retrieve data from the depths of the corporate file systems. However, because they were dependent on others in MIS departments to provide these tools and services for them, a wide spectrum of users who only wanted to do their job more efficiently felt ill at ease.

The advent of the personal computer changed all this. More than any other factor, it offered people a way to increase productivity and become more sophisticated about performing their job. They began to experiment, using their personal computers to create private databases, personalize programs, do word processing, and manage their time. They could now perform certain types of analysis quickly instead of using a host computer to debug the input, correct errors in messy programming languages, and wait for the computer to schedule their task or job for processing for what might be a 30-second model calculation. In a large system, this process could take an inexperienced user anywhere from a few hours to several days.

Like the minicomputers before, the personal computer became another link in the distribution of computing power out to the user's desktop. Minicomputers as well as mainframes become hosts for supporting linked personal computers.

IBM Legitimizes the PC

Corporations did not begin to use personal computers extensively as terminal replacements until IBM formally entered the arena in 1981 with the introduction of the IBM PC. But at that time another industry transition began to occur: the personal computer became a legitimate business and data processing tool supplementing the central computing environment. This trend continued, and new concepts of providing computer services and tools to users on a separate computer arose. Mainframe software developer companies began to incorporate operation and extension of system software subsets out to the personal computer. These changes required designers to define how services could be presented and delivered to the personal computer user and how data could be transferred between the two.

◤ THE EVOLUTION OF END-USER ENVIRONMENTS

End-user environments are created when people begin to use personal computers (or other terminals) in their jobs. These environments consist of individuals that depend on computers in some form to accomplish their daily business tasks. They either use computers directly or are the recipients of information from computers that enables them to perform their business activities.

The end-user environments changed because technology and business evolution presented a persuasive force for change. Resistance to change is often rooted in fear. As people overcome these fears, acceptance of new alternatives becomes easier. Ironically, the greatest resistance to personal computer usage as a tool for business centered around how the personal computer could be tied in with multimillion-dollar data centers that were constructed to support a large amount of processing activity and movement of large volumes of data. The environment changed because some of these data centers become obstacles to the very thing technology was supposed to improve: business efficiency.

End users quickly realized that personalizing computing power provided flexibility to perform the kind of analysis, statistical and otherwise, that supports business. Standalone activity on personal computers increased as rapidly as the expansion of installed personal computers in corporations. By the end of this decade, millions of personal computers will exist in businesses.

So what about change? Data processing management, responsible for holding together the computing facilities that process business data, must somehow sanely cope with the demands from users. Most good management starts with the nature of the business and deals first with issues that can be handled internally.

Coping With Change

End users used the personal computer along with the electronic spreadsheet, such as VisiCalc, to make working with data eas-

ier. Besides converting the personal computer from an amusing
toy to a useful business machine, the spreadsheet enabled users
to eliminate tedious hand calculations. Budgets, forecasts, statistical analysis, and what-if calculations became less complex and
less time consuming. The "grunt work" factor was drastically
reduced to an automated mechanical activity.

Demand for more functionality gave birth to word processing
software that enabled better and easier letter and memorandum
creation. This occurred because users progressed to another level
of need. Databasing evolved from a need to insulate oneself from
the complicated host databases that never seemed designed for
general access by nonprogrammers. End users collected and
managed project-, market-, or corporate-related data in their own
cosmos for their own private needs. These phenomena further
widened the already growing separation between standalone personal computers and central hosts.

Users realize that they were limited in capability as long as
data and applications remained local. Demands of the business
required access to corporate data — data that represented more
current information than they could create, data that the corporation maintained and updated on a regular basis. Like a love-
hate relationship, users who once resisted being connected to the
host now found the opposite: resistance from data processing
management to allow them to be connected.

Links Begin to Develop

User needs created pressure to move the personal computer from
a standalone unit to host connection. Following Figure 2-1
clockwise, you follow the progression of use of the personal
computer, not the course of linking.

Initially, personal computers were not connected with sophisticated link products to the host. *Protocol converters,* products
that translate one form of code or protocol to another, were used
as one type of linking mechanism. Other connection forms
allowed a personal computer to mimic, or *emulate,* another terminal. Users could only read the host data with a personal com-

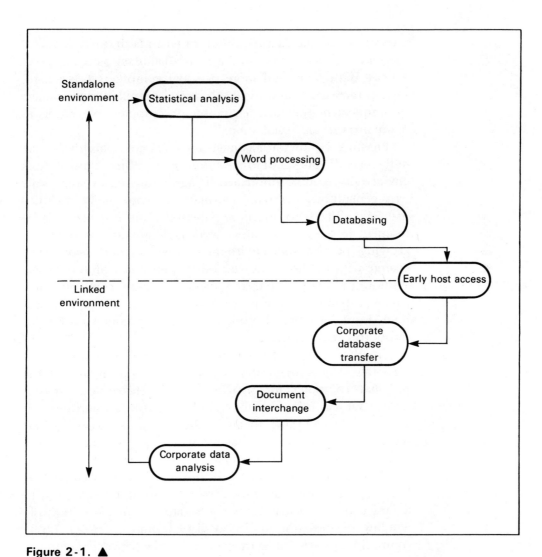

Figure 2-1. ▲

*The evolution of
workstation-to-host
applications*

puter but could not transfer it to their desktops. A personal computer connected to the host with such products was simply an expensive personal computer being used as a dumb terminal to access the host.

Environments changed to require *linked capability*, a means of connecting to a host and enabling data transfer, because user access to corporate data requires transfer in both directions. End users now expect access to corporate databases as a matter of course. With more and more personal computers being used, there is increasing pressure to accommodate links and to manage the implementation of such personal computer integration to maintain a secure installation.

Figure 2-1 shows a document interchange capability as part of the overall concept of *office automation*. Office automation is any activity such as automated filing or calendaring that deals with general office activities normally done manually. To automate the office is to minimize paperwork and provide an environment in which most office work is done with computers. A growing part of this environment involves document interchange with the host and with other users attached to the host. Without linking personal computers to the host, complete interchange capability is not possible, nor is it possible to achieve a high degree of efficient automation. Link products evolved to satisfy this requirement as well.

Finally, in Figure 2-1, note that analysis is performed on corporate data both at the host for large models and at the personal computer for smaller subsets. Hence, the linking process returns full circle for complete usefulness, starting with the personal computer in an isolated mode, to accessing and retrieving data in a host-attached mode, to disconnecting and performing further activities in a standalone manner once again.

Many variations occurred as users quickly moved up the learning curve, and fear of using personal computers gave way to a larger list of demands. Some variations included multiple window sessions (the ability to display more than one single computing process at a time on a single personal computer screen), integrated spreadsheets (such as Lotus 1-2-3), icons (graphic figure representations for routine processes such as a garbage can for deleting old files) for easier personal computer usage, and graphics for data representation, to name just a few. What used to be the features of only the most sophisticated host software systems can now usually be installed as a personal computer package.

Connecting to multiple hosts simultaneously can also be achieved. Evolving products permit this capability, which becomes even more powerful in certain situations in which the personal computer can process data while transferring data from the attached host. When this occurs, windowing becomes a natural evolution in personal computer usage.

◀ EXTERNAL ISSUES

External issues influencing changes in the end-user environment include dealing with the visibility of electronic capabilities beyond the corporate walls: providing capabilities that people have come to expect. Individuals and corporations have become accustomed to knowing that having a personal computer gives them access to a wide variety of services and data. They expect to be able to freely use the personal computer to access them.

The corporate treasurer, for example, expects to be able to use the personal computer to monitor funds activity at the company's commercial banker. The person responsible for trust accounts expects to be able to link into a host and manage that day's trust accounts unencumbered by another organization. People are being conditioned to expect and utilize home banking facilities from their own living rooms by simply turning on their personal computers and entering certain access information to pay bills and transfer monies between accounts.

The entire external arena for using personal computers is changing as connection into hosts create real possibilities about what can be done. It is an arena that offers exciting changes in how you do your business and spend your discretionary time.

Take, for example, the ability to connect over telephone lines to other databases such as *Dow-Jones* for stock information or *The Source* for general information on products, companies, and so on. Public libraries in some states offer a connection service for a fee. Time-sharing companies for years made their business dependent on external customers connecting to their systems for storing data, executing programs, and paying for specialized services that are too expensive to install and maintain on the customers' own computers for limited use. Companies like ADP, Tymshare, Boeing Computer Services, and McAuto are only a few that provide such service. They too must cope with managing the attachment of, and services for, personal computers accessing systems over telephone lines.

This is only the tip of the iceberg. The financial community helped people overcome fears of performing transactions such as check cashing and deposit with automated teller machines (ATMs). Charge accounts may be paid via ATMs. And television and radio commercials have again done an amazing job of conditioning the public over its fear of electronic money changers. An entire generation of high school and college students are acclimated to working with keyboards and electronic devices. A great deal of change is on the horizon. You will be able to do home banking and loan processing as well as take advantage of many other consumer-oriented services by using your personal computer connected to host company systems.

Companies are also realizing that they do not need to permit processing to be done by other entities. Using banks as an example again, corporations are demanding to do their own portfolio management, update their own personnel/payroll applications, and manage their own cash activities. All these applications use a personal computer to download files and upload changes for processing.

The environment requires attention to systems and how these links are selected and integrated. It requires an understanding of services, expectations, and resources to support such systems and personal computers. The environment is changing because competition and costs are demanding it to change. Communications and integration of personal computers at a system level are mandated by economics, customer satisfaction, and a need to deliver services, information, and applications across a wider geographical spectrum. A whole issue of continuous processing is surfacing in situations in which personal computer access is available.

◥ THE DOMINANT ISSUES

In the short term, several key aspects of personal computer integration cannot be ignored:

- Host processing capacity to service linked personal computers
- Data upload and download requirements
- Cross-application and service usage
- Securing host-based data and programs
- Servicing and maintaining linked personal computers.

Relative to host processing, it is sometimes overlooked that even though these are personal computers, linking requires resources both for physical access and for processing. It is easy to forget that connection usually ends at the host. A host system can be overloaded if it is not properly planned and managed.

A great deal depends on how many personal computers will be linked to a host. Are they linked from remote locations through modems over telephone lines, or are they directly connected to communications controllers and mixed with other terminals? How much active on-line connection is required for host access? What is the frequency and volume of data transfer? What amount of host offloading is expected? Given all these factors, there may be a distinct difference in host capacity usage.

As you see in Figure 2-2, every host reaches a level of saturation based upon resource demands. Assuming for the moment that the only variable is attachment of terminals and personal computers, curve B typifies environments in which all attached personal computers require constant servicing for interactive work or data transfer. In certain circumstances this can approach 60 to 70 percent of an entire host system's resources very quickly. If a lesser percentage, say 30 to 40 percent, needs to be connected periodically, some other curve (A) is more accurate. It is imperative to understand the activity and role of linked personal computers relative to the business and applications serviced.

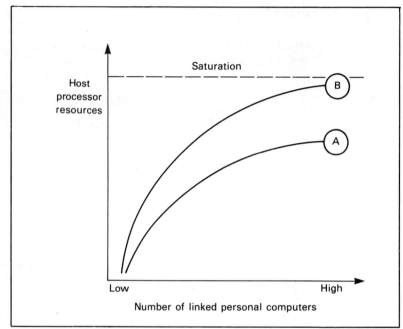

Figure 2-2. ▶

Host capacity usage versus attached personal computers

Data Quantity

Data upload or download requirements must be defined, estimated, and projected relative to existing and planned systems for end-user needs. Different design and link selection criteria prevail, depending upon the extent to which they are required. Issues of uploading tend to address levels of security protection and potential database corruption at the host. More complex system network and integration issues abound if data must be available across widespread applications or correlated with other data. However, uploading into corporate databases is not a new practice; many companies have used on-line data entry processes directly into host systems for years.

Cross-application and service usage means how to make data and other capabilities available to personal computers across various applications that need the same data and how to supply different services using the same data. It is easy to visualize a single application or service working with different types of data. Similarly, the same data can be used across different applications. At times it is important to view data within the context of several situations. Windowing can help here, but it is essential to design the systems so that multiple linked personal computers can have system access, just as terminals do. What this means is that a single personal computer can access more than one host and simultaneously look at the data. Obviously, security systems and processes are essential, which leads to the next point.

Security

Securing host-based data and programs is an ongoing issue. Data must be protected according to its importance, not by its location. Centralized host-based security systems help control data access and dispersement, but it may be appropriate to impose other levels of security that are attendant with linked personal computers. Linking intelligent workstations into hosts presents many variables to be considered. This issue is treated in more depth in Chapter 5.

Maintenance

Servicing and maintaining links are essential for good data center operation. The issue is one of how it is carried out within the confines of the service philosophy of the organization. Is the data processing installation capable of its own maintenance, are they vendor dependent, or is there a third-party service organization that supplies assistance? Do vendors offer 800-number telephone assistance, and are proper diagnostics available to isolate the problem or record valuable problem logging? Answers to these questions are essential as organizations progress through the learning curve of link usage, increase the number of operational links, and expand the design of links into their networks and applications.

◥ LONG-TERM ISSUES

As services and applications become distributed to end users, they must be designed with distributed systems in mind, including applications and databases. Not all users in a data processing organization are internal. Many services are delivered to external users, which may be other corporations or consumers in the retail market. As personal computers become more widespread outside the corporate environment, the demand increases for capabilities that permit the personal computer to transact general day-to-day business. Links are required to provide such delivery capabilities.

One crucial question concerns how personal computers should interrelate not only with a single host but also with entire systems driven by a core of hosts. How must configurations be designed to provide redundant backup, continuous processing, alternate routing, transparent database access, and a secure environment against nonauthorized users? Are these link-related issues? These issues, which incorporate links as a part of the process, appear when intelligent workstations are permitted to access hosts. Hence, they must be considered when integration uses links.

The dominant long-term issues with personal computers and hosts go beyond designing configurations and selecting links. They include planning a framework to support services defined by the business corporate strategy. This framework must provide for future additions of personal computers, product upgrades, information flow, system compatibilities, network expansions, multiple networks, technology obsolescence, and future product incorporation.

Effects on Existing Networks

Effects on existing networks take many forms. To support the addition of personal computers, network capacity must be sufficient to handle the flow of data and information between personal computers and to and from hosts. Capacity to handle peak loads or continuous volume transfers is a critical design factor. The network is a resource that dispenses information across a wider area of users. Workstations connected within a local area access a broader network, which, in turn, is driven by a series of host computers. Links become points within the network serviced transparently by large computer systems.

Personal computers are a resource requiring other resources for servicing. When disconnected and operating as standalone units, they are self-contained and require no additional external support. But when actively connected to a host or network, the degree of resources required depends on the transaction type performed, the data transfer volume and frequency, line speed, and the available host capacity, to name just a few factors. The number of actively connected personal computers used for data transfer and on-line access affects resource sharing as well. It is the mix and percentage of data transfer within a given period that is significant over and above the total number of connected personal computers because ratios of connected personal computers to total PCs varies with the environment.

The major effects on the network come from the types of applications these personal computers support and execute. The application and the information flow determine what the network must do to service the computer. Many existing networks are designed to connect and service data requests to and from dumb terminals. Because workstations have internal memory and auxiliary data storage in the form of floppy and hard disks, data requests result in a larger volume of data from the host than might normally be required by dumb terminals. A line and a computer access port are thus tied up for the duration of the transfer, even though the user may need only a portion of the data.

Today, more and more people are using personal computers instead of dumb terminals and are connecting them to a host, which in general means that larger hosts are needed. A never-ending circle is resulting: more personal computers are being host-connected so that end users can perform independent work without using host facilities. The host must handle the data transfers, however, which means that it must service these users. Consequently, the host is moving toward a role of database manager and traffic director to ensure servicing. In turn, this results in host resources shifting from processing to handling and fulfilling data requests. The addition of personal computers requires that at some point host resources be upgraded to keep pace with the network attached to drive these user machines.

◤ THE NEW ROLE OF MIS

MIS adjusts to its new role by accepting the inevitability of personal computers as business tools and the applicability of links to integrate them into the business process and data processing systems. MIS departments must understand how personal computers can help their business and must identify their specific problems associated with connecting them to hosts. No longer is MIS in a position to stonewall personal computer introduction or usage; it must now facilitate such integration in a useful way. Users are still requesting service, only in different forms. They want access to systems and files that previously only MIS could access and write applications against.

MIS is becoming more cognizant and knowledgeable about business plans, anticipated services, projected growth, and a myriad of other nontechnical issues that help make better decisions. It is no longer just a question of designing and implementing software applications on schedule. The MIS executive must be aware of where the business is headed so that major software systems can be designed, expanded, and modified to support future services. These services must include the incorporation of personal computers as the primary access terminal. MIS can no longer be concerned about simply providing end users with applications and computing facilities but now must supply a framework that is critical to business success within a corporation.

Factors Affecting Management

Similarly, a company's systems analysts, network managers, technical support personnel, and software programmers are in roles of supporting efficient operations and service delivery to end users and personal computers. Their activities are increasingly complicated by the introduction and evolution of many communications options and protocols designed for different capabilities and business needs. Simply keeping current on the variety of cabling systems and linking options for personal computers is a full-time assignment in itself. Such skills and expertise must be organized to address the basic communications foundations of networks upon which data is transferred between applications.

In the past, management and organization were established to address specific aspects of a data processing installation. Network managers monitored network traffic without regard to the business or type of application; database management concerned itself with housing corporate data, backup, and recovery; and, more often than not, operations management remained responsible for resource planning and host performance without getting involved in application planning or business strategy. This system must change as personal computers become more dominant and play a larger role in defining applications. It is essential that these groups operate in concert to manage data centers expanding and to get smarter in using technology.

Changes in Attitude

MIS must adjust in both attitude and in organization to its new role of supplying and monitoring computing services. It must accept a cooperative role with the knowledge that efficient systems cannot be addressed in an isolated way. No longer can applications be defined without operations and database management getting involved to ensure proper resource availability, security, and efficient execution. Organizationally, management structures must reinforce a systems approach. Responsible parties must clearly understand the business's purpose and scope and cooperate to address services and personal computer integration in a systems manner.

A clear methodology and approach is essential and desirable. Once issues and problems are defined, the organization can address personal-computer-to-host integration by defining and implementing the correct solution.

◣ WHERE DO WE GO FROM HERE?

The rest of this book concentrates on how to start thinking about workstation integration and implementing personal-computer-to-host links. Guidelines, thoughts, and suggestions help MIS executive management understand the major link integration issues. These issues create a knowledge about what to expect in expanding their service networks and what their technical management is coping with in trying to make all of those personal computers useful. From this book, you should get a perspective on what limitations exist from a business standpoint and what they mean.

If you are in systems analysis or technical management, you can assess your situation regardless of where you are in the process of integrating links. You can organize how to select links, learn how to plan for their introduction, and learn how to create link network approaches.

The factors involved vary, depending on an organization's ability to adjust to business climate and technology. No one specific methodology is applicable and correct across all organizations in different industries. For successful integration to take place in a predictable and measurable way, any organization's approach should remain constant and methodical.

3 Micro-Mainframe Link Categories

▼ GETTING STARTED WITH LINKS
▼ DIRECT CONNECTION VERSUS REMOTE CONNECTION
▼ LINK FACTORS
▼ TERMINAL EMULATION
▼ FILE TRANSFER SOFTWARE
▼ DATABASE INTERFACES
▼ FILE SERVERS
▼ LOCAL AREA NETWORKS (LANS)
▼ FINDING SOLUTIONS

If you consider the wide range of micro-mainframe link products and multiple options available, you can quickly become confused and disoriented in attempting to choose one over the other. If you have been entrusted with the responsibility of connecting personal computers and workstations into hosts, you may wonder how and where to start. The questions often come faster than the answers. What do you look for? Whom do you call? Which products are the best? How do you find vendors? Which periodicals, trade journals, or magazines are good to read for information? Which should you read?

◥ GETTING STARTED WITH LINKS

The first problem is where to start. In some cases it's just a matter of becoming educated about the basics:

- The types of existing micro-mainframe links
- What different products offer
- What functions various products support
- Product sophistication levels
- General price ranges.

In short, the initial approach is simply to learn about the industry, become familiar with various products, and learn the terminology. The second problem involves knowing what products to select for a given installation, application, and network. This entails knowing what problems are to be solved and approaching them from a solution viewpoint. This chapter is devoted to the first problem.

Why Categories Are Important

Using categories makes it easier to consider micro-mainframe links with respect to applications. You can quickly converge on a group of products that satisfy your business and technical requirements and then sort product claims of various vendors within a category.

The type of solution is more important than the product itself. There are an incredibly large number of products that all do the same thing on the market. Developing categories is a first step toward selecting a product. It also helps you focus on products pertinent to the business need. Link selection is a process of elimination and definition.

Once categories are defined, you can order and weight factors that are critical to your business and data center needs as you see them. You'll find that discussions with vendors become more productive, describing what problem must be solved is easier, and ranking features becomes second nature. You can then take the top three or six products, compare their functions and features, and decide how they meet the perceived needs of the business and your users.

◤ DIRECT CONNECTION VERSUS REMOTE CONNECTION

Direct connection consists of attaching a personal computer to some controller by using a coaxial cable. A personal computer is usually directly connected if it is within 2000 feet of the controller.

If the personal computer is not physically near the data center controller and cannot be attached directly with a cable, remote connection is used. It communicates with a host via a modem, using telephone lines. The user (or the modem) dials a telephone number that accesses a host; hence, remote attachment.

In some circumstances, it is not possible to connect directly. For example, personal computers in a home can only communicate to a host over telephone lines. Direct connection generally provides faster data transfer. Remote connection offers flexibility in attaching to different hosts in different geographical locations.

Remote connection is generally asynchronous; a single character of data, preceded and followed by control information, is transmitted at a time. In synchronous transmission, a group of characters, say 256, is sent at a time, in a continuous stream. IBM supports asynchronous communications and pioneered synchronous communications with its popular 3270 terminal series. Computer vendors such as DEC and Hewlett-Packard use asynchronous terminal communication as the primary mode, although not exclusively, because of their own system and terminal design.

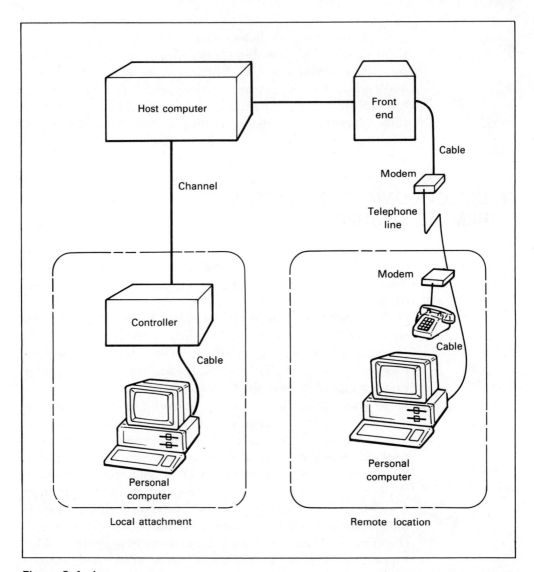

Figure 3-1. ▲

*Local versus
remote attachment
IBM environment*

The IBM Connection

Figure 3-1 shows the difference between a local and remote attached personal computer in an IBM environment. This diagram uses generic representation; vendor names and technical details are purposefully absent. For local host attachment, a controller that supports certain types of terminal equipment is shown. The controller in Figure 3-1 is local to the host and is attached to a channel or adapter. The personal computer is directly linked to the controller with a cable and, because of other installed hardware and software, appears to the controller and host as a recognized terminal.

For a remotely located personal computer, the host may have a connected front-end communications unit that supports a variety of lines. These may be high-speed lines transferring thousands of characters of data at a time or normal telephone lines connected via modems. The personal computer is connected to the modem with a cable. The modem communicates across a telephone line to another modem at the other end, which, in turn, connects directly to the front end. In this way, a remotely located personal computer can be linked to a host.

The Non-IBM Connection

Figure 3-2 demonstrates local and remote attachment in a non-IBM situation such as one in which DEC equipment is used. In such an environment, controllers and front ends tend to be integrated as adapters. Thus local attachment can occur if the personal computer is directly connected to one of these adapters. Software must be installed on the personal computer to emulate supported terminals. Similarly, personal computers can be remotely attached via modems communicating to adapter channels. Other techniques and equipment can eliminate the problem of using a single channel per modem; however, they will not be elaborated upon at this point.

MIS management doesn't always have a choice in the location of its users; it must design systems to provide services to where those users are located. This is even more true in today's society as personal computer users expect to be able to rely on today's telecommunications technology and "reach out and touch" their computing services.

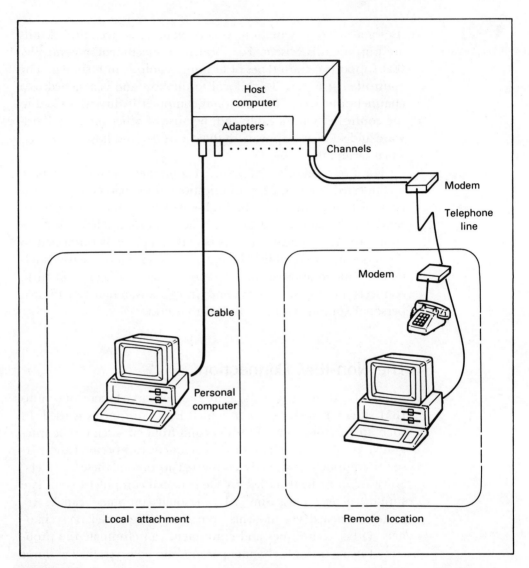

Figure 3-2. ▲

*Local versus
remote attachment,
non-IBM
environment*

◤ LINK FACTORS

These system designs affect product considerations in terms of function, user response time, efficiency, and cost. It is here that decisions must be made on how demands of remote and local users are to be addressed. The type of link products selected are greatly influenced by present and future usage profiles that depend on many factors, including:

- Type of data transfer
- Transfer frequency
- Number of remote versus local users
- Available host capacity
- Personal computer user growth
- Local and remote printing needs
- Simultaneous active, on-line connectivity.

Connectivity consists of physically providing the protocol to attach a terminal device to a host; in itself, it is no longer the issue, as many products are available for this purpose. The issue is how to accomplish connectivity within the network systems.

For example, to illustrate the point, let's assume for the moment that a particular installation must service a set of remote users. If this user set is not very large, say less than 25 or 50, it is possible to allocate each user a modem and have a counterpart modem at the host end into which the users can dial a telephone number and connect. Figure 3-3 profiles such a situation. If the number of remote users with personal computers is expected to increase over the next six to twelve months, however, then it may be wiser and more cost effective to consider an approach other than providing each user with a modem. Although this seems trivial, it does point out that future growth must be given careful thought.

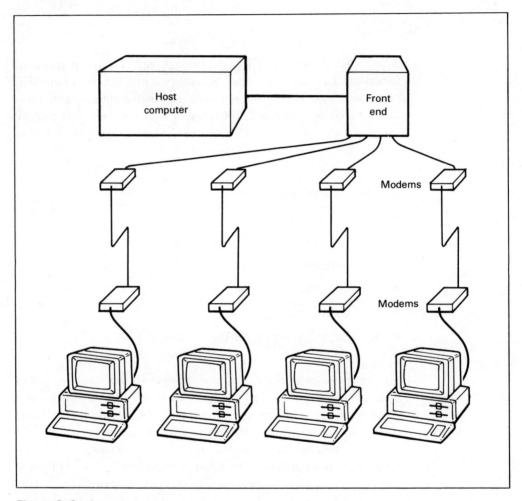

Figure 3-3. ▲

Remote personal computers attached by modems

Multiplexing

Figure 3-4 displays one way of connecting a large number of personal computers with a host. In this diagram, linking is accomplished by using a more traditional method of connection that focuses on multiplexing a number of connected sessions to a host across a given set of telephone lines. These multiplexers statistically allocate portions of data traffic across a single line;

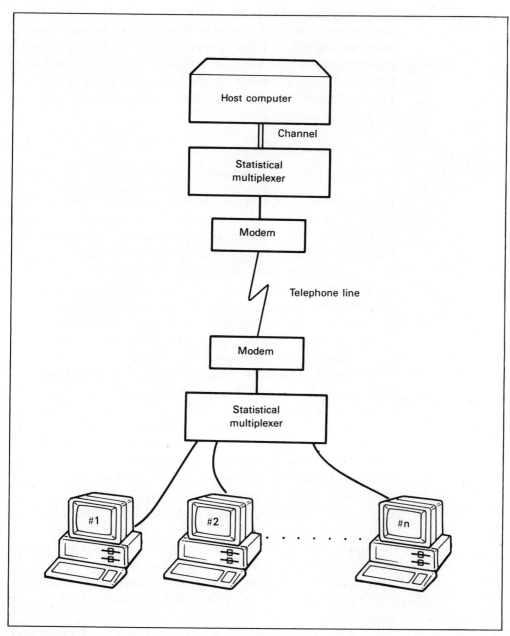

Figure 3-4. ▲

*Personal computer
linking via modem
and statistical
multiplexer*

thus, personal computer users need not be aware that others are using the same line. This technique eliminates the one-modem-and-user-per-channel requirement shown previously in Figure 3-2. Clearly, the solutions shown in Figures 3-3 and 3-4 offer advantages and disadvantages along with different cost and usage breakpoints.

External Considerations

When personal computers are directly attached to the host either via adapters or control units, certain factors must be considered. With direct connection, limiting distances are important for link hardware. As pointed out earlier, attachment distances generally cannot exceed 2000 feet. This distance factor must be known. In an IBM environment, mixing personal computers on the same control unit as 327X terminals can cause controller performance changes, depending on the type of user personal computer activity taking place—factors such as number of single transaction queries, data transfer frequency, and volume.

For remote attachment, primary external considerations center around telephone line reliability and cost. Standard analog telephone lines are most frequently used with attached modems at speeds ranging from 300 baud to 2400 baud. As data transmission speed increases, however, it is more likely that data transmission errors will occur. Also, the longer the transmission time for a file transfer at low speed, the higher the chances for a transmission error because of lengthy connection time. If a line is "dirty" or "noisy," there is a high probability that errors will occur during transmission.

So what about links in the remote case? Selection is based on the link product's ability to sense a data error. If an error occurs, some products may require an entire data retransmission while others can commence from the point of failure. Management must determine and decide what type of transmission will be the norm and if it can be satisfied across analog lines. Line quality provided by the telephone companies continues to improve as new technology emerges, but remote links via modems should have error-detection capability.

The Digital Option

If you have absolute requirements for guaranteed line reliability and availability, a digital data set (DDS) line that is dedicated to your data transmission needs is available from telephone companies. How the DDS line is installed between two points is based on the area codes and phone number prefix between points. Line speeds can range between 9600 baud and 56 Kbaud. In many states, the number of hours a line can be unavailable is guaranteed not to exceed a level measured in hours per year (generally under 5). Remote link attachment can be implemented across these lines as previously illustrated in Figure 3-3. Of course, if a construction crew runs a backhoe through the line, it can be lost for days. So it is advisable that a few analog dial-up modems be available for emergencies.

The Bottom Line

What are you willing to pay for high availability transmission in remote situations? DDS lines carry an installation charge plus a monthly ongoing fixed fee. The higher the rated transmission speed, the higher the monthly fee. Although these charges may go down over time, demand for such lines has kept these fees reasonably steady. Others will contend these are the costs of doing business and are cheap when compared to the possibility of lost data. But what if there is a requirement for more than 1, 2, or 10 lines? Maybe even 30? Link products can help by being efficient. If a link on an analog line is not efficient, the business pays in excessive line charges every time data is transferred, for the life of the product.

Capacity and Resources

Host capacity and available resources to support personal computer attachment must be monitored and projected. There's been a great deal of discussion about the amount of processing personal computers can remove from hosts (offloading). Regardless of whether this is 10 percent or 90 percent, the host must spend some amount of time acknowledging and servicing these users. Because of the nature of the evolving industry, the host is becoming a vehicle for:

- Storing and managing corporate data
- Executing large application systems
- Servicing communications networks and terminal systems.

For personal computers to offload work from host processors, they must perform useful functions that would normally be executed at the host. These functions use host-stored data. For offloading to be effective and productive, this same equivalent function must be done at the personal computer with data from the host. How efficiently this is done depends on the remote and local connection issues discussed above.

The remote and direct-connect relationship to systems is another question. Knowing the ratio of directly connected personal computers to remotely connected computers does not supply the answer. It is only a small measure of how host capacity may need to support activity. Different types of links must supply particular functionality, which in turn depends on the application system for interfacing and the way in which linking takes place.

◥ TERMINAL EMULATION

Before personal computers, host computers — whether from IBM, DEC, Prime, Wang, Burroughs, Sperry-Univac, NCR, Hewlett-Packard, or any number of other computer manufacturers — did support connection to specific terminal types that the host vendor provided. Even the screen displays and keyboards varied from vendor to vendor.

The important factor, however, is not the hardware but the actual terminal protocols used to communicate with the host. Given simulation of protocols at the user end, the host need never be aware of what is on the other end, let alone the type of terminal device. If these protocols look like what the host computer is accustomed to seeing, then the host presumes it is talking to a standard terminal that it recognizes.

By imitating, or *emulating*, these terminal communication protocols, nonstandard devices can be connected to the host. Early link products enabled personal computers to communicate to host computers by emulating the protocols used for connection. In the case of DEC, the protocols are those for primarily the VT/52 and VT/100 terminals; in the case of IBM, mainly for the 3270, 5251, and 3101. The current standard in terminal emulation is Digital Communications Associates' IRMA product for IBM 327X emulation. Emulators can be designed to address products communicating in either synchronous or asynchronous mode. The terminal type and mode of transmission to be supported determine the mode of emulation.

There are many different types and levels of emulators. From the end-user or terminal level, the basic terminal and protocols must be emulated for complete connection and usability. Technically, terminal emulator manufacturers must provide interfaces between the keyboard and display as well as map the codes that govern the terminal device buffer and keystroke scan into the personal computer in a way that makes them analogous to normal terminal operation. So the lowest level of emulator makes a personal computer appear as a dumb terminal recognizable in every way to a host. Figure 3-5 shows a simple generic terminal emulator.

The advantage of using a terminal emulator is that it is simple and straightforward. The connection conforms to standard host requirements, and MIS can maintain existing installation procedures for host access. The cost of an emulator offering synchronous transmission ranges from $800 to $1600 per personal computer. Software for asynchrnous transmission emulation links is around $100 to $300 per personal computer. The limitations are that expensive personal computers are transformed into inexpensive dumb terminals for host access. In addition, asynchronous operation is a very slow method of terminal emulation. The person using the terminal is limited to what can be done

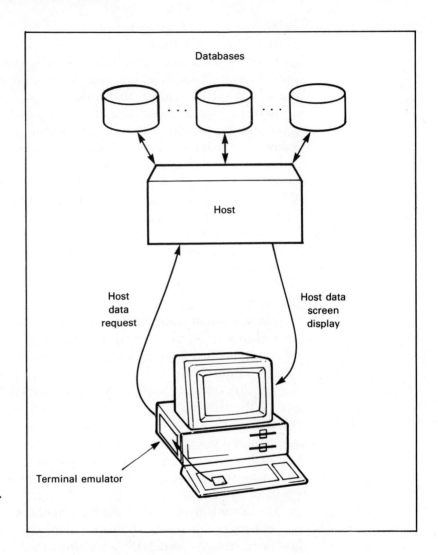

Figure 3-5. ▶

Simple terminal emulator link

with a personal computer when linked to the host. If database access is required, the user must also know how to access that database.

Early emulator products introduced in 1983 and 1984 in many cases did not allow you to switch dynamically between operation in personal computer mode and the host in terminal mode. These emulators required you to physically initiate a host disconnect before operating solely on the personal computer. For example, if you were working with a Multiplan spreadsheet and wanted to retrieve data from the host, you had to perform at least a five-step process. First, end the Multiplan session and initiate a terminal emulation mode. Second, set up and initiate a data transfer from the host. Third, end the emulation mode after data transfer is complete. Fourth, convert the data format to that of Multiplan. Fifth, restart Multiplan and load the converted data.

Specific terminal emulation had also been incorporated as part of the hardware. As these products matured, and systems orientation and user needs evolved for enhancing emulators, additional capability began to appear.

Advanced Features

Terminal emulators began to incorporate single "hot" key switching between sessions, allowing you to swap between a host activity and personal computer sessions. As an example, the five-step process described above gave way to a more efficient and easy process. You do not have to exit Multiplan to initiate a multistep process for data transfer. Instead, you touch a single key that places the Multiplan session in suspended mode and starts the emulation session. This is possible because some emulator products have coprocessor capability. You then initiate a data transfer, specify the application (Multiplan) destination, and the data is transmitted and reformatted automatically. Touch a single key again, and the Multiplan session returns.

Windowing, as described in Chapter 2, allows you to view multiple sessions. Windows can also offer the potential of viewing activity associated with simultaneously connecting to more than one host. In addition, emulation for specific types of terminals is loadable directly from a floppy disk.

Other capabilities have also emerged that permit file transfer to the personal computer by bypassing specific terminal screen formats and addressing the transmission of data directly to and from user-generated applications. IRMA, 3270-PLUS from CXI, and LinkUp from Information Technologies transfer data to the host in IBM file formats or from the host into the user's personal computer files.

Data can also be retrieved in formats usable by a spreadsheet application without performing transmission specifically designed for the emulated terminal's screen format. Products exist that provide all of the above capability regardless of whether the host computer is IBM or non-IBM. For example, in the IBM market such products as Lotus/Answer and dBase/Answer from Informatics General selectively extract host data and transfer it in formats directly usable by Lotus and dBase. Similarly, Hewlett-Packard's Application/Link used in conjunction with its financial report generator extracts data from the Hewlett-Packard host IMAGE database and converts it for use in VisiCalc, Lotus, and other selected spreadsheets.

Protocol Converters

As mentioned earlier, different types and levels of emulators exist. A large number of protocol converters have been installed and continue to find a market, particularly in the IBM world. In this environment, front-end processors and control units are prevalent, and terminal devices accessing this equipment must provide protocols consistent with their interfaces. Again, in the IBM environment where synchronous transmission is prevalent, protocol converters are highly useful for permitting host access by asynchronous devices in synchronous mode. In such a case, the protocol converter essentially emulates a control unit. Figure 3-6 displays how such a configuration appears to the host and how personal computers are connected. Access is via direct attachment or dial-up.

The converter makes the translation between asynchronous to synchronous for compatibility with the host front end. In this case, the personal computer need only contain an asynchronous communications adapter. These protocol converters can be used either with IBM's Binary Synchronous Communications (BSC) or SNA/SDLC (Systems Network Architecture/Synchronous Data Link Control).

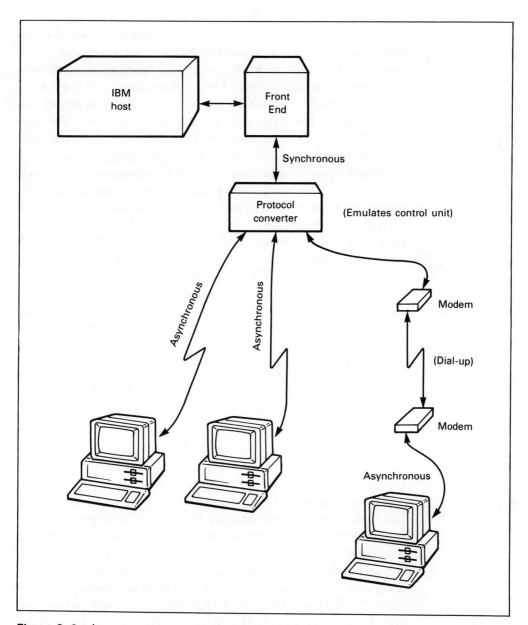

Figure 3-6. ▲

*Protocol converter
as control unit
emulator*

Although some say that protocol converters are not as desirable as other emulation methods, converters are considerations for situations in which user sites are remote and may require only infrequent host connection. Their advantage is that they are a relatively inexpensive way to provide dial-up capability for remote users. Their cost may be shared across a multiple user base. However, protocol converters are limited in their capabilities and do not offer very many functions.

Finally, another level of emulation involves products that are inserted into the personal computer and permit it to emulate the control unit itself. Useful primarily in the IBM environment, such devices allow a personal computer to connect directly into a host front end by using synchronous modems. These products serve two purposes: one, they permit protocols to be addressed equivalent to the control-unit-to-host front end; two, they provide specific terminal device emulation to the user. These products, although more expensive ($1200 and up per personal computer) are advantageous in remote areas supporting few users that require relatively little host connection. Figure 3-7 displays such an emulator.

Additional Products

As terminal varieties evolved, additional emulator products were introduced. A series of vendor terminals have become industry standards for the manufacturer as well as the link vendor. Emulator manufacturers provide software-loadable personalities for link hardware to minimize their own exposure to product redesign, preserve their customers' initial link hardware investment, maintain the flexibility to emulate future terminals and enhancements, and provide additional functionality as required. Examples of industry terminal standards include IBM's 3277/78/79, IBM's 3101, and DEC's VT/52 and 100. Others that are evolving include IBM's 3270 PC. In the graphics arena, standards that exist include DEC's VT/125/240 and the Tektronix 4010/12/14. Several others may be considered standards, depending on how "standard" is defined. We define standard as those having the highest visible market share—those that are the most widely used and accepted.

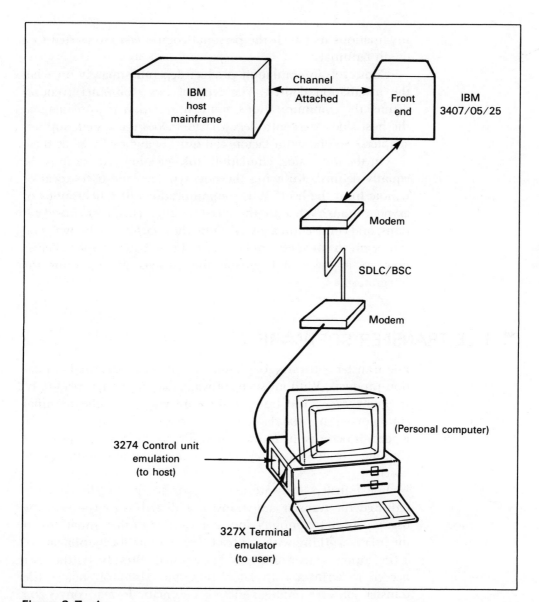

Figure 3-7. ▲

Control unit/
terminal emulator

Emulator links are most appropriate for use when management wants to provide only basic host access. They should be used when it is not necessary to allow sophisticated interaction with host applications beyond read-only and should be used only in situations in which the personal computer is converted to a dumb terminal.

Choice of an emulation product depends squarely on what the installation desires. The type of host computer (vendor) defines the communications and configuration requirements at the host side. Are controllers a factor? Does the system support adapters? So one set of factors can quickly and easily be defined.

On the other side, emulation link selection criteria must be equally defined. Knowing the host type, are the users local or remote from the host? Will communications be synchronous or asynchronous? What are the speed requirements, cost considerations, and connection activity? Once these factors are known, you can begin to consider emulation products. Later chapters define how to manage and pursue the process of planning the integration.

◥ FILE TRANSFER SOFTWARE

File transfer software goes hand in hand with terminal emulation products. Without such software, data transfer is read-only. In many cases, file transfer software is part of the terminal emulator — if not standard, as an optional capability that may be loaded. It permits the movement of files to and from the personal computer, or downloading (from the host) and uploading (to the host).

File transfers software allows users to specify the data file required for transfer and transfer it directly — as is — into the user's personal computer for later work. In other situations, if the user is working with a spreadsheet or other local application, a file format conversion may be required. Previously, the user needed to write a conversion program. Many of today's file transfer software products include automatic format conversion as specified by the user. For example, the DIF (Data Interchange Format) used by VisiCalc and by many other popular personal computer applications is a standard conversion option, as are other popular spreadsheet formats such as WKS (Lotus 1-2-3) and SYLK (Multiplan).

In a variety of situations, file transfer software requires a host-based portion for selective data extraction. This selection and transfer type is more sophisticated and is discussed later. There are instances, however, when software is resident on the host because of the nature of the transfer process. In some cases, for example, the software is "packetized" to enhance the time of total transfer. Packets of records are then sent to the host where they are, in turn, broken down from the packets into the original configuration format. The effect of this type of file transfer is observed in elapsed transfer time for large data files. The effects on small file sizes may not justify the cost of such packages.

File transfer software is necessary when data transfer requirements exceed the usefulness of limited screen displays. In other words, it is necessary when data must be downloaded in reasonably large quantities for local personal computer processing — quantities much larger than are justifiably feasible in screen-size segments only. The host may not be required for any additional service in processing this downloaded data. An example is transferring financial branch office data to be used in a spreadsheet for planning and projection analysis. There may be no requirement for processing or uploading the data to the host. Consequently, the selected transfer software and its role relative to the host is dictated by the purpose it is to serve.

Advantages and Disadvantages

There are advantages and limitations to using these products. File transfer software can be quite generic in its use and applied across binary, text, or ASCII data. Format conversions may still be required for specific applications, but the more standard are generally included.

A limitation may arise with packages that group data in packets. During asynchronous transmission, start and stop bits are used to determine the beginning and end of a transmission of data. Products that group data in packets may inadvertently create a combination of bits that represent a start or stop indicator, which may prematurely terminate a transmission. There are ways to overcome such situations, depending on the hardware equipment used and the particular package selected. Other limitations depend upon the design of the transfer package relative to transfer efficiency and speed. This becomes a comparison situation when selecting among various products.

Many emulation products contain or offer file transfer software. It may still be advisable to consider other packages in situations involving unique transfer needs or an unusual combination of nonstandard host and personal computer equipment. A complete file transfer system that far surpasses that available with emulation products may be necessary. The cost range varies, depending on whether host software is required and the sophistication level of the package selected.

A great deal also depends on the features supplied by the file transfer package. Such features include security access capability as well as vendor operating systems and application database supported. In some cases the file transfer software requires a portion resident at the host and one portion in the personal computer. The pricing structure is split accordingly between the two parts. An example of such products is RELAY from VM Personal Computing. Simple file transfer capability can be purchased for under $300 for a personal computer. Other file transfer systems range between $800 and $2300 per personal computer for DEC, Burroughs, H-P, and IBM systems, depending on the number of personal computers and operating systems support. More sophisticated transfer systems range up to and exceed $25,000 (which includes a set number of supported workstations), depending on their functionality. RELAY, for example, falls in this latter category.

Application Integrated Interface

Application integrated interface links are sometimes referred to as integrated software links. This means that the micro-mainframe link is specifically a part of the application software that resides on the host computer. As part of the software, link initiation for data transfer is transparent to the user, data is converted to prespecified formats to and from the host, and emulation capability is included. When you purchase the system, you buy the link that is part of the package. When you request data, you do not know how the transfer is implemented, only that the data is presented to you in a form usable by the application. Examples of such links include McCormack & Dodge's PCLink and MSA's PeachLink.

These links, although they use specific terminal emulation products, are generally vendor specific to host application software. In some cases, the personal computer software portion is a subset of its host counterpart. In other cases, the host application system may use a link for compatible movement of data into personal computer productivity tool spreadsheets like Lotus 1-2-3 or Symphony, and Multiplan.

These links embed terminal emulation as part of the system, incorporate file transfer and data reformatting to move data to and from the application, and simplify the user interface by which data requests are made. This greatly simplifies the complexities of retrieving data from a database management system. As an example, assume the host-based system is a financial general ledger package. The personal computer user desires to download data into a Lotus spreadsheet from this host system; however, the data resides in the database used by the financial package. A vendor of such a system provides a user interface that permits the user to define and recall the required data without knowing the internal database structure and the Lotus spreadsheet format to which data is loaded. The user queries for the data on the personal computer; the host system retrieves and consolidates the data from the database and then transfers and reformats the data into the proper rows and columns. Figure 3-8 diagrams such an integrated link.

Considering such a link capability makes sense in at least two situations. The first is one in which a customer already uses a particular vendor's host application software and it is necessary to transfer data to a personal-computer-resident subset of that same software. If the vendor offers an application-integrated link designed specifically for that application, you should definitely consider it, especially if it includes file transfer and data refor-

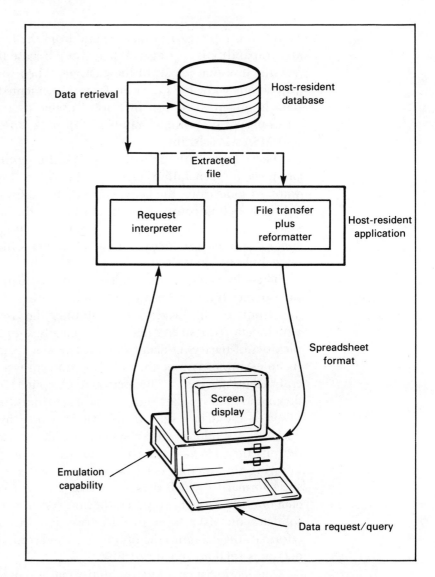

Figure 3-8. ▶

Application integrated link

matting. The second situation is one in which it is appropriate to implement a fully integrated application set and the link capability is a contained subset function; that is, a full systems approach that includes workstation communications.

The advantage is that you can use a single vendor for delivery, installation, and system support. The major limitation is that such a vendor's expertise is usually in developing the software application, not the link. If you want better link capability, for any number of reasons at a future time, you may have very few choices. Your vendor may not immediately support future link technology enhancements.

These application links are much more expensive than emulation or file transfer because of the value added of the application into which they are designed. If MIS and the users require a certain application, there may be no choice but to pay for the system and pay the price of the attendant link. If the application is already installed and personal computer access is required, management may again have no choice but to pay the price.

However, an application vendor eager to entice customers to its higher-priced, higher-margin host software may include links ostensibly free with the purchase of the host product. This situation is expected to become the norm in the future. Prices for these systems can average $25,000 to $50,000 with a specified number of personal computer links configured into the system, say 10. In some cases, as stated, additional personal computer links can range from free to $2500, not including spreadsheet software.

◥ DATABASE INTERFACES

All of the links described thus far rarely offer users any capability that would enhance or help host database access. These links provide very little to the user (except some application interface links) for easy, simple host database access and retrieval. The user must understand the manner in which databases are stored at the host and the record structure governing data storage. Vendors that confronted this personal computer access situation were those offering databases on the host themselves. These vendors include Cullinet and IDMS, Software AG and ADABAS, CINCOM and TOTAL, Hewlett-Packard and IMAGE, to name just a few.

Installations are paying more attention to using relational structure techniques for storing data rather than record formats, although a large number of such record-keeping databases are currently in use. Also, many users have developed their own local databases and would like to supplement them with more comprehensive data that can only be found at the host. So users are expecting to retrieve data on a selective basis rather than by total files. Consequently, products are evolving that permit users to extract data selectively without requiring them to know specifically how data is stored at the host and in what formats.

Database interface products allow data transfer between databases and personal computers, or among host databases. They permit a database subset to be downloaded to a personal computer for manipulation, update, and review without concerning users with the particular system's DBMS dictionary. Host access is, however, provided by means of a terminal emulation access capability that runs on the personal computer. Examples of some of these databases include Cullinet's GoldenGate, Software AG's Natural/Link, and Informatics General's Answer/DB. Figure 3-9 portrays a database interface link.

What about total integration across databases, applications, and hosts? Eventually the industry will see a merging of these particular links as local personal computer databases become more sophisticated and relational. Their association with the structures on the host, although not necessarily identical, will begin to look conceptually alike. You can expect to load subsets of the host database to a workstation and see very little difference with that on the host. MIS will be able to download subsets and know that they correspond to the system and productivity applications that the end users are working with at their stations. This is a natural evolution that will take time.

Advantages and Disadvantages

The advantages of database interface links are obvious. First, if a database is implemented, it provides a compatible method of data transfer to the user. Second, the software and hardware link

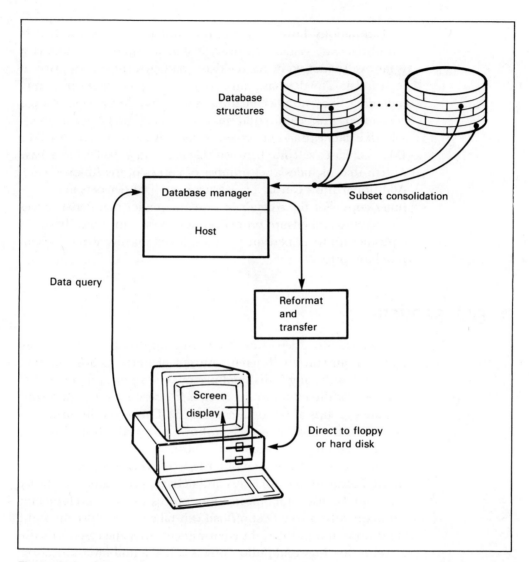

Figure 3-9. ▲

Database interface link

is supported by the database vendor, along with its interfaces to any productivity software. Finally, local personal-computer-hosted databases may one day conform to the same structure as the host's, making a total mirror image transfer of a subset possible.

Limitations, however, are in the implementation cost. Unless a host database system is already installed, incremental link cost is far overshadowed by the database management system price, at least today. The database can easily exceed $100,000 in price and include a fixed number of links, say 10, while the cost of each additional link connection may approach $2000. Conversely, selective data extraction products, such as Answer/DB on IBM's IMS database, sell for between $20,000 and $50,000 for a base system that includes a set number of copies of the link software. Additional links can be priced at up to $600 per personal computer copy. For these database systems, vendor maintenance fees are necessary to ensure proper service; these can typically cost a customer up to 12 percent per year, based on the current system purchase price.

◣ FILE SERVERS

File servers are a departure from other approaches because they represent an entirely different concept of micro-to-host linking. Rather than having individual personal computers linked either remotely or directly into the host, a file server collects and consolidates groups of personal computers. The server, in turn, connects into the host. Figure 3-10 shows pictorially how this type of a configuration appears to the host.

One notable distinction of a file server is that it provides centralized local storage for users and delivers processing capability that can be used for application processing or development. Consequently, a true host offload can take place under the right conditions and in the right environment. In some cases, this file server technology and philosophy is called a mid-layer processor. If implemented properly, file servers can provide users non-host interim processing capability, storage for large file and data downloads from the host, and insulation from system unavailability of the host computer. When users must directly access the host, most file servers offer a feature known as pass-through that enables the personal computer to connect to the host, supposedly without degradation. Hence, host access is preserved along with local operation.

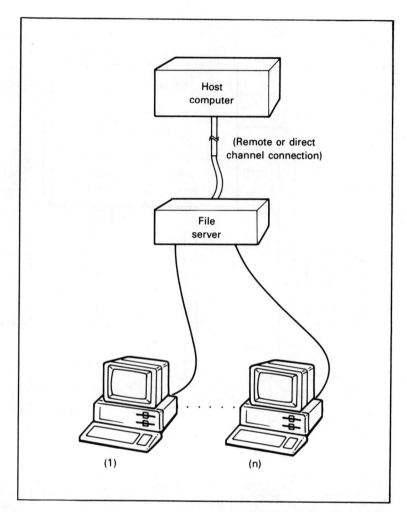

(Remote or direct channel connection)

Host computer

File server

(1)   (n)

Figure 3-10. ▶

File server configuration (1)

Figure 3-11 displays a detailed expansion of a pseudo file server. Simplistically, the server is managed by some operating system, contains a reasonably expandable memory capability that may range to several megabytes, supports a complement of direct access storage of several million megabytes, and can generally attach a tape drive for use in emergency backup and recovery situations. Typically optional is a redundant internal battery power supply that can be used if a power outage occurs. It is

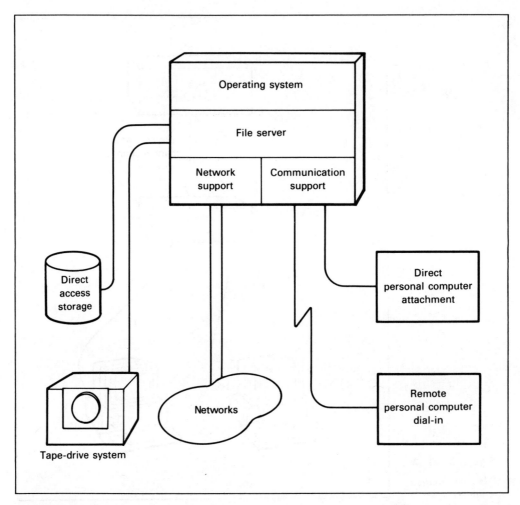

Figure 3-11. ▲

*File server
configuration (2)*

intended to sustain server operation up to 30 minutes, primarily
to initiate an emergency backup. Terminal emulation capability
is contained on the file server for use by all attached personal
computers, and other mutually usable software can be contained
on the file server as well.

A file server's role relative to users is to provide processing
and data transfer capabilities that under normal operation are

generally provided by a host. The file server is expected to achieve a certain level of performance that may not be possible from the host because of other system demands on host resources. Hence, in certain circumstances file servers can be interposed between the host and the users to achieve an interactive and processing performance standard. Relative to the host, the file server can be viewed as a vehicle that frees the host from the constant servicing of user data transfer requests and other activities that distract the host from concentrated service of large processing requirements.

File servers are best viewed as a way to insulate a group of users whose work activities can, in fact, be isolated from the host. The server acts as a host gateway for processing file transfer up or down from the host to the end user.

When is such a file server technology useful and appropriate? This concept is very useful for creating nodes of users whose processing and data uploading and downloading requirements can be managed and predicted to a reasonable extent. The group of users can remain almost autonomous from actual host support, and periodic host requests by individual users will remain the exception rather than the rule during the normal course of the day.

File Server Applications

Let's profile two examples of environments suitable for a file server. The first entails a group of chemists, remote from the host, performing specific data analysis with the same scientific analysis routines regardless of the product laboratory data. Products differ and require test data on a regular daily basis. It is not possible to store all historical test data at the chemists' workbench; it must be databased at the host.

Beginning each day, appropriate tests can be predetermined for use by the chemists during that day's activity. It is possible to download a predefined set of data to the file server for access by all chemists. Tests can be run against the products and, if additional test data is required, the chemist may request data from the

the host through the file server for downloading. During the test period, the chemist performs all storage and processing of data at the server, not at the host. At the end of the day, server data is uploaded to the host database along with additional tests the chemists may have written to supplement the historical data.

Aside from downloading and uploading, analysis routines are resident and executed at the server along with specific routines that may be generated by the chemists. The chemists are, in effect, isolated from the host; they perform all day with little host interaction. Security can be maintained within that group of individuals using the specific file server, and redundancy can be achieved by adding a second server for a backup if necessary. Data backup can be achieved via a separate tape system driven by the server.

The second example is a financial institution that permits corporate customers to perform their own daily portfolio analysis. At the beginning of each day, the host downloads the portfolio files to the server, which allows customer dial-up. Customers access their own private data and manage their business for the day. At day's end, the server uploads changed files into a host area for later updating into the master database system. The data download is predictable, customers need not access host data directly, and usage and access is restricted to the server in question. Most customer data modifications resemble data entry, and files that are uploaded automatically undergo host audit trail generation and reconciliation.

Advantages and Disadvantages

Advantages of servers are that they offload personal computer to host linking, support LANs (local area networks, described later), offload host processing requirements, and offer another alternative to security levels. Regarding the latter, most servers provide for log-on identification, password protection, and file authorization for file access. This is in addition to that which is already installed and implemented on the host.

The disadvantages of file servers center around the fact that they require a certain level of expertise to maintain the system's operation and identify failures to the vendor for proper servicing. The server may be in an area where data processing and communications expertise is not available, such as in a financial users department. If the product should fail or encounter operational problems, there must be some level of expertise to define the problem and possibly help to correct the situation.

The Bottom Line

Servers are initially a great deal more expensive when compared to other micro link products such as terminal emulation directly connected into the host. Their relative cost can be argued quite heavily, depending on business objectives, long- and short-term factors, and expected product life. For now, let's disregard the natural price erosion that will occur over time as technology improves and volume decreases manufacturing costs as installations and server shipments increase. Let's look at today's comparison under today's microscope.

First, let's take the argument for the system cost as a disadvantage. Prices range from a low of $10,000 to as high as $50,000. These prices depend on the operating system license fee, megabytes of main storage, megabytes of external direct access storage, tape drive size (megabytes), network and communications port support, and terminal emulation support, not to mention application software that might be available. They do not include additional cable costs, use of a LAN, or other factors related to the general environment, which may include remote operation support costs. On a direct comparison basis, it seems they call for a substantially higher initial cash outlay.

However, let's assume that your kid (age 5, of course) wants a truck, but not the cheap one made of plastic for $2.95. No, not on your life. It's got to be the one painted with bright red colors, made of high-grade steel sturdy enough for dropping and pushing through those dirt hills. Price tag: $49.95. Depending on the situation at the time (and the kid's temperament), you just may get by with the $2.95 truck, and it may be the best truck for you, given how it will be used over a very short time. On the other hand, the steel truck will certainly last much longer, probably not break as easily, and may even last until your offspring enters junior high. So the $49.95 investment measured over these factors and time may be the most sound investment. Such may be the case with file servers.

The following key items must be weighed when considering the cost of a server architecture and implementation:

- Expected operational life
- Number of attached personal computers
- Projected growth of server system
- Degree of host offloading
- Reduction in data transfer costs
  Line time if remote
  Host service capacity
- Server capacity expansion
- Personal computer configurations
  With hard disk (10 Mb, 20 Mb, or greater)
  Floppy disks only
- Shared resource usage
  Storage
  Printers
  Application software
  Multiple host access.

Each item can be defined and evaluated relative to the business activity and services it needs to support, then ranked according to its importance. This information can then be translated into costs, and related to the configuration.

When you consider these factors, the cost of a file server may not be as unattractive over the long term as it may initially seem. Also bear in mind that a minicomputer can be used to fulfill the same purpose, although it too carries the same disadvantages described earlier.

◥ LOCAL AREA NETWORKS (LANS)

Local area networks have been talked about and used in various forms for some time, even though they are not as widespread as vendors hoped. The LAN industry is prime for growth and is experiencing long-awaited expansion as users become more familiar with LAN capabilities and application software and services evolve to support LANs. These products clearly and most definitely have a role in linking personal computers to hosts and servicing the needs of end users in more than one type of environment. IBM's 1986 introductions in the area of connectivity also display a reliance on LAN technology as a means of tying systems together. IBM acknowledges the dispersion of processing to end users, and is offering products such as its own token-ring LAN to spur this growth.

The real key is how company management goes about defining the need for LAN technology and how it selects the approach that contributes most to business needs and future expansion. How are they used? What types exist? What capabilities do they offer? What applications are designed for LANs? What form of LAN should be chosen? Before proceeding into this arena, answering these questions and more is critical.

When discussing specific products, many distinctions separate LANs. Each distinction is peculiar to the way the vendor addresses the actual technical connectivity, expandability, performance, and function. This book does not provide an in-depth analysis of LAN technology. This section briefly provides some background on the types of LANs and the considerations of planning their use from a business as opposed to technical perspective. Consequently, it does not discuss or contrast the merits of token ring versus other forms of LANs, nor does it discuss effects from any one particular vendor's market presence.

First, we hear a lot about baseband, broadband, wide-area, and now limited-area networks (LmANs). This can be confusing, and unless you are a confident and capable system designer or network specialist, you can feel intimidated just discussing this technology. So let's provide you with enough information to differentiate all of these types. This way, at least you will understand their roles relative to your own company needs and the geographical distribution of your users and services. In particular, you can think of these technologies in terms of the present and future growth of the kind of installation you wish to provide and the kind of budget you know makes the most sense for your company, both short and long term.

LANs connect workstations so that they can communicate to each other. LANs can be connected in several topologies, including a star, ring, or bus (some refer to this as a backbone), as shown in Figure 3-12. For now, we will not portray a different configuration for baseband and broadband to display the different hardware required.

Baseband LANs

Without getting into the technical details, a baseband LAN connects workstations with standard twisted pairs of wire similar to those used to wire telephones. It carries information on the wire in digital formats so that no digital/analog or analog/digital conversion is required. All data is sent at the same frequency, so special equipment at either end is not necessary to convert from one frequency to another.

These network types are typically less expensive and easier to install than other LAN configurations; they perform at high speeds approaching 10 Mb per second, which makes them useful where high-speed transmission is desirable. Their data transmission range is generally limited to between 3000 and 6000 feet unless special pieces of equipment called "repeaters" are used to regenerate the data signal during transmission. A second disadvantage is that such a system is more susceptible to noise-created errors because the cable and wire are not shielded.

Broadband LANs

Broadband LANs connect workstations together using coaxial cable in much the same way as your cable TV works. The data

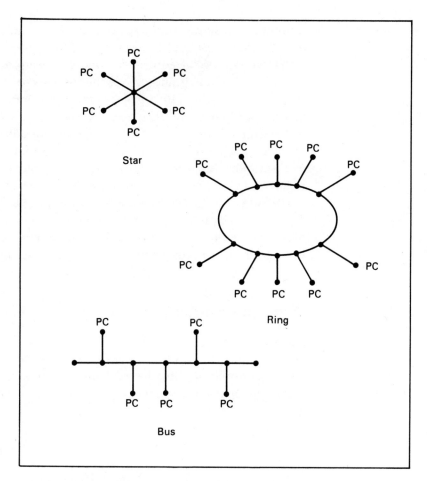

Figure 3-12. ▶

Star, ring, and bus LAN topologies

(in digital format) is converted at the point of transmission to an analog signal that is then sent across the cable at some frequency. The system divides the carrying capacity of the cable into multiple channels, each capable of supporting a different frequency. Thus, many different types of data, each with a different frequency, can be transmitted across the same cable. That is why broadband LANs are useful to companies that desire data and video conferencing across the same network. Baseband LANs cannot do this because the wire is not divided into multiple channels for carrying information. Performance is in the 2-Mb-per-second range, and because of radio frequency transmission technology, distance between workstations is measured in terms of miles (like 10 to 30) rather than in feet.

However, special equipment and hardware are required to condition the signals and decode the frequencies at the receiving end for broadband. This involves amplifiers, frequency splitters, and a "head end," a device used to receive the analog signal at one frequency and convert it to another. Broadband LANs are more expensive than baseband on an initial cost and per-workstation basis because of this extra equipment. The system, however, is less susceptible to noise than baseband.

Broadband is a good choice for developing a "backbone" or "spine" configuration with smaller baseband and broadband networks connected into this arrangement. The networks can be structured into compartments that support user needs.

Wide Area LANS

The easiest way to think of wideband LANs is to think in terms of very large distances (distances of several hundred miles) across which information must be transmitted. These distances do not make a great deal of economical sense for pure broadband LANs. They traverse users in different cities and counties over a wide geographical area; hence, wide-area networks.

The primary way to reach such widely dispersed users is via some form of network similar to a telephone switching station, or PBX (Private Branch Exchange). In essence, message-switching technology is used to network stations to each other. Only a modem and phone set need be available at the user end.

The obvious advantages lie in using technology that has been tested for many years and enhancing the usage of an existing PBX. The disadvantages will depend solely on the current installation and its technology use relative to PBXs, and whether the installed PBX offers sufficient capacity to meet the data transfer demands that may come with such a configuration. Installation planning must take into account the demands that will prevail over servicing widely dispersed users and the types of demands they impose on information need. Figure 3-13 shows how such a wide-area network would appear to the system.

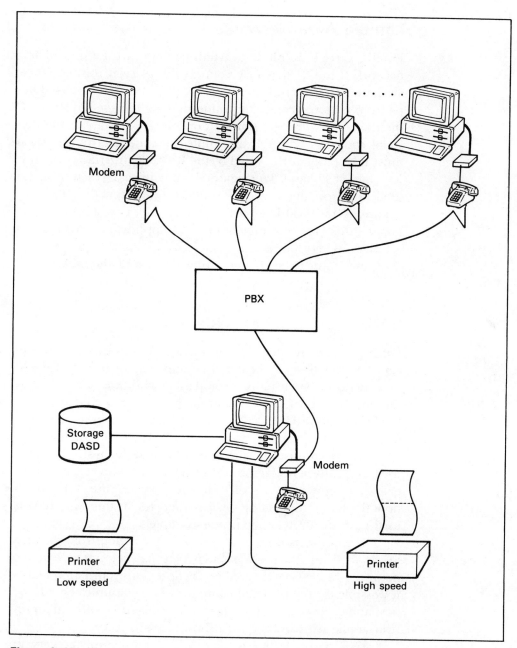

Figure 3-13. ▲

Wide-area network configuration

Limited Area Networks

Finally, there is an old but revitalized term called a limited-area network (LmAN) that may confuse things even further. These are networks that use twisted-pair wiring just like baseband but perform personal computer connection via the age-old RS-232C interface ports that are standard on every workstation and personal computer. LmANs are limited because data transmission must take place at the speed of the RS-232C interface, which is less than 9600 baud. Workstations can connect to each other via modems, providing a wide-area networking capability. In many situations, the 9600-baud limitation may not pose a big problem because this may be sufficient for most applications. Also, use of a LmAN is very inexpensive: they cost under $100 per personal computer connection, not counting the cost of the modem.

LAN/Host Connections

For personal computer access to occur, LANs must have a way to connect into hosts. Whether baseband, broadband, or LmAN, these networks are usually incompatible with those supported by the host. If it's DEC, you confront DECnet. For IBM it's SNA; for Prime, it's PRIMENET. Consequently, a gateway is needed to connect dissimilar network types. If LANs are of the same type and are compatible with each other and the host, a bridge is used. Basically, a bridge connects LANs of the same type, while a gateway connects LANs of different types. Figure 3-14 shows how these two connecting devices are used. In this case, IBM is used with the 3270 as the prime example.

The gateway is needed to make the translation from the protocols used on the LAN between personal computers and the network protocols recognized by the host. This translation makes it possible for the personal computers to communicate with the host and vice versa. So the gateway is necessary to interlink multiple connected workstations if host access is to occur.

LANs, particularly baseband LANs, are complementary to file servers in that the two can work in concert with each other

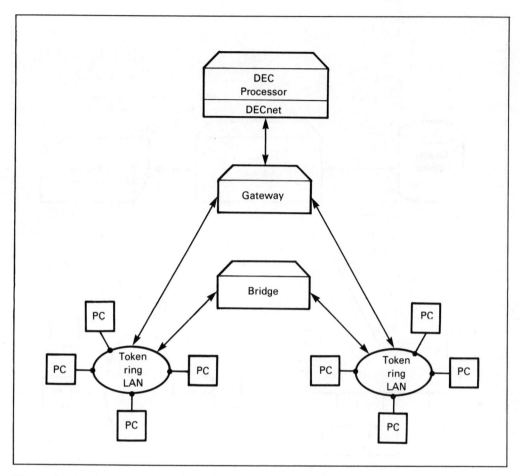

Figure 3-14. ▲

*Gateways and
bridges for
network-to-network
connection*

and fill a role that supplements host access in a number of ways. As stated earlier, file servers can act as gateways, provide local storage for data file download use and multiple sharing, provide shared resource usage for such peripherals as printers, and offer additional security features that complement those on the host.

In short, file servers used in conjunction with LANs can provide benefits associated with file server use and additional processing capability wholly supportive to the LAN. They may even

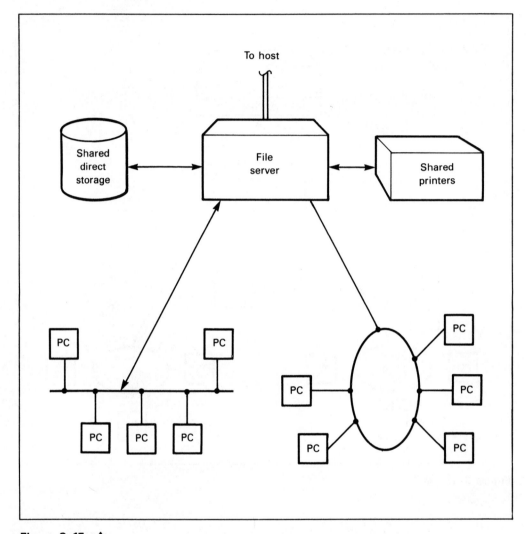

Figure 3-15. ▲

File server/LAN configuration

reduce the workstation or personal computer configuration required by the user. Figure 3-15 profiles use of a file server to support multiple LAN configurations. Different vendors market server and LAN-supported technology. However, the variety of offerings is increasing, and token ring may slowly evolve as an industry standard.

Typical LAN Applications

LANs are typically appropriate for considerations involving groups or departments of individuals that are in a single area and most often perform the same type of function; for example, in banks this may be a portfolio managment department, and in other companies it may be the cost accounting function. LANs should also be considered when it is desirable to isolate a particular group of individuals from access to hosts and maintain additional levels of security. In the latter case, such a use would probably involve a file server. Other situations may involve user groups that need to exchange or share similar data. One example may be the use of an electronic mailing system or a document interchange capability.

The largest LAN advantage is interuser communications without the drain of excessive host resources. The disadvantages, however, involve the choice of software to support LAN technology, security, and cost. Software applications for LANs play a large role in installation definition. What type of functions are supported and how will they be implemented within the LAN? These applications will greatly influence the LAN's effectiveness if it is to be used for more than simply communications peripheral sharing without the need to share files with multiple access.

Security is a consideration for LANs not linked to hosts via file servers that provide record and file locking or additional password protection. Costs are an issue when choosing a LAN, because there are hidden as well as direct costs. LAN connection costs will vary widely, depending on the number of personal computers connected, the LAN type chosen (broadband, and so forth), whether a disk server or file server is used, cost of the actual cable, and other salient aspects of selecting, operating, and implementing a LAN.

◥ FINDING SOLUTIONS

The important point about all of the categories discussed in this chapter are that there are a great many selection opportunities for planning and implementing a strategy to link workstations with hosts. Each category lends itself to a wide range of considerations and "beforehand" thought that must go into defining the appropriate network and mode of solution.

To be solution oriented implies that you have an interest in solving and removing problems. By just picking a link product without carefully thinking about what its ultimate use is to be may prove costly and tragic at a later date. If you view the linking or personal computer integration problem from an application and system viewpoint, you can minimize wasted motion toward the selection process. If you define the needs, compartmentalize solution possibilities, and view possible products within categories and combinations of categories, you can open a variety of ways to build a framework that you can expand upon as time and needs dictate.

The rest of this book is concerned with helping management and those responsible for defining and implementing link integration systems ask the right questions and assimilate answers and restrictions into a usable plan and implementation philosophy. Our goal is not just to provide a framework but also to provide an understanding of the process by which such link integration must be managed.

4 Communications And the End User

❐ CONTEMPORARY COMMUNICATIONS
❐ THE NETWORK'S ROLE AND THE END USER

Let's talk about communications at a *personal* level, relative to what we can associate it with in our daily lives. We can almost see personal computers as a surrogate to personal interaction. When it comes right down to it, we are all used to talking with one another, although at times this is a rather difficult thing for us to do. So it is with personal computers linked to hosts: sometimes it is rather difficult to do.

The concept of communications has changed significantly in the last several decades. In the 1960s, communications simply meant having a dialogue between two or more people; it had nothing to do with computers. Few people thought of electronic transmission of data and information as we know it today. Yet today it is almost expected that we be able to reach into other databases for information that we need to do our jobs.

Why can't personal computers talk to each other in the same way? To communicate implies conveying to a person our thoughts and ideas, and exchanging information that contributes to our understanding of what we want and need. This takes place on a personal basis as well as at a business level, where information transfer is imperative.

75

◣ CONTEMPORARY COMMUNICATIONS

However, when the "electronic age" dawned, the word *communications* assumed an entirely different meaning. We began to view it in a kind of space-age world. We all wanted people to know that we understood what was happening in the world of computers and were not initimidated by the use of this word. The word *communications* took on the connotation of connecting machines together electronically so that information could be freely obtained and transferred.

Through the 1970s people began to become comfortable with computers. Terminals began appearing in banks, retail stores, and in business and office environments. When the personal computer exploded on the scene in the late 1970s and early 1980s, even children suddenly became computer literate. To most people, the word *communications* now means how to connect a system or workstation into other systems to access data.

When personal computers started to become everyday tools, we began to think of ways we could use them that would contribute to productivity in business and enjoyment in the home. Entire businesses evolved around just such applications. We became comfortable with the fact that a home or personal computer could provide access to information that before was only available to those who had special skills or authorization.

Beyond the horizon, technology is moving us toward voice recognition and verbal input that will bring us full cycle back to our most comfortable means of communications. As a start, we need only to witness the evolution of integrating voice communications with data to reduce overall equipment and communications costs and obtain improved line usage. It is this usage and data transfer efficiency that saves money.

Communications is changing, and we as end users expect current and reliable information when we request it. We want to access different systems and databases, and we expect to do so relatively freely and easily. In addition, we want to do this from our personal computers, which are what we have on our desktops, what we are familiar with, and what we find to be productive and flexible tools. With modems and telephone dial-up, we can access virtually any database anywhere.

How the Flow of Information
Is Changing

We have become conditioned to being able to obtain as much information as we want (which, however, does not necessarily mean as much as we need). Previously, all electronic data passed through an intermediary group that had the responsibility of generating programs to extract data from corporate databases. Computer systems were complex vehicles that did not lend themselves well to everyday end-user programming. The language of communicating instructions to computers was not friendly. Database structures and access rules, not to mention formats, were so complex that they required a skilled programmer to understand and extract data.

In addition, companies found it necessary to protect corporate database access for reasons of security, sabotage, and misuse. Obtaining data for your own use required you to have intimate knowledge of how to communicate with the host computer. This is the reason system programmers were so indispensible and paid so well. They kept the mystique (knowingly or unknowingly) so that no one else really knew what to do. They created the aura that only few came to understand and accept. Knowing what data you needed was one thing, but getting it required you to use a different and somewhat mysterious process altogether.

The process of obtaining information consisted of the following:

- Data specification — Defining what information the user wanted.

- Application specification — Defining what the program looks like to extract the information.

- Application development — Writing the application.

- Application test — Testing the application.

- Paper report — Providing the user with a listing of the requested data.

- User verification — Validating that the data provided is the data that was requested.

We can also summarize the process graphically, as shown in Figure 4-1.

You can modify these six steps, but the general idea is the same. Users never did have full control over how they obtain or manipulate data. The process always entailed a request to MIS management, and scheduling occurred based upon MIS priorities, never under user control. The end user initiated the data-gathering process, lost control over the activity to get the data, and then regained control over future access to the same data after the data access application software was delivered. In this

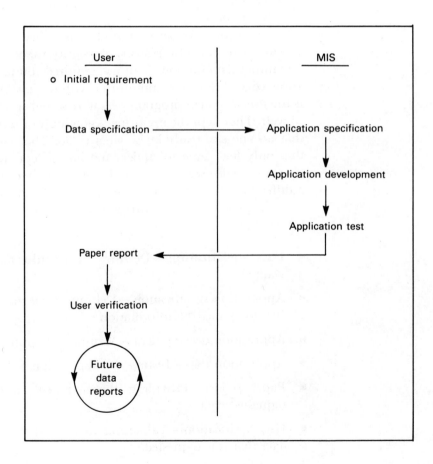

Figure 4-1. ▶

The information collection process

case, the micro-mainframe link and the communications vehicle happened to be the MIS department and its programmers.

By the very nature of its design, information flow had to be interrupted with a manual process. You can associate getting data from a host to talking with a foreign ambassador through an interpreter. The process can be slow and cumbersome, depending on how good your intermediary happens to be. Communications linking could not be an automatic action between the user and the host computer because there were no facilities that were capable of doing such interpreting. Hardware and software had not been created to permit linking.

Information Centers

Since the 1960s, bringing computing to end users has become essential. The evolution of technology and its effect on the availability of computing increased the demand by users to "roll their own" applications and develop and retrieve their own data. The concept of the information center, which was formally initiated in a marketing sense by IBM, answered this demand. Other computer vendors began to embrace the concept in an effort to provide their own customer base with equivalent capabilities. As a tool, the information center provided the power to meet end-user data access and development demand.

The information center utilizes an entirely separate computer to serve end users in an interactive manner (see Figure 4-2). Tools such as program generators, high-level languages, graphics packages, and analysis or decision support capability, which are placed on this host, offer users an environment in which they can develop their own applications. With an information center, a company can isolate end-user activity, release MIS from massive support burdens, and temporarily satisfy end-users' demands for control over their own destinies. Linkages are supplied to permit access to that specific system. Scheduling capabilities that allow jobs to be executed on some other possible system are added as an additional tool.

Although information centers enjoy wide industry usage,

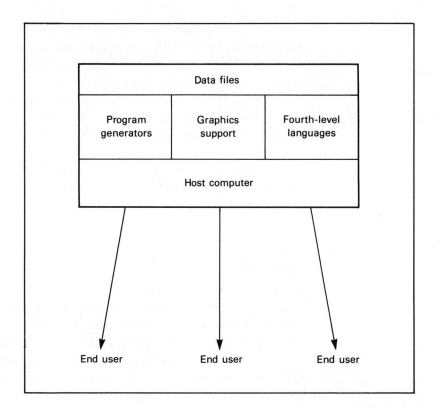

Figure 4-2. ▶

An information center

they are not links in their purest form and do not generally ease information flow to others than those designated to use the center. If the data that the user requires is not at the information center's host, there is little recourse but to go elsewhere. What an information center *does* do is to place an enormous amount of expensive system resources at users' fingertips. In many cases, there are still the problems of transferring data from some other host corporate database computer to the information center and of moving the data from the center to the user.

However, information flow is changing: users now know that somewhere there is data that can help them resolve problems, track business changes, and test hypotheses about new markets and products. They expect to access information at the point where it is resident. They no longer expect to have to make requests to MIS groups. They expect to define the type of information they need, know where to get it, and figure out how to use it. The micro-mainframe link plays a critical role in this process.

The Management Viewpoint

If we acknowledge that users do need data and that they are the best ones to decide what data they want, the question becomes: What is the best way to supply the information to the users, and how do we deliver it in an efficient and cost-effective way? The plethora of micro-mainframe link product options available does not help resolve the problem, particularly if the installation does not have an overall communications strategy. If management is attempting to satisfy end-user requirements as they arise without a definitive plan, confusion results, which compounds the problem of selecting and installing micro-mainframe links.

Data processing management and systems planning people look at linking issues in a different way. Management wants to satisfy end-user needs while dealing with problems of communications growth, security, database contamination, network flexibility, future upgrade ability, system resource utilization, and data file recovery and backup.

From management's vantage point, most information flow is *away* from the corporate database. Users access the system, transfer data to their workstations or personal computers, and transfer it back after they have made changes. However, if the retrieved data has been changed, management is skeptical and reluctant to permit unlimited uploading back into the original files without first scrutinizing the changes for integrity. You can't blame them for being concerned about a serious problem and wanting to maintain a system that is good for everyone. It's their job to make sure that everyone can have good data and that critical work is not negatively affected. Suppose that you made an error and loaded bad data over good. You would certainly be upset if MIS management said that they couldn't recover from the mishap. You would be even more angry if someone else destroyed your data and you couldn't recover.

This situation does not apply to all installations and environments. In some cases, it is desirable to upload data back to the host computer—for example, to update corporate data or for document processing once analysis is completed. For years we have used key entry and data entry systems to update files of master databases. Although you may call it by a different name, you are still using a form of host link to move data to the host. This information flow is from the end user to the corporate host database.

A system with one-way transfer partially satisfies the problem. By using a set of controls and established procedures, you can maintain flexibility on both sides. However, such controls should not create a bureaucratic structure that will deter users from using the system.

◥ THE NETWORK'S ROLE AND THE END USER

End users should never have to perceive a network or micro-mainframe link as a physical entity. It must remain a concept, not appear as some durable piece of equipment that must be used to perform a job. Beyond being familiar with simple access procedures, users should not have to know techniques for getting to certain information. Query is essential for user data access; it cannot be complicated with detailed language formats and still remain easy to use in a communications sense.

Successful businesses make it easy for users to access information to monitor and manage the business, track potential growth markets, and identify new business possibilities. The successful business develops a communications layer that remains independent of the application it serves. Thus, users can move data across this layer independent of the applications for which it is intended.

Networks can be expected to continue to grow and get larger, rarely decreasing in size or facility. The network (nodes and connections) always increases if the network is doing its job and supplying quality service to users. As users get accustomed to electronically moving about an organization, more applications arise, and the network becomes even more secondary and transparent to their needs. It becomes merely a conduit for movement and is taken for granted.

Links must conform to the standards and protocols the installation uses. There are many options to choose from, and, although there is industry hope that some standards will evolve, today's environment dictates that there be multiple links and networks. There are so many different corporate and end-user data access requirements that there must be a variety of link products. Until there is a standard (if ever) in the distant future, management is forced to wade through the design and link selection process. Their basic goal is to optimize information flow.

Performance demands on both the host and networks increase as such network expansion takes place. This expansion is governed both by available host resources and by personal computer connection demand. To connect personal computers and workstations to hosts and maintain acceptable user response time, the host must be able to service peak loading and a rising number of users. If the host offers no space capacity and resources, performance is almost certain to degrade as the network and connecting micro-mainframe links expand. If the network does not perform, usage and satisfaction decline.

Finally, networks never remain constant. End users find ways to navigate to information files and databases that are necessary for their jobs. Networks hardly ever remain static. In general, having on-line capabilities almost always calls for continually increasing service standards. The basic configuration of a network can remain the same, but the services, applications, data transfer, and tools available constantly change.

The network's role with regard to end users is beginning to become transparent. Information flow can occur and be directed to and from any location or stored for later use at any host. Micro-to-mainframe links are becoming integrated portions of these networks because they fill a need that deals with pure connectivity. The end user does not, and should not, care whether access is provided via Ethernet, bisynchronous lines, leased lines, DECnet, PRIMENET, SNA/SDLC, or asynchronous modems (to name just a few). These are only system-level considerations.

The End-User Viewpoint

End users view a network system as an easy-to-navigate highway to a final destination. The highway should appear like an interstate with optional turn-offs rather than a secondary road with stop signs, directional lights, and stoplights at which decisions must be continually made. This is not much different from today's users dealing with such factors as file size, time to transmit across lines, alternates to schedule and process transmission, errors encountered during transmission, or how to recover damaged data sets.

End users look at their workstations and personal computers as processing tools that should provide them with a means to circumnavigate the information globe. They look at their workstations and say "What do I need to do today? What do I want it to do? If I can't do it all at my own desktop, where do I need to go?" Their decision processes are focused on the desktop tool at hand, not on the network.

◥ SUMMARY

As Figure 4-3 illustrates, end users view network systems as an amorphous cloud, which they enter and leave with ease. Data center management must decide how to attach them to the network. That same management must decide (although often with strong user input to guide them) how the database is structured and what access is available. Systems individuals and those responsible for the operation of the network system concern themselves with aspects of data flow and host loads.

Having seen many management and technical activities regarding micro-mainframe links and the businesses they support, we can assure you that there are ways to size and develop the task of integrating personal computers without sacrificing timeliness and cost.

A methodical approach is appropriate where it can be applied. We admit that there are instances in which the best approach is to install several link types, choose one that works

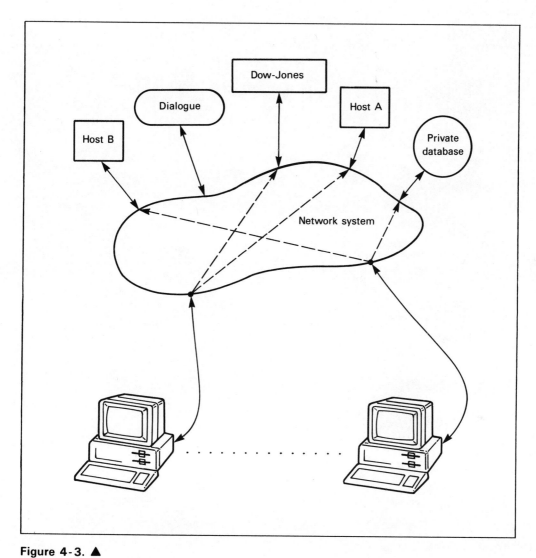

Figure 4-3. ▲

*The end user's
view of a network
system*

the best for your needs, and stabilize (not necessarily standardize)
on that choice. The difference involves a seeding approach to
addressing integration versus a planned staged development. We
treat both as appropriate in this book.

5 Assessing Integration Needs

❚ ASSESSING NEEDS
❚ LINKING SUCCESS FACTORS
❚ HOST/WORKSTATION APPLICATIONS
❚ PROFILING PERSONAL-COMPUTER-TO-HOST
  CONNECTION
❚ THE EVOLVING HOST ROLE
❚ DATA INTEGRITY, SECURITY, AND CONTROL

If you already know your PC and system integration needs, you can skip directly to the next chapter, which is devoted to planning approaches for personal computer integration. However, if you are just beginning the assessment process and need to develop a representative profile of what workstation integration needs exist in your organization, then you should read this chapter.

❚ ASSESSING NEEDS

There are two schools of thought. One says you don't have to assess needs but instead permit growth and allow issues to resolve themselves over time. This management theory sometimes works, if the organization provides enough time and dollars. However, in many situations, this type of expansion occurs unsuccessfully.

The second school of thought says you can control growth by servicing priority needs first. It doesn't mean that you resist user demands; rather, you tackle the assessment of needs in areas and departments that express an immediate requirement for linking personal computers—end-user computing. Begin your penetration here, experiment a little, and learn what works best before proliferating it all over. The opposite of unchecked growth, this approach lets you keep the process bounded. You can assess your needs on a smaller scale, knowing what the ground rules are for integration into the rest of the business.

Issues of keeping your link and data processing operation efficient and cost effective are another matter entirely. Usually, you have a system that services users because it is necessary. You often haven't had time to optimize it for peak performance, but it runs. Keeping up with user demands is difficult enough without concerning yourself with fine-tuning the system or identifying areas where money is wasted.

If your job is to manage and operate data centers and contain costs, you have probably assumed a position of responsibility for correcting a poorly operated and organized situation. You often say, "Why did they do it this way? It doesn't make sense." In a case like this, you need to put structure around the situation. You need to organize your approach and establish a process by which you and your people can bring about change. It is this process that is important.

Though unencumbered growth doesn't work on a large scale, it can be successful in specific areas if you closely monitor it. Unencumbered growth never works if the area permitted to grow unchecked cannot be insulated from the rest of the data processing community, and if it directly affects host operations. Situations like this create a negative rippling effect on performance, response time, throughput, and host capacity.

Assessing personal computer integration needs requires stepping back, observing what exists, and paying attention to the types of business and user activity that are occurring. You should look at personal computer integration from the totality of the organization and data transfer systems that are currently operating. In some cases, you must be compatibile with existing systems; in others, you may need to change some systems to accommodate the integration. Ultimately, you need a foundation to encompass existing, changed, and new systems.

Figure 5-1 provides a process flow of determining your needs and the key questions to answer. It can guide you in your assessment and help you put a framework around determining your needs within a set of given business and system knowns. Note that when you define your business needs, you actually have two options. The first is that if the needs for the application don't fit your existing business plans, you can go through another evaluation. Second, and often forgotten, is that you can reevaluate your existing business plans. Sometimes the application needs are the reality that makes you reconsider your posture in other areas. Don't be afraid if this happens to you.

So what do you do and how do you proceed within the process framework illustrated?

A Time for Addressing Personal Computer Integration

Your time to actively confront and address host integration is now. Actively confront it methodically. Don't just pick link products here and there, test them, and guess they'll work all right. Find answers to the questions that make your whole approach a process of solution, not tolerance.

If you want to point to your data center and its handling of personal-computer-to-host linking as a showcase, you have to start with some commitment and enthusiasm. It's a matter of taking charge and not reacting to the pressures of a situation with haphazard solutions that don't provide a framework. If you aren't careful, sooner or later you can find yourself out of control. That's when your boss strolls into your office to ask what you're doing about this end-user computing situation. Then what do you say? We're still looking at it? Action brings about solutions.

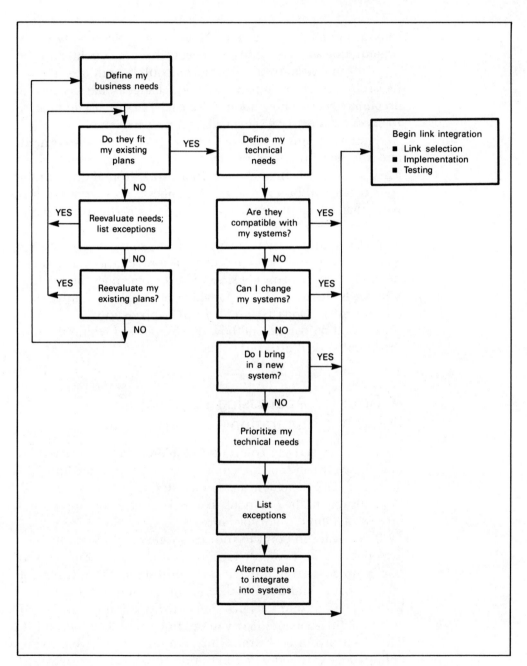

Figure 5-1. ▲

*Approach for
assessing needs*

Determine	What applications exist What works today What is needed tomorrow
Review	How users interrelate with the host How users process data with the host
Understand	Where the business is moving How this affects personal computer connectivity What communications are required
Assimilate	What resource requirements are needed for the business (people and communications)
Identify	What role personal computers play How personal computer usage is growing What host systems are intended with this growth
Define	How data interchange takes place across software applications What data integrity issues exist What security steps are necessary
Develop	An approach satisfying personal flexibility A process for expanding personal computer growth

Table 5-1. ▲

Active steps in solving end-user problems

Table 5-1 identifies steps that you can take to solve end-user computing problems.

Millions of standalone personal computers and workstations are in the business community and are used as an adjunct to host processing. Standalone stations that do not connect to any host are distributed computing tools on the user's desktop that go nowhere. These stations are integral to the business. But for them to become a cohesive part of your overall data processing operation, they must access the same databases and file systems as directly connected dumb terminals. It's like a spider web that grows larger and larger.

Personal computers are scattered about doing useful work, but they would be more effective if they were integrally woven into the fabric of your entire data processing system. You have at your fingertips a tool that users are clamoring to use. You don't even have to sell them on the idea. Whether they need it or not, they want to use it. The timing is perfect: you have 100 percent user support. Grab that support and run.

To integrate these workstations, you must pay attention to communications. Every micro-mainframe link, LAN, or file server is a communications product that in itself starts to become a network. This part is your contribution to end-user computing.

Communications Costs Are Critical

Communications costs are a critical part of the data processing budget. Their importance continues to increase because almost everything that is done involves communications in one form or another. Voice communications, data communications, and micro-mainframe links are all percentages of this budget. As the industry continues to progress to distributed computing, communications and information transfer costs become increasingly important business issues.

Communications is a natural process as businesses increase sales coverage, open branch offices, automate production facilities and laboratory environments, and service other companies. Large cost efficiencies can be achieved with good analysis and network design. Expenditures for hardware, software, and services to implement a cohesive design can pay for themselves in 6 to 18 months simply from the savings in ongoing operational costs. The payback time varies, depending on the situation and, of course, on the nature of the business and how end users must be serviced.

You know that the cost of transferring data is increasing and that this trend is ongoing. But how you measure this increasing part of your data processing expenses depends largely on what you include as a communications "cost." For example, some companies only discuss the cost of transmitting data, while others consider only voice telecommunications costs. But telecommunications costs cannot be contained strictly to direct costs of your particular data center. There are also the costs of telephone lines, ongoing charges for using these lines, and so on.

Overall, there is a much broader definition of communications costs in today's computing environment. Anything that contributes to the need to move data is a cost of communications. This includes micro-mainframe links, personal computers, dumb terminals, desktop systems, integrated voice/data systems, use of public networks like Telenet, and modems. Personal computers and terminals are included in this definition because they directly affect the need for connection into hosts and service for data transfer, no matter how trivial. When you consider all of this, your total communications cost increases are very large.

In 1983, 1984, and 1985, given this broader definition, end-user communications costs ranged between 10 percent and 20 percent of the total data processing budget. The spread is largely due to the size of the business and the dispersement of users across a geographical area. Even if this percentage does not grow over the next five years (and it is projected to do so by almost all market research companies), the number of dollars continues to be significant because total company data processing budgets are increasing. This is true because it has always been true. It is the cost of doing business.

Issues of Scale

One key to success in assessing requirements for linking personal computers and workstations into hosts is to keep things in perspective. For example, the analysis and needs for a company with several hosts operating 600 dumb terminals and 200 personal computers is different from those of a company with a single host operating 10 personal computers. Issues and concerns of the latter are no less significant, but the solution changes.

Depending on your stage and particular needs, what is important to your company differs from what is critical to another, even in the same industry. Figure 5-2 shows a hypothetical situation in which company size can affect various factors in linking personal computers. The triangle for each company

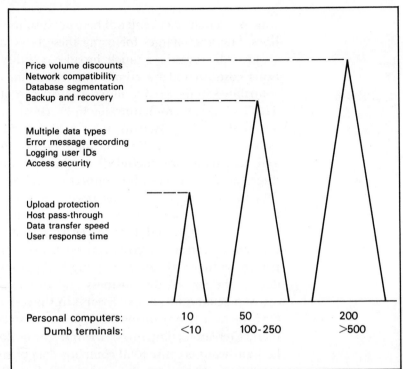

Figure 5-2. ▶

Relative importance of issues across customer size

merely suggests that response time and access security are important in the 10-PC company, while database segmentation may not be. The 200-PC company also finds discounts and network compatibility important, although they are not factors for the other companies. Your company can have an entirely different list of factors.

◥ LINKING SUCCESS FACTORS

Companies that take time to address personal computer linking into hosts and networks in a cohesive way are companies that know a planned approach is the only way to maintain an orderly installation of additional personal computers. They also know that cost control is achievable when it is known how growth is planned, how link integration products are selected, and how personal-computer-to-host linkages are implemented. It is imperative that you know the personal computer integration options considered and the long-term expectations for a particular linkage approach.

Determining Business Services

You should also determine the business services that personal computer links support. In some cases, you can't always have the luxury of beginning from scratch because businesses don't always start with a plan. Some ongoing services may be obsolete, and you may have to start other new services. But for the purposes of our example, let's start with a clean slate.

As an example of a business service, a company wants to permit external corporate customers in a time-sharing mode to access and download their company's personnel files into a remote personal computer for review and update. The files are then uploaded to the host for production processing. Your job is to provide the links, maintain reliable and error-free transmission, provide security preventing other company file access, and establish procedures and precautions to prevent uploads from destroying master data files. Start by realizing that your host links support remote personal computer access.

Another type of business service allows internal end-user financial people to load specialized data to their own desktops. The type of service can be restricted to a specific database segment that can be placed in a temporary host file before downloading. Security is important, but perhaps not quite as important as in the previous example. In some cases, you can expand on a service in such a way that it makes an old service obsolete. This is particularly true if you must implement links for personal computer usage where dumb terminals previously constituted the only data access. Application system changes and modified procedures can become so drastic that they render dumb terminal access almost useless.

Technical Versus Business Review

It is a mistake to develop a personal computer integration plan by starting out with product technical reviews. Too many companies allow technical personnel to decide how to integrate personal computers. Not surprisingly, the first reaction of technical people is to do what they do best: look at product technical specifications only.

Technical evaluations are important, but their worth is limited unless they're kept in context with the rest of the situation. You must define what these link products are expected to support. If a personal computer integration strategy or plan doesn't support the business, it won't work.

First, determine what business services the workstations or personal computers are expected to be a part of in the overall scheme of things. Are the services intended primarily to improve the productivity of the company's own internal people? Or are they money-generating fee services available to outside individuals or companies?

A Functional Linking Approach

If the point of the system is to enhance operation, productivity, and efficiency of the company's internal people, then identify what services are the most logical to address. Let's use an example: a manufacturing company wants more efficient market and sales analysis. Currently, analysis takes place on standalone personal computers. Each month, branch sales reports are submitted in various formats. Data is keyed into a standalone personal computer. Later, it is reentered into the host system for use by other departments, such as production control, to schedule next month's production. A market forecaster uses the sales data from the host, not the same standalone PC data used by market-sales analysis, in concert with historical host-based sales data for analysis and trending. Figure 5-3 illustrates how sales data might be consolidated into a host system.

In this case, the issues are obvious and quite simple. From a business standpoint, the data must be consistent across all corporate departments. Performance is not the issue, but verifiable data

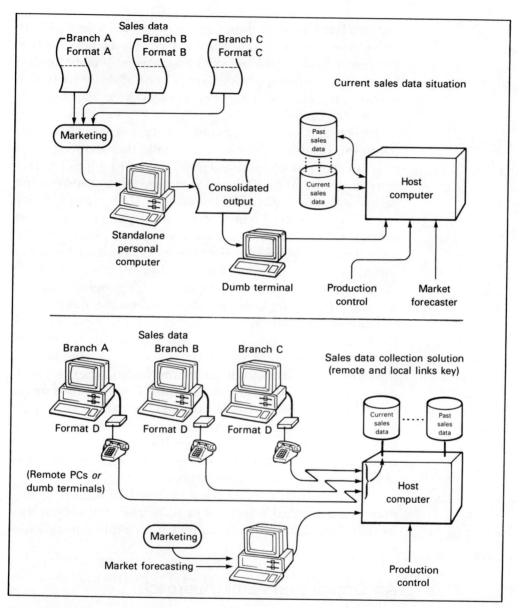

Figure 5-3. ▲

Consolidating various sales data into a host

and timeliness is. Reporting formats must be standardized, and data should only have to be entered once into the host database. Procedures for accessing and storing updates must be established, because some existing branches are late or update themselves. As a result, reports and associated analysis from the data will become more reliable.

Remote and local micro-mainframe links are key elements in transforming a fragmented sales data collection and usage environment into one of consistency and organized approach. Data entry errors are minimized and contained at the source, while data is kept current across the corporation. If data entry is late, it is unavailable to all who need access, not to just a few. You push control of the situation back to the host where you can centralize and contain access and security procedures. The host becomes a vortex for collecting and distributing data.

What does this example have to do with personal computer linking? The answer concerns what data you are linking. You enhance productivity and have successful host links only if the end business results are favorable. Now that all data is contained in the same place in the same formats, you can develop network linkages and select products to implement the personal-computer-to-host connection consistently. Users can then see the same data as everyone else. If templates are written to interface host data to different personal computer application packages, they only have to be done once. You improve the overall smoothness of the business operation along with the timeliness of sales reporting and management.

In this example, the variable of unusual data formats is eliminated. You can deal with types of links instead of various data formats. You can concentrate on personal computer integration.

An Organization Link Approach

In many cases a specific department, division, or function is the automation focus. It must be dealt with as an integral part of the data processing picture. If it isn't, there is a good probability that whatever is defined is not consistent with future corporate plans.

Addressing these internal services includes

- Reliability expectations
- Tolerable system outage periods
- Usability
- Maintenance requirements
- Flexibility.

The needs of your internal personnel and department groups that use host databases and services must be treated with the same regard as external organizations to whom you supply the same capabilities.

Let's use another company example for this second point. This example involves automating the specific divisional laboratory described earlier with over 60 graphic personal computers for scientific research and data analysis. Again, you must assess the business needs for the linking system, not the technical needs at this point. Your first questions involve understanding what business requirements must be satisfied with the overall system. What is the nature of the business, and what are the key elements that the system must support?

Always remember that links are part of the network. Because these links are integral to the host itself, to perform as efficiently as the rest of the system, you must establish the links' role with respect to the host and the defined end-user services. You cannot arbitrarily decide how you can connect end users to the host without first identifying how they are going to interact with each other and the host. Know what your users expect the host to do and how they intend their data to be used.

In this laboratory automation project, there are four specified and necessary business goals:

1. Automate the process of selecting and running tests of chemical products.

2. Automate the process of collecting and retrieving product analysis data.

3. Reduce the costs associated with cataloging and librarying product data and status.

4. Maintain high reliability and availability for production.

You can translate these goals into the following key objectives:

- Provide selective test retrieval and downloading for execution of product tests.

- Collect data directly from the test instruments into the workstations.

- Upload data from the workstations to the hosts at random periods.

- Provide preliminary data analysis at each chemist's workstation.

- Guarantee complete data transfer reliability and data integrity.

Figure 5-4 shows how each goal can be converted into one or more action items. Each item, in turn, affects your network design and link hardware and software selection.

With the exception of the host and the workstation, this is a classic application of the micro-mainframe link technology to a group of technical users that could care less about the type of link used, just as long as it works. In fact, this is an excellent example to demonstrate the next part of the issues that cannot be overlooked: user requirements.

In this example, users are not computer literate, nor did they wish to be. Because of this, their requirements for communications and data transfer include

- Easy procedures for data selection and transfer.

- Preset command lists to be used without expert knowledge.

- Notification when data transfers are completed.

- Automatic data retransmission upon any errors without user intervention.

- Notification if data errors occurred and retransmission did not succeed.

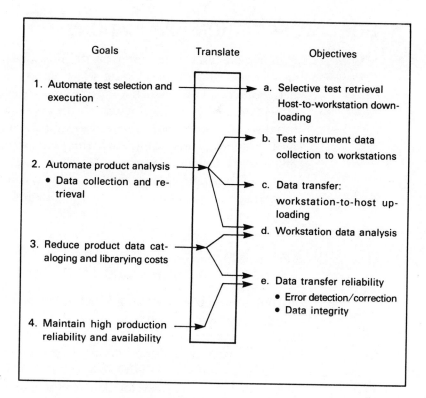

Goals   Translate   Objectives

1. Automate test selection and execution

2. Automate product analysis
   • Data collection and retrieval

3. Reduce product data cataloging and librarying costs

4. Maintain high production reliability and availability

a. Selective test retrieval Host-to-workstation downloading

b. Test instrument data collection to workstations

c. Data transfer: workstation-to-host uploading

d. Workstation data analysis

e. Data transfer reliability
   • Error detection/correction
   • Data integrity

Figure 5-4. ▶

Translating goals into link objectives

The business services analysis process includes

- Sizing what services are to be delivered.

- Basic cost parameters.

- What existing data processing structures must be conformed to.

- What level of users are addressed.

- What needs these users have relative to the ongoing nature of the final linkage solution.

This sounds like it applies to systems design and analysis as opposed to simply choosing link technology, and it does. You cannot develop a consistent, overall micro-to-mainframe link plan without applying fundamental concepts to assess the environment in which these links are installed and perform.

◣ HOST/WORKSTATION APPLICATIONS

Applications and expectations at the host and the workstation are not the same. In developing selection criteria for link products, you must know which applications are run on the host and which are used at the workstation. If the applications on the personal computer are tools intended to supplement activity on the host, then you must know how this will occur and what the relationship between the two is. Hosts are still the largest single source of computing power, but their role is changing. You need to know how personal computers are to interface with these hosts and how users interact with both.

Personal Computer and Host Roles

If you differentiate processing expectations between the host and the end-user workstation, you can determine what roles the host and the workstation play in the overall scheme of things. Define what applications and tools are used. You know that users analyze and process data relative to specific files or data sets. This means that your users develop data for use with existing applications such as spreadsheets, graphics representations, or word processing. What type of business activity takes place at the workstation dictates not only what kind of linkages and performance are necessary but also indicates what future application requirements are probable. The learning curve and maturing process of the people and their use of the system always create new ways to use the system. Expect your users to be satisfied with their capabilities until they master the tools at their disposal.

This is the easy part. Users will find new ways to use these tools, and your link network should be designed to support them. If you don't anticipate this, you can be faced with a review and upgrade of your link plan sooner than you think.

Link-to-Host Connection Time

It is imperative for you to know approximately what percentage of the time host connection is required and what is done during that time. Connection to the host tells you how much you must be concerned about sufficient host processing power and resources to drive your personal computer links. The estimated connection time and the intensity of user activity during that time provide insight into how much work your host is doing just to support your linked users. Even if your users are not actively connected, they initiate activities that require host processing. Consider these activities as a load on the host as well.

There is always a division between host connection for interactive processing and standalone activity. For example, the personal computer can be used almost 100 percent of the time in a standalone fashion, except when it is connected into a host database for very short periods of time. If this is the case, an ordinary modem with communications software is sufficient. You can even add file transfer software for downloading files. Look closely, however, for this can be just the beginning. If users access databases, seeking data for sophisticated analysis, you should anticipate the possibility that more sophisticated analysis applications will soon be required — necessitating more elaborate data retrieval and host linking products.

However, let's assume that users connect to the host 100 percent of the time. They access host databases and files, execute host applications, and set up host applications with data that is keyed directly from the desktop. Eventually, they will discover the tremendous benefits of performing some preliminary activity on the personal computer. They can do setup locally, schedule jobs for submission to the host, and use data supplemented by that on the host. You should assess the information types being transferred, the activity type being performed with this information, and the nature of the data transfer — all require certain forms of links.

◤ PROFILING PERSONAL-COMPUTER-TO-HOST CONNECTION

Figure 5-5 profiles several different personal-computer-to-host connection time situations. First of all, although the personal computer can be actively connected to the host 100 percent of the time, the user never works at the personal computer 100 percent of the time. During an eight-hour day, people take breaks, have

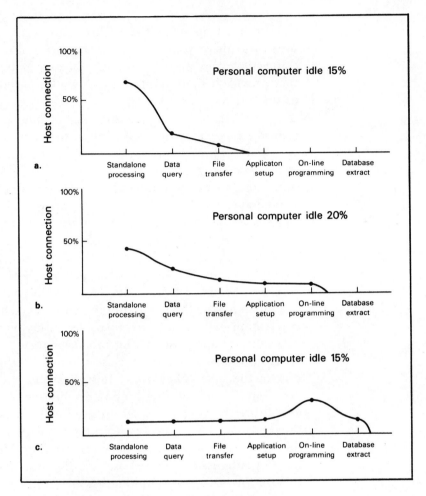

Figure 5-5. ▶

Link connection to host time

lunch, attend meetings, think, and sometimes just stare at the screen. Consequently, each of the illustrations in Figure 5-5 accounts for personal computer idle time.

The vertical scale represents the actual percentage of connection to the host, and the horizontal scale lists activities that could be taking place within the environment. These have been selected as an example; you can profile different activities.

Figure 5-5a profiles a user whose personal computer is used

primarily in a standalone mode. The user doesn't require much interaction with the host; any connection is simply to select and obtain data. In this case, we estimate that during an 8-hour period, the user is operational on the personal computer 5.6 hours per day and is idle another 1.2 hours. For less than an hour (48 minutes) the user is in emulation mode to perform data query. Data transfer is required less than 30 minutes a day. What this profile tells you is that you do need emulation, but that your data transfer host servicing is minimal. This can be a profile for users in sales forecasting or financial evaluation. If this profile applies to 100 personal computers, you have to consider the overall loading effect on the host and the peak times when it occurs. However, if you have only 5 personal computers, your concerns are not as critical unless the host is already overloaded and any additional servicing becomes a problem.

Figure 5-5b shows a user connection profile changing in terms of activity. In this case, users depend on the host to provide data, and they interact more with the host for query and application execution. Our example shows that the typical user requires host servicing and connection 40 percent of the 8-hour day (3.2 hours). The other 40 percent of the time is spent analyzing data in a standalone mode. Such a profile can be characteristic of individuals performing production management or market data analysis, to name just two. Host interaction is high; connectivity for interactive servicing is emphasized, and there is a large dependence on emulation.

Finally, Figure 5-5c is characteristic of programmers or modelers that address large data files or develop new applications for use by others. The personal computer is used in a standalone mode less than one hour a day because most of the data and tools needed are resident at the host. There can even be a relational database in which data resides, requiring special micro-mainframe link interfacing provided only by that vendor. For 30 percent of the time (2.4 hours) the user requires host resources to query, search, and transfer data. An additional 45 percent of the time (3.6 hours), tools (on-line programming and application set-up) require direct use of the host.

As these illustrations show, you can be connected to the host all of the time, but you never use the connection 100 percent of the day. This factor must be considered when you select links and manage your host resource capacity.

Financial Spreadsheet Example

As an example, consider users who perform financial analysis with spreadsheets. Because of what they do, their spreadsheets are large. Each sheet contains 70 line entries, and there are spreadsheets for each of seven profit centers. The spreadsheet is structured on a monthly basis for 18-month periods that the user can review on a monthly or quarterly basis, and each entry is 10 characters. The line definition itself is 25 characters. Ultimately, these separate sheets are all consolidated into a single sheet and together are stored at the host.

From a total data standpoint, each sheet, including the consolidated one, contains 1750 characters of line definition plus 12,600 characters (70 lines × 18 months × 10 characters/line) for a total of 14,350 characters per sheet. Assuming a 1200-baud transmission speed with a transfer efficiency of 85 percent due to overhead, each sheet requires about 2 minutes for transfer to the host. This totals 15 minutes for all 8 sheets, which is not a large amount of data or time in this case. Higher-speed lines, of course, can reduce transfer time even further (Figure 5-6).

At higher transmission speeds, transfer time is decreased. Each additional spreadsheet of the same size increases total transmission another 2 minutes. The point is that the smallest amount of data at low transfer speeds consumes significant time when you are waiting to do something else. Think about how long it takes with even larger data files.

In this case, most all of the work can be done locally at the workstation and transmitted to the host. Sometimes it is desirable to download the data from the host into the workstation for additional updating and analysis. The issue here is not discontinuing the activity at the workstation but efficiently moving the data to and from the host. If possible, it is better to merge all of

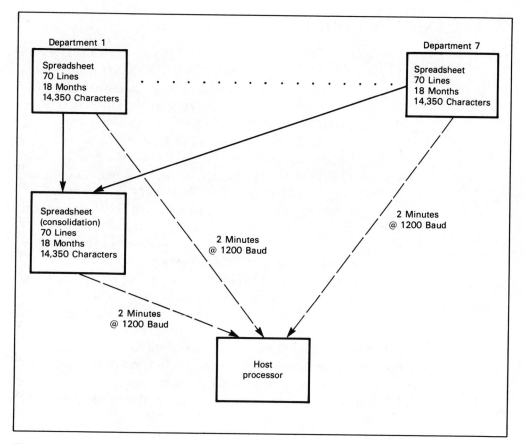

Figure 5-6. ▲

Spreadsheet and host transfer time

the spreadsheets into the consolidated sheet before host transfer, particularly if only the consolidated sheet resides at the host. This is a linking issue because it affects data volume being transferred; it also affects where sheet merging takes place. Although a simple example to comprehend, it demonstrates that links are a part of the issues in developing micro-host linking strategies. The example should provoke thought on linking and its role relative to the total process.

◥ THE EVOLVING HOST ROLE

The host is becoming a central data repository that manages and controls the flow of data and information to and from destinations upon request. Users initiate requests to retrieve data from various parts of the company and geography. The host is a processing vehicle for large applications that require extremely large data files or banks of information that cannot today be conveniently handled at a user's desktop. Because the host can store voluminous amounts of data, it is ideal for maintaining and authorizing the information flow away from its own core.

Communications networks and links that connect into this host become arteries attached to vast amounts of data. The host is becoming a traffic manager whose main purpose is to drive the links and networks to which it attaches.

Your host is not an unlimited fountain of resources, either. As personal computers connect into hosts, they require resources and capacity, either from the network or from the host. If personal computers are directly connected to the host, a direct drain is inevitable. This drain takes place when the host services data transfer. If personal computers are linked indirectly to the host via LANs, the drain is on total resources available to the entire LAN. If capacity is insufficient or unavailable to the entire LAN system, all workstations connected to the LAN are negatively affected, and end-user performance can degrade.

The applications that you run at the host are those that cannot be economically or practically executed on today's personal computers. For you to adequately assess integration needs, you must define which applications need to run on the host and which can be executed on the workstation. Such a division of labor affects the type of links that become candidates for consideration. This example is restricted to situations in which workstations already exist or are being added. The premise is that you evaluate what applications might make the personal computers more productive and examine how they should be linked.

◥ Data Transfer Requirements

Data transfer requirements directly affect the following:

- Information access
- User performance
- Satisfaction levels.

If information access is read only, terminal emulation links such as DCA's IRMA, CXI's ConnectWare, or ITI's LinkUp are the best choice. They're relatively simple, easy to install, and fulfill basic connection needs. If access requires data downloading, the links you select must be able to handle the transfer volume adequately. You also need to select file transfer software if it is not included. High-speed bulk data transfers can be the most effective and cost efficient if the situation calls for a very large volume of data transmission.

You may decide to transfer entire application programs for execution at the workstation. In these instances, you should make sure that the type of transfer taking place does not mistakenly change any of the transferred bytes of information (more about this later).

In some situations, the personal computer need not be connected to the host except when it is necessary to perform data transfer. Many products on the market permit automatic host disconnect when the personal computer works in a standalone mode. Aside from the three previously mentioned micro-mainframe link vendors, emulation product vendors that permit automatic host disconnect when not in data transfer mode include AST Research, Attachmate, and Forte. When such a product is used, the host does not continually look to see if the workstation needs servicing but instead waits to be signaled that a data transfer is requested. This reduces the active drain on the host for polling to see if there is any need or request for data service.

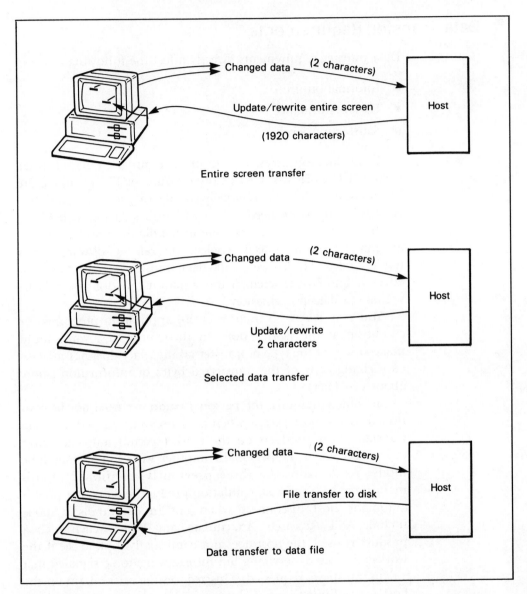

Figure 5-7. ▲

Data transfer forms

Performance Considerations

When links are used, user response time is a direct result of the activity on the host, the host's ability to service interactive requests, and what the user is doing. The host governs this performance.

Link performance is also sometimes considered synonymous with data transfer volume, frequency, and type. It is the link that transfers data. Different link products offer different transfer speeds, although many of these speeds are standard — 1200 baud or 9600 baud. All of the vendors mentioned that supply remote connecting (via modem) host links support these speeds.

Coaxial connecting links (direct to a host terminal control unit) allow for data transfer speeds in excess of 9600 baud up to 19,200 baud. These include CXI's coaxial products as well as ITI's and AST Research's, to name a few. Such speeds are achieved through the design and implementation of the host connection and protocol exchange. You can expect other factors to improve throughput efficiency at these speeds, based on how the transfer software groups data to transfer a byte or character of information. This throughput is the most important factor in measuring link performance.

Some links group or block data in sizes consistent with screen displays, transferring one screen image at a time. Other links provide transfer of only selected data that is changed in the screen display itself. Visually, the difference between transferring an entire screen and sending only changed information is the difference between rewriting an entire screen display versus instantaneous update. Still other links use specialized file transfer software that transmit the data directly to a data file on the workstation. Once transferred, data can be displayed on the screen in any format desired. Performance depends on users' needs and satisfactory acceptance levels. You must scrutinize the link design to know how data is sent only if these factors are important to your application's performance. Figure 5-7 illustrates the options.

Sizing Data Transfer Volume

It is essential to have an estimate of the typical or average data transfer volume that can occur. You also need a safety factor for misjudgments when estimating. Be sure to allow excess capacity to ensure that you have not underestimated transfer needs. An estimate can tell you how much data you think you are going to move between the host and attached personal computers. Make such an estimate to make sure that the links you select meet this volume. You don't want a link that takes forever to move 10,000 characters of data. An estimate should include a practical expected average and a maximum peak that the micro-mainframe links are expected to handle each day. If you are planning a network of links, an estimate tells if the host can handle the capacity and if your network (LAN or otherwise) can support the traffic.

The data volume estimate need not be exact, but it must represent a best guess. With it, you can begin to size the requirements for data transfer. You can construct scenarios that profile what the link system must address before you spend any money or procure equipment. In essence, the data volume estimate is the beginning of a model that can be used later to simulate and estimate changes and additions to the data transfer process.

Volume is important. If the volume of data being transferred is under 100 bytes, the use of any link product (including a modem) is more than sufficient, because transfer even at the lowest speed takes only seconds. For example, if the volume includes files that exceed 1000 records at 80 characters per record, then transmission takes about 9 minutes at 1200 baud.

The best approach is not to think of volume as a complex term. Performance can be a complex issue, but for now think of it as a simple problem consisting of workstations and data transfer volume. As shown in the next illustration, you can divide volume transfer across workstations. Volume can be either low or high. The installation and the number of workstations can be thought of in relative terms as well—either few or many. The point is to keep things in perspective. However, it is sometimes difficult to estimate the volume of data traffic without having performed any measurements. The service being instituted may be new, so there may be no volume precedents. A situation like this requires your best educated estimate of how you think users will operate.

Keep in mind the present workstation base and how it is going to change. Referring to the illustration below, assume that you have a few workstations across which there is low transfer volume (point A):

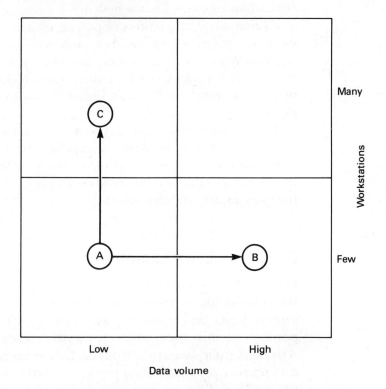

Is it anticipated that the number of workstations is going to increase while the transfer volume remains relatively unchanged across each personal computer (point C)? Or is it more probable that the number of workstations will be constant over the next few months, but that data transfer volume will increase dramatically over each personal computer (point B)?

Data Transfer Frequency

Data transfer frequency is another major criterion. Assume you can transfer 100,000 bytes easily and tolerably once a day. But if the requirement calls for transfers of this size every hour across 20 or 30 workstations, then an altogether different philosophy is required. Aside from physical links, you need a process to manage the transfer operation, assuming that it is not random.

As Figure 5-8 shows, data transfer frequency dramatically effects host capacity. For the host that services 20, 50, or 250 personal computers, the process of polling each personal computer for requests, retrieving the data, and scheduling the transfer demands resources. If the transfer frequencies are extensive, then you should consider other host alternatives. If the situation isn't monitored, transfer loads from workstations can exceed the host capacity.

Data transfer frequency, coupled with transfer volume, are critical factors that you model in capacity estimates. These estimates are important in sizing the capacity of link networks to ensure sufficient growth for addition of personal computers and increases in data transfer volume.

Scientific Case Example

Let's look at the scientific laboratory example discussed earlier. We consider the percentage of active workstations, peak and average loads, and transfer speeds. (The data is simplified for purposes of this discussion.) Of the 60 stations connected, 40 actively transfer data to and from the host at any given time. The data transfer per workstation averages 15,000 bytes six times per day, or 3.6 million bytes in a single eight-hour period.

At 9600 baud and an 85 percent transfer efficiency rate, total transfer time is approximately 59 minutes for the 3.6 million bytes. Again, this is not a major factor unless a high percentage of these stations coincidentally transfer data at exactly the same time. At 1200 baud, the transfer time takes eight times as long (almost eight hours for the same transfer). Despite the host performance and the dedication to interactive response, line speed

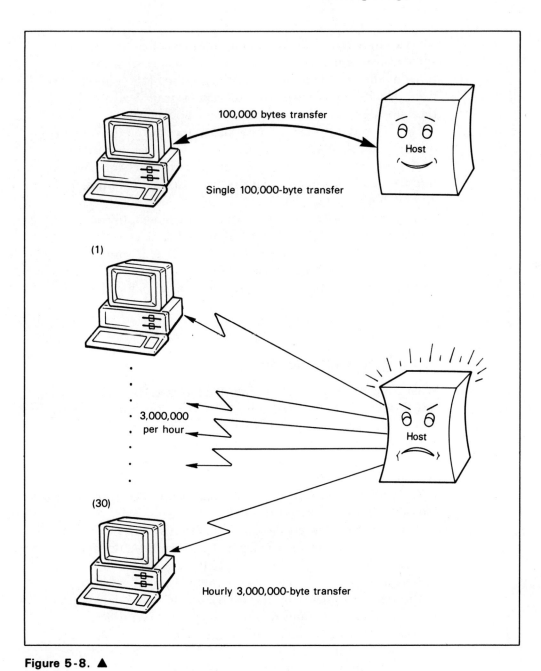

Figure 5-8. ▲

*Degree of transfer
volume*

plays an important role in tying up host resources. If your high-speed transfer links can operate at 19,200 bits per second, transfer time for this data becomes almost negligible. File transfer software that is very efficient can alleviate a great deal of transfer time stress by not tying up the lines or host ports.

In this example, stations are added as they are needed, and the transfer requirements remain about the same. Data transfer and host load are predictable, and any percentage change in the transfer load is measurable. This permits capacity planning to be an ongoing activity.

Note also that because station additions cause a linear rise in data transfer, the effect is easily monitored as new workstations are added and frequency and volume change. This simplifies the task of estimating when service becomes degraded or at what point a different approach is necessary for servicing the workstations.

Data Type Considerations

What kind of data is being transferred? Data is classified as ASCII, text, or binary. As Figure 5-9 shows, depending on how data is stored at the host, it sometimes is necessary to write a translation program to reformat the data after transfer for input into a workstation application. This is not unusual and is not a monumental task. In many cases, reformatting routines already exist. In many more cases, the personal computer application itself can translate downloaded data.

For example, Hewlett-Packard's financial system permits the user to selectively retrieve data from H-P's own IMAGE database, download it to workstations via H-P's Report Facility, and automatically reformat the data for use in Lotus 1-2-3 or other applications designated by the user. Format conversion is performed automatically and requires no user intervention.

Know the kind of data being transferred, what applications use it, and how it is used. If at all possible, perform the translation at the host before transfer to the personal computer, because the host offers greater processing resources for this trivial chore.

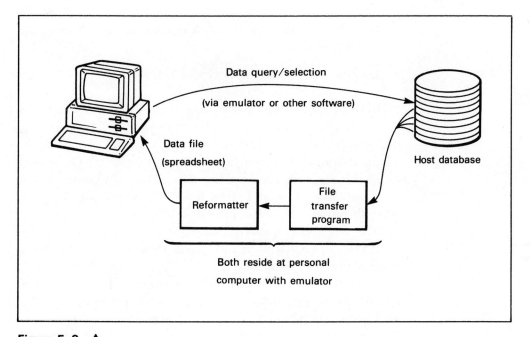

Figure 5-9. ▲

Translating host-retrieved data

Consider maintaining data at the host consistent with the form used on the personal computers.

◥ DATA INTEGRITY, SECURITY, AND CONTROL

Data integrity, security, and control are often discussed in reference to the state of data and some relationship to its transmission to, from, and among personal computers. These terms are primarily used when discussing issues related to uploading and downloading data between hosts and personal computers and in connection with access to a mainframe by a remote terminal or personal computer.

Each of these terms can be defined as follows:

- Integrity — state of being unimpaired; rigid adherence to a code of behavior.

- Security—freedom from risk or danger; freedom from doubt, anxiety, or fear.

- Control—exercising authority or influence over.

In assessing security needs, you must determine whether or not the data is sensitive. Data should be protected because of its importance, not its location. In today's world, access can be obtained from almost anywhere there is a telephone. The reasoning is simple: once you have transferred data to a personal computer, you have lost control of it for all intents and purposes. Once the data is away from the host and its more sophisticated security systems, almost anyone can view, use, or manipulate the data. You can display it on a PC screen or merely take the disk to another personal computer.

Users have to solve their own security problems; products cannot. Many products work with micro-mainframe links to deter access, encrypt data, and monitor successful access attempts. But the user must take responsibility for implementing these products, enforcing their use, and installing and adhering to policies and procedures for protecting the data.

Access Control to Secure Micro-Mainframe Links

A number of products are used to secure micro-mainframe links. Many user organizations, especially banks, government agencies, and utility companies, use access control software that can be purchased and installed on mainframes.

These software packages "challenge" terminals trying to gain access to the mainframe by requesting a user identification (USERID) and a password. The correct responses allow users access into the host processor, but the users are further restricted to particular programs, data, or both, according to their security level. In addition to access control, this software also records audit trails to determine which users have successfully accessed the data as well as those who have made unsuccessful access attempts.

Other mainframe software system features include the ability to assign different modes that simplify installation. These modes include the following:

- *Monitor mode* is used by a system administrator to observe and monitor user accesses and other system manipulations such as data file access.

- *Warning mode* warns users that what they are trying to do now is permitted, but will be precluded in the future.

- *Prevent mode*, the most severe of the three, actually stops actions attempted by the user against host data systems.

Leading security access software control systems include RAC-F (IBM Corporation, Armonk, New York), ACF-2 (Cambridge Systems, Los Altos, California), and Top Secret (CGA Allen, Division of Computer Associates Incorporated, Holmdel, New Jersey). These are the leading control systems in the IBM arena.

Dial-Back Devices for Securing Access

Another type of product that can be used to secure micro-mainframe links is the dial-back (or call-back) system—a hardware device that front-ends the host to be protected. A remote user calls the host computer, which asks for a USERID and password. Upon a correct response, the host system instructs the caller to hang up. The host then calls the telephone number associated with the USERID and password, which it has stored in memory.

While this device does have limitations in that it is highly restricted to specific telephone numbers, research by the Alec Group (San Jose, California) indicates that users are adopting these dial-back systems at a brisk pace. Surveys conducted by this organization show that the installation base for such dial-back products increased 33 percent in 1985 over 1984. This trend is expected to continue (possibly at a lower rate) through the rest of this decade as users seek to secure against unauthorized access via links. These devices are easily understood and implemented in a computer network environment.

Integrity as an Issue

One serious problem that confronts users is the possibility that data can be contaminated or destroyed accidentally or maliciously. This is the primary argument against allowing personal computer users to upload data from their private databases into corporate files. Most data processing installations want to validate data before updating the master files, and they generally want to do so in a batch processing environment. The rationale is that proper procedures must be used to ensure that the data being uploaded is valid.

While this is probably true for catching gross alphanumeric errors, transpositions, and field violations, it is highly unlikely that you can quickly detect data that is purposefully contrived or fabricated. There is no easy way to know that a diligent saboteur did not develop a special data stream, undetected by the smartest verification procedures. Establishing a rigid code of behavior for input data can help, but it is not the only answer. The issue is the integrity of actual data files, data authorization of specific levels of system access by persons, and specific authorization to access different hosts.

Computer installations routinely perform data entry and validation before uploading. It all started with key entry systems. There is very little difference in this data entry situation and that of uploading from personal computers, except that the speed of performing the update with micro-mainframe links is faster. In fact, micro-mainframe links are often an integral part of all key entry systems.

If the object is to destroy data, there are many ways to accomplish that in most data processing installations without using a micro-mainframe link. To talk of a micro-mainframe link as creating a data integrity issue is a red herring. The links do not create the integrity issues; it is the lack of safeguards on the hosts that permit them to be used as such. When links are implemented and uploading is allowed, appropriate procedures must be instituted to minimize the possibility that data corruption can occur, and if it does, that it can easily be recovered from.

The key to maintaining data integrity is to create an environment that allows integrity to be achieved through a natural process and protect it through early warning and preestablished recovery procedures. If data is damaged, it is essential that proper recovery procedures to the most recent level be instituted as soon as possible. Procedures must exist that permit selective updates to be introduced from an audit or trace capability designed into the system at the host level. In addition, users must employ systematic back-up routines and have workable contingency plans.

The micro-mainframe link is a tool; it does not create data integrity problems itself. Links cannot, conversely, correct integrity problems.

Securing Access

Security, as the definition suggests, is knowing that data is accurate and that it is available only to those with a need to know. MIS management must ensure host system security without complicating access procedures of legitimate users. Like anything else, security can range to extremes. Clearly, if the host does not operate any top-level security system, it is very difficult to monitor activity except when the data is known to be violated. The key is to institute a system that combines prevention, authorization, and access deterrent. Most major vendors such as DEC, H-P, IBM, and Data General provide security systems either as an adjunct to or as a part of the operating system. Also, many third-party companies supply independent security systems. Figure 5-10 shows an "onion" approach to the types of system levels that must be secured, and in what order. The protection concept is in the outer layers.

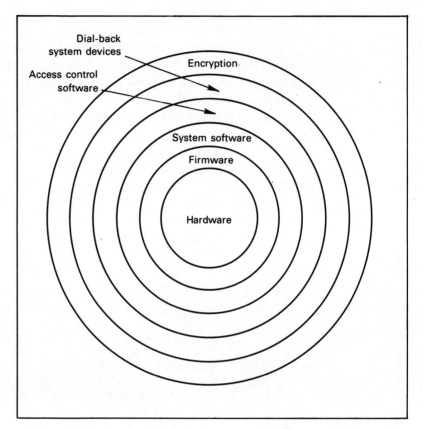

Figure 5-10. ▶

Onion approach to security (courtesy the Alec Group, San Jose, California)

Securing Host Access

There are at least two forms of securing host access, neither of which is dependent upon a micro-mainframe link.

- Recognition of the terminal device requesting access.
- Recognition of the identity of the individual at the other end seeking access.

The latter is becoming known as "seeing through" to the user identity, regardless of the micro-mainframe link employed.

Recognition of the terminal device is trivial; it does not discriminate against the user at the other end. Its effectiveness is limited, but it is still used in some installations. Validating user identity is a much more effective means of protection, and various algorithms are used to implement this recognition. They include the normal user identification keyword, password, and perhaps an additional level of access authorization. Other more sophisticated capabilities are marketed that include the use of random access numbers and special hardware cards containing user data. In addition, biometric devices, those that recognize a characteristic of the person (such as a retinal pattern, palmprint, fingerprint, and so forth) are now being used primarily in government and defense-oriented industries. Financial institutions such as banks are also a prime market for these products.

If the host system supports interactive access, then it is imperative to set company policy regarding host access. To assess integration needs, you must determine what applications and data are totally untouchable by dial-up or other forms of remote personal computer access. Once you know this, you can examine options for protecting the system and database segments.

Controlling Data Dispersement

Exercising authority over who gets what data is always a crucial issue. Users do not disagree that such authority or control is necessary, but they may differ on how it should be administered and enforced. If data is contained all in the same files, it is more difficult to discriminate access. If a database is used to categorize data as well as store it, then the lines of isolation are more apparent.

To control data availability effectively is to prevent data from becoming known where it is not supposed to be known. This is especially important in today's banking and finance industry, where corporations perform their own payroll and personnel updating and corporate treasurers manage their own portfolios. Banks can ill afford to allow their clients to view data from competing companies or even to have it known that such a breach of security could occur. The financial institution must guarantee absolutely that all data is secure and accurate. This is especially true when the equipment used to access bank files is a personal computer downloading data from the host via some remote linking capability.

Encryption

Once host access is authorized, the next issue concerns downloading the data to the user. Data encryption is an extreme form of protection that can be used to secure data before or during its transmission to or from the personal computer.

This example explains how encryption is applied in most user installations. A cryptosystem consists of the following components:

- Algorithm—a formula used to encipher the text
- Key—the starting point or input into the algorithim
- Hardware or software—used for the encryption process.

Identical encryption equipment is normally located at either end of the circuit to be secured. Before encoding a message, the user receives a key that is used to set the algorithm. A message, or plain text, is entered and then encrypted (scrambled) using the algorithm set by the key. This results in cipher text that is unintelligible and can be sent over the communications link. After the cipher text is received at the other end, the receiver sets the algorithm using the appropriate key, reverses the encryption process, and decrypts the cipher text back into plain text.

A number of algorithms are used today, the most common of which is the Data Encryption Standard (DES) promulgated by the National Bureau of Standards. Other systems include the public key and a number of proprietary cryptosystems.

Theoretically, individuals who do not know the encryption key cannot decrypt the data for viewing or other use. However, once the data is decrypted, it is available to anyone who has access to the personal computer on which the data is resident. Also, duplicate files reside at the personal computer, one decrypted and the other encrypted. When data is uploaded to the host, the data file is reencrypted before transfer, and the original source is deleted. Many users leave the decrypted files on their personal computer, which defeats the process.

If a network is used with a file server, the data is encrypted and stored on the local file server. Once decrypted, it is available in plain text on the file server to all connected users. The network of personal computer users can view the data as if they had access to the authorized personal computer requesting the data. This is a problem not yet solved with today's software.

Security of data and access control is a technical and company-culture issue that must be addressed with an overall plan. Important to remember is not to overlay so many access and downloading restrictions that the process becomes tedious to use. If this is the case, it only stimulates users to find ways around the system and to beat the process. Keep things simple and understandable. By all means, make sure that data files can be recovered if a violation or corruption occurs.

◥ SUMMARY

This chapter covered a great deal of information. It should leave you with an organized list of issues that you can reflect on before, during, or after assessing your own personal computer integration needs. The point of the chapter is to let you know that the problems you are asked to resolve are not trivial and that you needn't feel bad if some people have made you feel that they are. It can be very disconcerting if you have been asked to take on this task when you have never confronted integration before. The questions and confusion can seem overwhelming at times.

Rest assured that you are not alone. The only way to maintain control of the situation is to organize an approach, as we pointed out earlier. An approach keeps you focused and maintains a course for action and solution. Table 5-2 shows a chart of the major considerations for sizing your needs. It places them in

	Business	Technical	Business and Technical
Organize an approach			X
Establish a process			X
Monitor link growth/activity			X
Identify needs			
■ Department	X		
■ Functional	X		
■ Organizational	X		
Define business services/needs	X		
Service priority needs first	X		
Standardize where possible	X		
Define user activity	X		
Cost/budget limitations	X		
Template development		X	
User performance requirements		X	
Data type considerations		X	
User logon audit trails		X	
Host pass-through		X	
Error message recording		X	
Link usability		X	
Service diagnostics		X	
Network compatibility		X	
Host-to-PC connection time		X	
Backup and recovery		X	
Upload protection		X	
Download requirements		X	
Tolerable system outages			X
Reliability expectations			X
Maintenance/service			X
Information access			X

Table 5-2. ▲

Personal computer integration assessment issues

	Business	Technical	Business and Technical
Upgrade/expansion			X
Existing database structures			X
Host/PC applications			X
Sizing data transfer			X
■ Volume			X
■ Frequency			X
File transfer vs. selective extract			X
Security access control			X
Data encryption			X
Host requirements			
■ Available performance			X
■ Resource capacity			X
■ Throughput requirements			X
■ User response time levels			X
■ Application/tool needs			X

Table 5-2. ▲

Personal computer integration assessment issues (continued)

an order that allows you to use them as a reference and guide. It helps to realize which factors are purely business or technical and which are both. Depending on your own unique and particular situation, you can ignore some of these factors entirely.

Remember what is said so many times: the more things change, the more they stay the same. You think that your needs are different and unique from anyone else's. But you can find that it is always a given that the same issues prevail in all installations confronting personal-computer-to-host integration. The factors that affect link network design and product selection remain constant, with few exceptions.

Table 5-2 is divided into six groups. Of the six, one deals only with pure business-oriented issues that form the basis of developing a start on assessing your integration needs. Two groups' issues are technical in nature, and three groups relate to issues that have both technical and business effects in one form or another.

Establishing an approach, implementing a process, and monitoring link activities are fundamental to your success. If you start haphazardly, you can expect to end up with more confusion and difficulty in selecting the products that can best do the job. You need an organized method both in the business and in the technical evaluations to know what you are looking at and how things can change over time. The business issues relate to identifying your needs and cost limitations for implementing links. Why are you doing this? What do you expect to solve? These are fundamental questions.

The issues identified as technical in nature relate to the kinds of system and operational restrictions with which you are confronted. If you don't have answers to these, then you must decide if they are pertinent or have no effect on the final integration outcome. You may very well say that you don't need to concern yourself with several issues that are listed in the chart. If you feel this is true, then it is key that you yourself have an answer to why; otherwise, you may be fooling yourself when it comes time to implement your link network.

Finally, items marked as business and technical are those that have a bearing and influence on the performance and operation of the business as well as on the end user. For example, host capacity can be purely a technical consideration: you either have enough host capacity or you don't. However, if you do not have spare processing capacity, you should either limit the number of links to be connected or contemplate a larger host processor. This becomes a business decision. Similarly, maintenance and service are classified as a business-technical issue. You have to decide how your company is going to handle this area. If you decide to rely on your own capability, then service diagnostics are essential and represent a technical issue. Either way, you need to have diagnostics for your own ongoing operational purposes.

This chapter gives you a good start on qualifying your integration needs. There is no replacement for thinking about and organizing what you need to do and how you proceed.

6

Planning Approaches To Workstation Integration

An organized approach to integrating personal computers doesn't have to take months. The quicker you can assimilate all that you need to do, the better. Once you understand the business services, applications, data requirements, user activity, and projected growth, you can begin to formulate ideas about how integration can take place. Today's technology offers many avenues to explore.

The approach you take to integration is limited by the amount of risk your company is willing to accept and by the priority of problems you need to address. Risk is associated with the leading edge — the need or desire to either use new technology or wait for software that is not yet fully developed.

Not every company can be the first recipient of early-stage technology. Not every customer wants to be a trial site for a new concept. For example, customers of the first LANs in 1983 encountered a tremendous lack of software, reliability, problem diagnosis, and problems never before foreseen in data processing. These pioneering customers greatly influenced the ultimate designs of the products they used. However, some of these early customers became disenchanted and have still not fully accepted the benefits of this technology. Others felt they began too early, but that they learned a lot about integration.

◥ A LITTLE HISTORY

Today's workstation integration is substantially different from what was done in the 1970s. Intelligent workstations did not exist then, and data processing management had to use dumb terminals that accessed, but were not able to transfer, host data. So if you think you have done this before, think back again to what you really did.

When you added more terminals to service users, the process was straightforward. You knew the host processing power. You knew what percentage batch job processing consumed of the total host processing performance and how much remained to support on-line, interactive terminal activity. You developed rules of thumb over the years that dictated when you added additional hosts. This usually consisted of knowing that the host became saturated with a specific mix of interactive terminals and batch activity. When this point approached, you considered an additional host.

◥ SIZING HOST TERMINAL CAPACITY

Even if the host were dedicated to driving only on-line terminal activity, a number existed for each host and model that specified when the host system was saturated in terms of total connected terminals, when no more host power existed. (Other host factors affected this decision as well, but these factors are too technical to discuss here.)

For a given level of system, you could accurately predict at what point user terminal response time would deteriorate to unacceptable levels after a given number of interactive terminals were connected (see Figure 6-1). This curve varied and its shape changed, depending on the size of the host. Adjusting other system parameters also affected the shape of the curve. Data processing managers controlled resource management.

There were also other approaches. For example, a generally ineffective but often used practice involved connecting more terminals than the host could possibly service adequately. Management limited, with the host, the number of users who could be simultaneously interactive at one time. You installed, say, 100 terminals, but enabled only 64 to be actively connected to the host at any time. If you were not one of the first 64 users, you could not access the host. Although this represents one way around the problem, dedicated individuals soon learned how to circumvent this process. Because data wasn't being transferred all over the place with dumb terminals, as the data processing manager, you could control access with an iron hand.

You could also project user growth in on-line terminals to be added and estimate batch processing increases. You could pinpoint down to the quarter and month when you would require more host processing power. When you knew a new processor

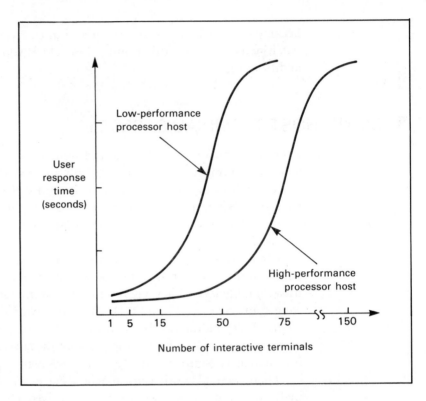

Figure 6-1. ▶

Terminal response time per host size

needed to be added, you planned accordingly. When a host was required, you generally enjoyed an abundance of capacity for a while, until workload absorbed the excess.

As the data processing manager, you primarily addressed terminal additions linearly—every terminal was connected to a controller that, in turn, was connected to the host. For our purposes, think of each terminal consuming a fixed set of host resources. Every terminal that was added required this same amount of resources. Consequently, you knew that adding a fixed number of terminals required an equivalent number of controllers and would eventually use up host processing power. The mental process, in a structured format, appeared as shown in the following illustration.

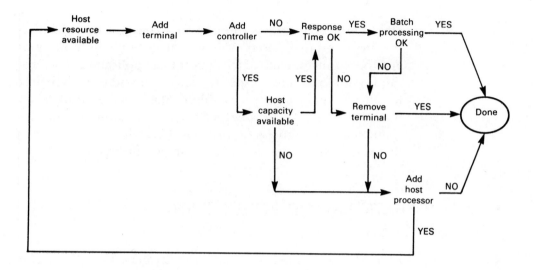

Effects of Personal Computers on Sizing

What's different in today's environment is that the arithmetic is no longer simple. Personal computers can perform thousands of activities or remain dormant (be standalone) with respect to the host. In essence, their drain on the host is as unpredictable as their use is predictable. They may retrieve host data, transfer large files, or operate standalone with physical host access capability. The load placed on the host varies, making it difficult to fix the usage of resources at any given moment.

You can no longer add up the number of terminals and personal computers connected to the host and easily determine the resources required to drive them. The situation becomes even more complicated as you add LANs, gateways, bridges, and file servers. The host is truly becoming a storage medium and system traffic director. Today's personal computer networks and link arrays bear little resemblance in operation to those of the early 1970s. Instead of directing the computing power of the host on centrally located data, users bring the data to their own desktop computers and applications.

Calculating the effect of this is difficult at best, and it is almost impossible unless you separately consider the activities of the user or group of users. You must first define the application and the resources required to support that application. Then you can begin to put into perspective what host resources are needed for that particular purpose. Taking the previous illustration, note that replacing *terminal* with *personal computer* does not change the flow process; it increases the additional information that you need in your decisions, as shown in Figure 6-2.

◤ CONSIDERATIONS AND INTEGRATION APPROACHES

Look at new methods for approaching workstation integration. Look at new products that offer you an opportunity to grow a system rather than just present a fix for today's problems. All too often, a product you may select to resolve a specific problem can't be used in another similar set of circumstances. If you choose products to solve particular problems, your micro-mainframe links will proliferate throughout your organization without any set pattern. Instead, look at products based on how they can be integrated together. Evaluate your problems as a whole and think of the system to be developed.

Choose vendors that satisfy your needs today and that can continue to support you as you grow. If the company is small, get acquainted with its management and understand their plans for product development and approach to customer support. You can have a great deal of influence on the company's product line. However, if the company is not financially sound, you may risk having an orphan product with no support. Look at big companies as well. What is their past performance? What is your past experience with them? In this embryonic industry, you are building a relationship beyond buying link products. In a sense, the company is the product because the company decides, with your help, what further products to develop. This is a very important aspect of today's market: most link vendors have only been in business since 1983.

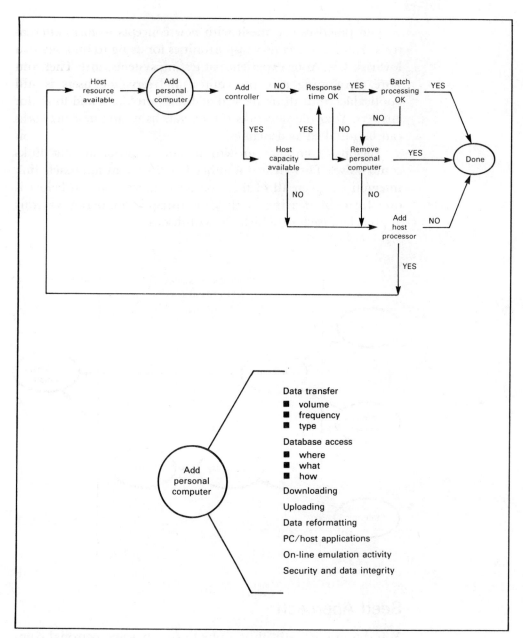

Figure 6-2. ▲

*Decision process
with personal
computers*

Old practices can mesh with new concepts to form alternatives. You can inject new opportunities for using technology in a low-risk way. Your experience at testing systems, installing software, developing new procedures, and servicing users is still applicable. Your thinking still addresses problems and looks for answers. Your old networks can operate as is, and new networks can be installed as demanded.

Personal computer growth became a problem that links could solve. This created another issue: how to approach link integration, given all of these product choices. Shown below is one form of dealing with link integration using various approaches, each of which we will discuss:

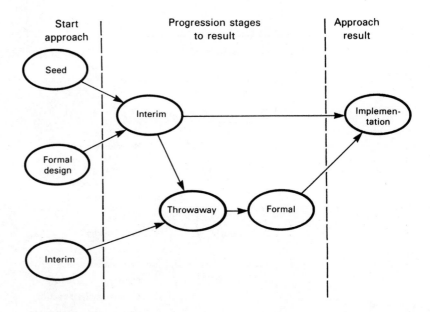

Seed Approach

You can use the seed philosophy to supply some personal computers to users and permit host access to selected areas or users. With this approach, watch carefully what applications are used on these seeds. Know what types of data are transferred and the frequency and volume of transfers to and from the host; then note patterns that occur. As these patterns evolve, you seed additional personal computers in the same departments to see if these patterns are consistent across all the users in the same area.

You have now formed a core or population density that can be quite informative about the ways that these workstations can be used in your business. It may sound rather clinical, like some experiment, but it is an experiment. The patterns that begin to emerge aren't dots in a picture; they are realities of how people begin to interact with the host.

Now you can develop a plan about how to fully integrate other personal computers in each area and how to supply resources to service each group. You have measured information about how and when the loads occur and what applications are being run at the personal computer and host. Expect more demands for connectivity and requests for additional tools for the personal computer as you progress.

Advantages and Disadvantages   The advantage of the seed approach is it gives you a chance to observe slowly and carefully and without great risk how personal computers can be constructively used in the business. It lets you decide where these systems should be placed. You have an opportunity to control the dispersement and set the guidelines. In the seed approach, *you* determine where the personal computers go. You retain control of a process that can quickly exceed management's ability to cope with transitions in the working area.

The disadvantage of the seed approach is that you do not know how the experiment can evolve. There is risk that personal computers will be used only for the most obvious tasks, such as word processing memos or trivial spreadsheet models. Although these tasks increase users' productivity, you can do the same thing by using dumb terminals in a host-based spreadsheet and text processing system. Ideally, the seed approach should generate curiosity and creativity from users to exploit what the host can offer.

Formal Design Approach

Another approach is the formal design. In this situation, you attempt to define all the existing parameters of the environment and plan ahead for the complete integration of all workstations throughout the company. If your company is large (several hundred or more personal computers), this task can be monumental. In small to medium-sized companies (25 to 250 personal computers), this task becomes manageable. Variations of this approach concentrate on specific departments or functions.

The formal design is a conscientious effort to establish quite clearly the data center's goals and requirements for supporting personal computer integration. The goal of the business is to make a profit. In many companies this means that the data center must reduce expenses, maintain sufficient computing power at less expense, and operate in a reliable manner. The formal design takes these issues into consideration with the technical requirements. It requires that you understand host resources and how they will be used in the future. It also requires you to understand what you want your users to be doing in the long term and what applications and tools you expect to provide. It demands that you define what personal computer tools and host access are available today and if they support growth over the long term. You'll also have to identify personnel skills needed for supporting links.

The formal design process uses logic to arrive at how personal computers are connected into the host and how they are expected to communicate across multiple hosts, possibly from different vendors. You should account for:

- Business requirements
- Technical needs
- Hardware connection mandates
- Data transfer limitations
- Security process
- Database availability
- Inter- and intranetwork possibilities

- Backup and recovery procedures
- Integration definition:
  What the overall design will be
- Implementation costs:
  Initial
  Ongoing
- Implementation stages
- Checkpoints to follow:
  Progress
  Problem resolution
- Vendor product selection for prototype
- Pilot definition:
  Validate design
  Validate requirements
- Installation testing:
  Connection hardware and software.

Advantages and Disadvantages   The advantage of this approach is that it allows you to identify and define important items. It gives you an overall strategy and approach for directing personal computer integration. It permits you to adjust to changes in the business, the economy, or the technology.

A disadvantage is the time required to develop a formal plan. Personal computers are often introduced faster than you can assemble such a plan, and departments sometimes do whatever they choose while waiting. It isn't appropriate to tackle the linking needs of an entire corporation at once unless your corporate culture and organization are conducive to the task.

Interim Approach

A third approach is the "staged" or interim method. With this approach, you address personal computer integration from the viewpoint that your solution for connecting to the host will be eventually either incorporated into an overall communications network structure or thrown away in favor of a different solution altogether.

An interim approach is good for companies that want to develop an overall, more formal integration plan for the business but need a quick link solution today, regardless of what the integration structure ultimately becomes. If your company cannot spend significant time defining requirements and devising an overall plan because user demands and requirements dictate immediate solutions this approach may be right for you. There are distinct questions, as shown below, that characterize whether an interim approach is suitable:

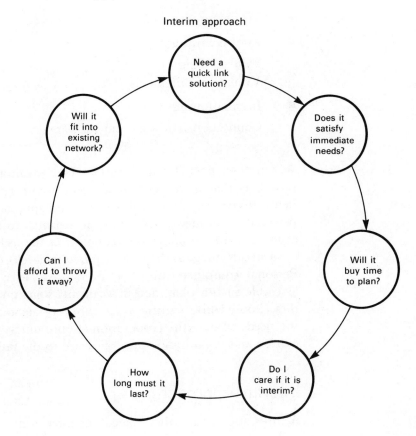

Interim approach

Interim-to-Formal

If you are in a company that wants a formal integration approach, the idea is to find ways to integrate personal computers that can be used with later network plans. Use safety and caution as you consider ways to perform the integration that can be used later and will fit company growth plans. This approach is for companies with low integration needs at the time — usually fewer than 20 personal computers. It is good for companies establishing their first real data processing center that have, up to now, operated with personal computers. It also works for companies that have very few (fewer than 10) personal computers and are just beginning to absorb more into their host.

You should select micro-mainframe link products — whether they are LANs, emulation links, or file servers — to be compatible with whatever direction your data processing center is most likely to take. You want to preserve your investment in these products and upwardly integrate them into your network. Therefore, select link products that will most likely be used in the new scheme.

Let's take an example: A company performing development on a DEC MicroVAX II VMS system required service for 10 users in the initial stages. Eventually, within 18 months, the plan called for a second MicroVAX II with VMS to support an additional 10 users. Local printers for each user were not required, nor were communications between personal computers at this stage. All such communications could be done via the host.

A great deal of uncertainty clouded the future use of a network LAN, and the company was not convinced that Ethernet was appropriate (or if a LAN was required at all). The solution involved direct connection of the personal computers with a VT/220 terminal emulator that could be used in a LAN environment. This option did not preclude use of Ethernet or any other LAN, yet it allowed immediate host access and data file transfer with personal computers. The company could use the same terminal emulation software with their final network plan, thus preserving its investment. All hardware and software acquired later, if necessary, would be *in addition to* the system, *not instead of* existing link products.

Advantages and Disadvantages   An interim-to-formal approach leaves you flexible to decide your ultimate processing needs and how they can be satisfied. You observe activities from the initial link connections. You make calculated investments, also in stages, until you define the one or two scenarios that your data processing needs dictate. This approach gives you time to learn about what you might do with your processing as well as time to understand the strengths and weaknesses of the interim integration solution. It allows you to be cautious and minimize expenditure while still supporting PC-to-host connection until you decide on the final design.

However, once an interim solution is installed, it can become permanent by default. If it takes too long to define the required network interconnection plan, you have to install your interim solution for every personal computer acquired. Eventually, this interim plan becomes your operating plan. To convert it into anything else becomes a bigger effort than originally conceived. Also, if what is anticipated in the network design is different from what actually occurs, the products selected to connect users to the host can become useless. In this case, you can't preserve any investment in hardware and software at all.

Interim as a Throwaway

In the second case of the interim approach (if you know that the solution will eventually be thrown away), goals are different. This approach is sometimes used by companies with hundreds of terminals, 50 to 300 personal computers or more, several hosts, and multiple department needs. Budgets and corporate attitudes can tolerate the notion of writing off hardware and software cost. It is an approach for companies that have a primary network standard, but who are encountering personal computer connection requests that don't immediately fit into the long-term scheme of things. Requests can be for host access or for personal computer networking that doesn't require host access.

Larger companies can solve user demands on a temporary basis and continue to grow along the plan and strategy established. It is not possible or cost effective for the company to devote excessive time to a request at hand if it is outside the ordinary or if it can be confined to a specific group of users that do not have a direct effect on host operations. In such a situation, the concern is not for a solution that can be upgraded into the network; it is of satisfying the user requirements quickly and economically.

The solution selected and implemented is eventually written off and discarded when the company finally gets around to including this group of users into the entire data processing process. Costs are not relevant.

Another example: A major West Coast bank was executing a computing decentralization strategy. It did not want to get immersed in problems of integrating handfuls of personal computer users (three to eight users) from various department functions across the company. These users basically only wanted to network personal computers within their departments. After careful consideration, an interim approach evolved. Several ways to connect systems were reviewed, an initial hardware and software investment was made, and ongoing support costs were added to the budget.

For every request involving similar needs, the bank selected and implemented a Corvus OmniNet for networking personal computers with a central hard disk for storage and common user access. Two individuals were trained for installing, testing, training users, supporting, and maintaining the system. These individuals installed the same equipment in response to each request. This equipment is expected to remain in place for about two years, when it will be removed in favor of more compatible host connection and networking access.

The bank benefits from several standpoints: user requests are satisfied; repeating solutions improves knowledge about its problems and installation; purchasing is consolidated for volume discounts; and user problems are serviced more efficiently if the problems across the base are similar. The bank expects to write the investment off in two years and feels that the investment today is well worth the time and aggravation to plan than to integrate these users piecemeal. Approximately 10 such OmniNets have been installed in 1985; another 10 or so are planned in 1986 unless the bank progresses sooner to a more elaborate LAN alternative.

Advantages and Disadvantages   The advantages to this type of interim approach are simple. The company never anticipates or cares if the adopted temporary solution is removed or integrated into the host network design. It serves a purpose and satisfies user needs as they exist at the time of the request. The cost of adopting such an approach is realistic for some companies; many more should probably consider it as well. The problem, however, is that too often the opinion is that if whatever is procured is not fully utilized, a poor decision has been made.

Sometimes an approach such as this one saves more time and money in the long term and gives you a chance to determine the optimal solution for your business. You should consider this decision carefully because the requirements vary for different companies. In our example, the bank did not require host access immediately and users were interconnected within their own environment. Another advantage is that because the solution is not likely to be integrated into the overall network, these users can be addressed later when you are ready with a linking plan that can be installed smoothly and in stages.

It is possible, given the design and plan, that the solution intended as a throwaway may actually be used in the end. Such a solution is not always tossed out, but when it is installed, it is never intended to be part of the final design.

One throwaway disadvantage is obviously cost. You make the decision that whatever money you are spending is to be written off. You decide that it is expendable money and the risk is that you have to do it all over again anyway. Another disadvantage is that when another host connection system is installed, users have to be retrained after they have become knowledgeable about the original system.

The obvious argument is that if the users keep the same applications, there should be no retraining or adjustment to new interfaces. With today's technology, however, no matter how hard we try to focus on retaining transparency to the user, there is always a change in procedures and processes. Today's technology simply does not allow a smooth transition to take place, although you can plan and hope for such a situation.

Figure 6-3 summarizes the advantages and disadvantages of each approach.

◤ ISSUES FOR INTEGRATING INTO EXISTING NETWORKS

If you don't have a system network installed, you can start with a clean slate and get organized. You can plan on what network is going to be basic to your company and anticipate the possibility that there can be more than one network. With so many evolving standards in the industry, having a multiple set of network protocols and standards is inevitable. The uncertainty of knowing which standards will be the most desirable and the most widely supported will continue through at least this decade. For example, there are Ethernet, IBM's SNA (System Network Architecture), Prime's PRIMENET, and Digital Equipment Corporations DECnet, to name just a few. There are also the X.25, X.400, and the ubiquitous IEEE 802.6 standards. Even within a given vendor's basic network, there are often several protocol levels supported. Link products must fit into these schemes.

There are many issues regarding linking personal computers to host mainframes and minicomputers, minicomputers linked to mainframes, and personal computers linked to other personal computers. The standards, protocols, and products begin to form layer upon layer of confusion that can distract the most serious architect and system designer.

If you have an information processing center with a network based on one or more of the protocols or designs listed above, the issues associated with linking personal computers into hosts will vary. You cannot delineate each and every problem encountered because different companies confront different usage patterns.

Approaches	Advantages	Disadvantages
Seed	■ Minimal risk ■ Control retained over workstation dispersement ■ Lets you set guidelines ■ Measure host effects ■ Identify emerging applications ■ Observe workstation usage ■ Slow/careful integration	■ Outcome uncertain ■ Potentially nothing creative evolves
Formal design	■ Important factors identified/defined ■ Develop overall strategy ■ Allows adjustment to change	■ Development time required ■ Difficult to keep pace with workstation installs ■ Departments do their own thing while waiting
Interim-to-formal	■ Flexibility to decide processing needs support for needs ■ Observe link integration ■ Calculated investments ■ Minimize initial expenditures ■ Step toward formal integration plan	■ Defaults to permanent solution ■ Conversion to anything else becomes difficult ■ Selected products don't satisfy final plan
Interim-to throwaway	■ Don't care about link solution ■ Is eventually discarded ■ Provides time to consider alternatives ■ Can be most economical decision in the long term ■ Satisfies immediate user link demands	■ Cost ■ Retraining after upgrade ■ Procedure changes ■ Technology does not yet provide smooth transition

Figure 6-3. ▲

Summary of link approaches

You can, however, identify important considerations for connecting personal computers into hosts that have established networking and protocol standards. These are

- Multiple host access within a given network.

- Host access across different networks.

- Access across different vendor hosts.

- Compatible and noncompatible personal computer integration.

- File transfer across multiple networks.

- Protocol conversion across vendor products.

- Problem detection and isolation.

- Network performance relative to the host.

These global issues are usually a part of integrating personal computers into existing networks. All information processing centers do not exhibit all of these traits. Large centers like Boeing Computer Services, General Motors, Hughes Aircraft, and Bank of America (to name just a few) confront all of them. You should identify which of these you confront today and which you are to deal with in the future as your needs change.

Multiple Host Access Within a Given Network

In many companies that process and transfer information, a single network infrastructure exists into which all added host computers interface. Eventually, by the year 2050, all host computers will communicate via a standard network infrastructure that permits connectivity from the personal computer level to the largest host mainframe. Public and private networks serving hundreds of thousands of users will be able to bridge to different information banks transparently and effortlessly.

For IBM, such a structure is called Systems Network Architecture (SNA). It provides for different layers of device-to-host interfacing. Varieties of network protocols are supported within a basic network architecture; the conceptual design forms a framework. Within this framework, these protocols define device communications between the network and host.

DEC offers its own infrastructure but also provides the capability to bridge its customers and equipment into the IBM environment. At this stage of the technology, DEC's full integration approach to systems can only be brought about by links, gateways, and bridges.

To put things into perspective, let's look at several examples.

IBM Connection Example

Figure 6-4 gives an example of how a network can be designed with IBM equipment. Each host can be in a different location yet still communicate over the same network. A personal computer can connect to a single host; however, it is also possible for a personal computer to access all three hosts.

Figure 6-4 is only a single example of host connection. Your link alternatives for connecting personal computers can also consist of the following options:

- Dial-up to each host using modems and file transfer software.

- Direct attachment via a coaxial connecting product to one host; dial-up remote access to the other hosts.

- A LAN providing an access highway for personal computers to hosts via gateways.

- A file server hosting personal computers and connecting to each host with high-speed lines.

What this example shows is that the host, although still an important part of the communications process, is basically moving information to end users. Its purpose is to process informa-

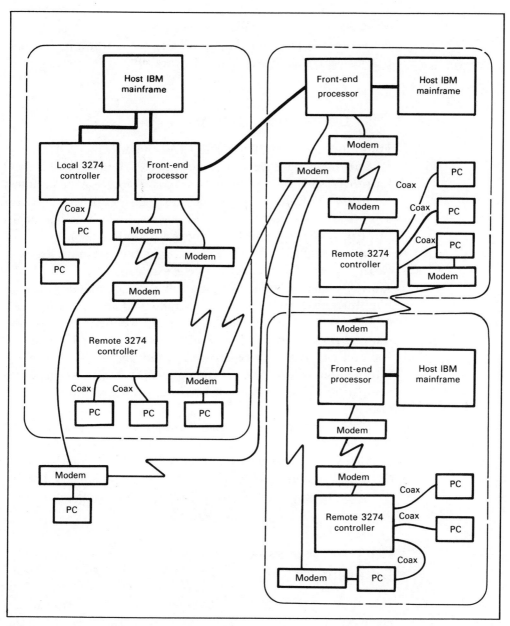

Figure 6-4. ▲

*IBM PC-host
network*

tion, execute applications, and manage databases. The network is the dominant force for the user, and the mainframe is a processing vehicle attached to the network.

DEC Connection Example

Figure 6-5 shows multiple DEC VAX hosts connected using a DECnet network. There are a multitude of options within DEC for providing end-user communications. For personal computers to access all hosts, you can use an Ethernet LAN. You can achieve multiple host access in other ways, including those identified in Figure 6-4 and listed above for IBM.

In either of the above examples, links can be connected via a variety of vendor products. These examples (IBM and DEC) show a framework for supporting link products and demonstrate how link products begin to form and integrate into a network framework. It's crucial that you maintain compatibility with the framework of the network and protocols supported. If you don't, you can encounter problems that negatively affect the flow of information to users that depend on data, and you can encounter compatibility issues when you expand to support future application needs.

Don't define or implement a complex solution to your problem immediately, and don't finesse the issue. Confront basic problems of integrating across multiple host configurations with as simple and straightforward a solution as possible. Whatever you design, expect it to remain for at least 24 months or longer.

Host Access Across Different Networks

If hosts are manufactured by the same vendor, then you can use gateways as a transition between differing networks. Once inside a given network, problems of access are simplified. The key is getting between the networks in a simple and easy way. Theoretically, the user never needs to know that cross-network access is occurring. The gateway, described in Chapter 3, is designed to solve incompatibility problems between different networks.

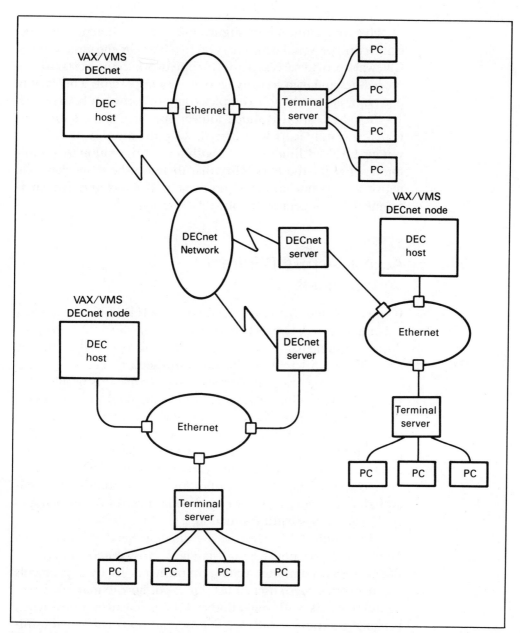

Figure 6-5. ▲

*DEC PC-host
network
(Ethernet LAN
configuration)*

The configuration in Figure 6-6 shows different networks connecting personal computers on two hosts by the same vendor. Gateways provide access across each network to the hosts. Access procedures and data security become very important. This is only one example; much more complex configurations can be designed.

Standardization is much touted, but there are situations in which it simply can't be achieved. Keep the number of different vendor LANs or link networks within a configuration to a minimum. Plan for the possibility that there can be more than one network type, but minimize how many. If the connecting environment is to operate reliably, this is crucial.

Access Across Different Vendor Hosts

If you are trying to access several hosts made by different vendors operating in separate networks, you have a different and more difficult problem to solve than permitting personal computer access across different vendor hosts in the same network. Companies and large users have been trying to solve this problem for years. The only solution so far is to add extra hardware to provide the electrical interfaces and software that performs data and protocol interfacing between the vendor operating systems. The products provide a bridge for customers that have users requiring access to different systems for various reasons. The users may need to access data, execute applications, or run tools that are not available to them on the personal computer. This can be especially true in a scientific situation.

The problem of access across different vendor hosts is the direct result of not having standard cross-vendor interfaces. Because each computer vendor implements its own protocols and network design, users must figure out how to make different equipment talk with one another. The problem is worse when personal computers want access to several hosts and when minicomputers impose an additional interim stage. The layers of interfacing and communications magnify integration issues and make your decision process difficult.

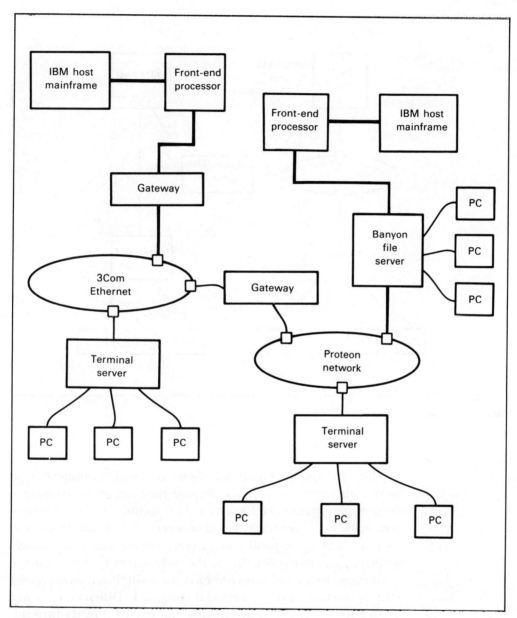

Figure 6-6. ▲

*Host-PC access
across different
LANs*

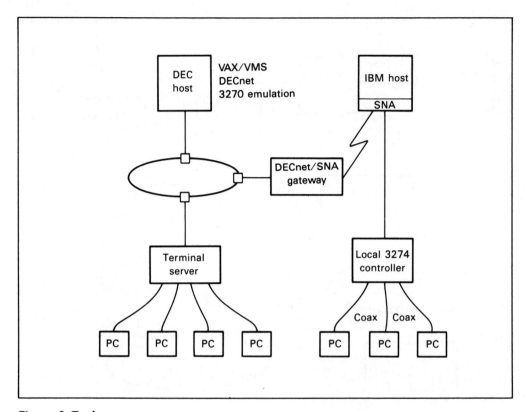

Figure 6-7. ▲

PC access to different vendor hosts

The example in Figure 6-7 shows personal computer access to two different vendor hosts. Because each vendor host observes its own terminal device formats and protocols, all of these terminals have to be emulated for host access. It is cumbersome for users to have to be proficient in every vendor's terminal screen formats, but sometimes this is the only solution. Some micro-mainframe link emulation products use a single hardware board that is inserted into the personal computer. Different terminal emulators are provided as software and loaded directly into the personal computer from a floppy disk. This gives the connecting board a "personality" that the host can recognize.

You have to recall that every vendor started by expecting to create its own market and customer base, which spurred growth. Now other vendors realize that additional markets and growth can be created by linking these systems together. Some host vendors have also realized that they can get additional growth by allowing their customer bases to access other host systems. Although technology is not yet at a stage in this area to make it easy and efficient for the customer to move freely across different hosts, it is evolving.

Most customers attempt to isolate different vendor hosts and keep their use restricted to the area or department they serve. In some cases this is not possible, and data transfer must be performed across hosts. In other cases users do not directly access the host but transfer data between hosts and use it on the host to which they are connected.

Several products permit users to access multiple hosts, access the same and different vendor hosts, and transfer data across hosts. For example, the Software Research Center offers a software product that allows such data movement across several different vendors' host computers, such as IBM, DEC, and WANG. Figure 6-8 shows how this company accomplishes inter-vendor host access and data transfer with its System Network Environment (SNE).

Although the inter-vendor problem can be solved, don't immediately rush to install modems and prepare all personal computer users for dial-in. Also, don't rush out and purchase emulators for quick installation and operation. You can exchange one set of problems for another. Have a plan in mind—if not on paper, at least in your head—for an approach to solve your linking issues instead of quickly finding products to do the job for now. You can create headaches later as you link more personal computers over time, especially in a multihost environment. This is more complicated if each host operates its own vendor-proprietary network.

◥ PERSONAL COMPUTER INTEGRATION: COMPATIBLE AND NONCOMPATIBLE

From early on, businesses encountered a mixture of different personal computer products. Personal computers ran on a variety of different operating systems, such as PC-DOS, CP/M, and CP/M-86. These were standalone systems and did not require

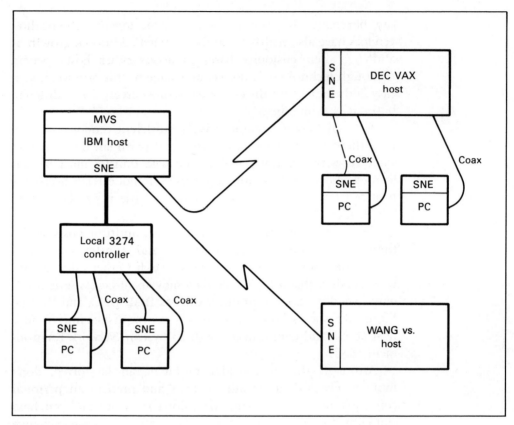

Figure 6-8. ▲

File transfer across different vendor host/PCs (SNE [System Network Environment] provides file transfer between vendor hosts)

host connection. The need for a standard operating system clearly did not exist at the time. Unfortunately, the personal computer add-on market did not evolve in the same way for this mixture of personal computer vendors as it did for IBM.

Most large customers have by now standardized on some personal computer type, likely IBM, and purchase only IBM or IBM-compatible systems. Apple's Macintosh computer is gaining presence in some organizations with specific needs. It is popular in markets in which the Macintosh's size and graphics capability are extremely useful. The Macintosh is also appearing in some scientific areas and in markets like desktop publishing, where ease of use is a primary consideration.

If your business uses a mixture of personal computers, your problems are concerned with physical connection, file transfer, and interpersonal computer communications. Your first question must be "Is it necessary for a user on one personal computer type to communicate directly with another on a totally incompatible personal computer?" If the answer is no, then you can decide if the users of each type of equipment can be isolated and addressed separately. If so, this eases the connectivity issue, and you can treat physical connection independently.You simply select, review, and prototype micro-mainframe links for interfacing that particular type of equipment.

If the answer is yes, you do need to interface personal computers that are not compatible, then you can determine if you can handle such communications through the host or directly between personal computer users. If each personal computer uses a different link or LAN to talk to the host, you can have problems. The common problem in interfacing unlike personal computers is file transfer. Personal computers that are not compatible, such as the IBM PC and the Macintosh, use different file formats. Transferring data between the two means that the data has to be formatted to be recognized by the machine. You must then develop templates to perform data translation so that transferred data can be transferred. Figure 6-9 shows a diagram, again using gateways, that connects noncompatible personal computers.

In such a mixed environment, you have to understand what the interplay is and how users work with the host. Don't try to force isolation among the users; the object is to treat all personal computers as if they are devices with singularly peculiar characteristics.

Fortunately, this kind of mixed situation is rare. Most companies standardize on either IBM or the Apple Macintosh. If your company is using both brands, they are probably being used for different applications. At the interface level, you don't care what the workstation is, only that it can transparently connect into your network.

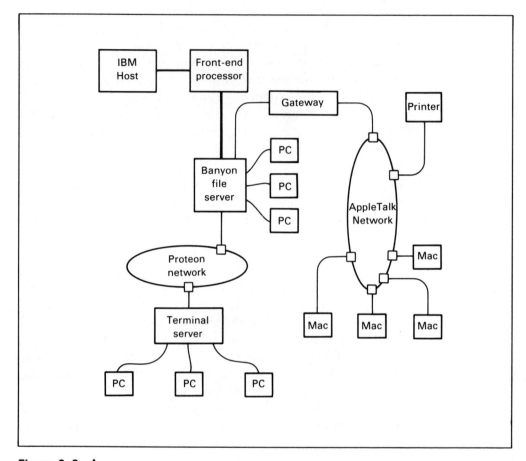

Figure 6-9. ▲

Gateways connecting noncompatible workstations

◥ FILE TRANSFER ACROSS MULTIPLE NETWORKS AND HOSTS

Part of this problem was addressed in previous discussions of personal computer access to different networks and hosts. Here we deal with physical data file transfer in addition to host access: the actual transmission of entire data files and information. Different networks, as you know, are implemented in different ways for communicating to personal computers, carrying data, and talking with hosts. Like the minicomputer and mainframe manufacturers, many of the networks designed by manufacturers are different because each vendor perceived specific market needs. Consequently, each LAN offers a distinct implementation and unique connection requirements.

Gateways, as pointed out earlier, are products that allow different networks to communicate. Their role is to translate between different networks so that data can be transferred back and forth. It is not easy to simplify cross-network access, but with precautions and procedures, you can transfer data in an organized way. Your users can be mobile between networks without having to know the technical details of how they got to where they wanted to go.

To travel back and forth between different networks, files usually have to be translated. If the vendor does not supply translation software, you must write it yourself or locate a third-party vendor who can. Recognize the obvious: different vendor host computers have different operating systems, and some hosts can operate under more than one operating system.

For example, an operating system called VMS is prevalent on DEC systems. IBM offers its large-processor system users both MVS (multiple virtual system) and VM (virtual machine). Both vendors have different operating and communications characteristics and manage and store data files in a different way. Also, if Unix, still another type of operating system, is operated on IBM and DEC systems in the same environment, the versions of Unix that are used in the different systems may often differ.

To transfer files and information between hosts, you must have software that can operate with whatever operating systems are involved. This software must translate data in accordance with the file structures supported by each vendor.

Protocol Conversion Across Vendor Products

Not all terminals and communications possibilities conform to the same technical protocols necessary to enable one to talk to the other. This is a traditional problem. Many times customers use a wide assortment of terminals. When personal computers are also used, the problem gets more complicated. Sometimes it is not only desirable but also sensible for you to have some of these terminals perform double duty and appear as other terminals to increase their useful life.

If heavy data transfer is not required, a hardware unit called a protocol converter can be an appropriate solution to the connection problem. Its capabilities are limited: it can only convert from one form of device protocol to another. Such a solution could be just what the doctor ordered in certain situations. The connection problem becomes one of pure technical protocol translation between one device and another.

Protocol converters do not have intelligence; they merely interface two dissimilar pieces of equipment. Unlike an emulator, a protocol converter offers no capability beyond pure connectivity. Each data processing installation generally supports several types of protocols, even more if a LAN is supported. To integrate personal computers, all these protocols must be exactly adhered to. Protocol converters can offer you a clean and simple solution.

Detecting and Isolating Problems

Serviceability and maintenance are two big concerns in today's market and in a rapidly expanding data center. Users are connecting into public and private networks, and data is being moved in all directions. Inside your own installation, your networks are expanding, supporting more personal computers, and using host performance.

You must be able to detect, isolate, and diagnose problems as quickly as possible for high network availability. (The term *network* is used here to apply even to a single personal-computer-to-host link.) Too many products on the market rely on diagnostics supplied by host computer vendors, and many supply no diagnostics at all. You will not always find problems in the hardware or software installed inside the personal computer. If a failure occurs in the personal computer, it is usually easy to identify; the corrective action usually is to replace the micro-link board with another. This is the easiest of problems to solve. The following illustration shows a simplified flow for determining link failure. Clearly, corrective action can involve the vendor, depending on how complex your links are.

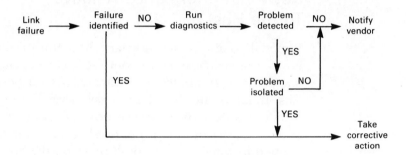

Your real complications involve situations in which failures occur in the network because of problems in the personal computer communications hardware. Operations management must identify where the source of the problem is, what caused it, and how to prevent it in the future. If there are 200 personal computers linked to the host, the problems quickly mushroom, and isolating them can be difficult or almost impossible.

Network diagnostics and system monitoring software are imperative. They are even more so if you have installed a variety of vendor products that must interface and communicate with one another. You cannot afford to invest a significant amount of money in equipment and network configurations and leave maintenance and operation to fate. If you don't have tools to help you, your exposure to lengthy problem periods can rise dramatically, particularly if you have no idea where to look for the solutions to the problems.

Be sure you know what the link vendor supplies as diagnostics. Establish a prototype check to see if the diagnostics perform and do what the vendor claims. Test to see if the diagnostics do what you want them to do and satisfy *your* requirements. If the vendor does not supply diagnostics, you should know what is recommended for problem resolution and what other products can do the job of detecting and isolating failures.

Network Performance Relative To the Host

Personal computer networks and host links can drain all of a host's spare capacity and resources. It is deceiving how much a few personal computers can demand from a host, especially if data transfers are very large—say, several hundred thousand bytes of data at a time for each personal computer. This volume of data transfer in itself is not overly demanding unless transfers are frequent and occur at peak times on the host—times when the processor is engaged in heavy resource usage that prevent it from providing optimal service to your on-line users.

Going back to earlier discussions, recall that you must establish and project the data transfer volume, the kind of activities taking place at the personal computer, what host service is expected, and what type of turnaround response time is required from the host. Understand how the system is to grow as more applications and users are added. You will have to tune the host to optimize the system for distributing its resource allocation based on the projected workload. No matter what you do, you can never ignore performance tuning.

You cannot expect to establish a network or extensive personal-computer-to-host links without any effects on the host. Although these effects can be small, depending on what is being done, as the users become more comfortable and explore other uses, demand can sneak up on you faster than you anticipated. All of a sudden your only option may be to add another host processor. With the proper planning, you can often avoid this very expensive proposition. At the very least, anticipate when an upgrade or host addition must be made and prepare financially for its introduction.

◥ SOLVING INCOMPATIBLE INTEGRATION ISSUES

Every time you combine different hardware and software products, the problem of incompatibility arises. Sometimes you even encounter a problem within a single vendor's product line. Hosting personal computers accentuates the problem because you have to address the various types of manufacturers' products that perform the same function and connection, but do so in different ways. You need not be concerned with how these products have implemented the process of connection, only with whether you can interchange or upgrade them.

A more important issue is that products that link personal computers to a host must process protocols and handle errors in a way that is consistent with existing networks. It's hard to know this before you install the product and see how it interacts with the existing systems.

Direct/Remote Host Connection

If being compatible with another micro-mainframe link standard like IRMA is important, are you sure that the product you selected is fully compatible? If IRMA or any other link is your standard and you are considering a new vendor link, satisfy yourself that software can be loaded and used on the new link. It's all right to have a variety of link products installed, provided different data transfer conversions aren't required at the host for each one. The key to link compatibility is at the software level—at the application level. If this remains transparent to the user, then the link hardware is irrelevant.

File Servers and LANs

The same logic described above is true for more sophisticated linking product strategies using file servers and LANs. Every vendor of a link handles things in a slightly different way from those products that they are competing against. Variations occur in the most compatible situations unless the product is a direct copy. LANs and file servers are no different; they too must interface with what you already have in operation. In some cases, variations will appear only in the interface presented to the user. If you are going to connect devices, make sure that protocol handling for device emulation conforms to system host vendor standards. It must be consistent across vendor links.

Across LANs, incompatibilities are masked with gateways. If you use a gateway, ensure with the vendor that the particular network LAN in question is in fact supported. Be sure you know how the LAN is supported and if there are any prerequisites to interfacing that you must satisfy before operation. Ask to speak with several customers who have the products installed in environments similar to yours. If the vendor does not have such customers, ask for reference accounts that you can speak with about their experience.

The time you spend in identifying potential exposures and nuances of operation is a small price to pay, considering the size of investment in a LAN or file server. This price encompasses dollars, time, and resources. If you acquire the link and it does not satisfy your needs, you have wasted the precious time of your people and have a product that cannot be returned to the vendor. It is difficult to tell management that you have made an error and will have to try a new method.

The greatest problem with dissimilar LANs and links is the lack of standards across these products. Unfortunately, the burden falls on the user. If you aren't careful, you can end up with a very costly and, possibly, unusable situation that simply requires more dollars and time to fix. Getting incompatible networks together can become a nightmare of large proportions.

There are no easy solutions for the compatibility problem. All that can help you is knowledge about what you need to do, how you want to do it, and unmerciful probing of the manufacturer about link capabilities. You cannot afford to do a blind install based strictly and solely on the literature that you read. You can get by with this if you are only using emulation products and the investment in one or two such links is small relative to the total cost of the system. However, with LANs and network gateways the cost and investment are much greater and the consequences of incompatibility are of a greater magnitude.

◢ DEVELOPING AN INITIAL NETWORK

There are two ways to go about establishing a micro-mainframe link network: top down and bottom up. There are many solutions to the same problem; it is the *approach* to the solution that is important.

When you go through the top-down process, you must assess all of the activities and needs of the users and business as described earlier in this book. You must consider the total system to be installed as well as the growth expectations associated with expanding and modifying the system over time as business and user needs change.

The other option is from the bottom up. Identify the specific user needs of what is necessary at this moment to link the personal computer to the host. Look at the problem of linking from the standpoint of what you can do today with today's technology to link that particular personal computer into the host, whatever the host may be. Decide if an IRMA, Forte, CXI, or ITI emulation board can do the job. Is file transfer software necessary? Do you care about transfer speed? Are more extensive departmental LAN systems required and, if so, which ones can you rely upon? Straightforward questions and answers characterize the bottom-up process.

The purpose of the bottom-up approach is to determine what you can do today with the technology at hand, regardless of the long-term plan. You decide if the solution can be used as you approach the implementation of your overall integration plan. If it can, maybe you have a winner. The following illustration shows how to converge on your initial network and link options from two points of view.

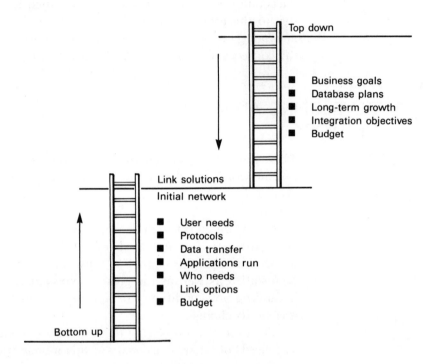

Two Alternate Initial Link Examples

Let's use another example: A bank needed to provide access to a host for its trust management. The data required could be identified and segmented. It could be isolated and downloaded very conveniently to users without affecting others on the host system. Looking from the top down, the bank knew that ultimately it would require a network and server structure to facilitate data movement to other users within the department, and eventually to external customers. From the bottom up, the bank needed to give access to personal computer users in the trust department immediately so that they could perform their functions more efficiently. The bank required a link solution that remained both cost effective (economical) and usable in the completed network.

Using the bottom-up approach, the bank selected DCA's IRMA product with file transfer software for direct connection to the host. IRMA is a PC-installed board that provides full IBM 3278 terminal emulation and connects directly to the control unit. Thus, users of IRMA could access other systems on the host beyond the trust information. For a LAN, they chose Micro Tempus' Tempus Link to interface all of the local personal computers in that department into the host. Tempus Link offers a wide set of capabilities, including the ability to generate applications cohesively at the host and at the personal computer. An interface at both ends facilitates building applications with the link interfaces in mind. Once this is done, data transfer becomes a natural part of the application. As a link interface, Tempus Link permits data to be transferred via emulation hardware products from a number of vendors.

Tempus Link supports a variety of 3278 emulation boards, including DCA's IRMA product, so the selected bottom-up solution remained compatible and usable. As remote personal computer users were permitted access, DCA's IRMALine provided a natural extension that gave a fully compatible system. The bank is now tuning the system to optimize performance when downloading, and uploading occurs at the end of each day.

In this example, another alternative for the long-term solution was to provide a file server local to the users of the trust department. A separate file server serviced external user access. From the bottom up, DCA IRMA boards were installed in the personal computers for direct host access. These interfaced with the selected file server. Data was downloaded to the server once each day; users worked off the server and rarely needed host access. External users operated in the same way, although remotely to the server. At the end of the day, users transferred data to the server and a controlled host update took place. As in the previous case, the solution defined here offers both a short-term and a long-term solution.

◥ SUMMARY OF LINK APPROACHES

To develop an initial link network, it is important to consider both ends of the program:

- What would you like to have operational in the future?

- What do you need to do right now to satisfy user access demand?

A plan that takes six months to implement does not work when users need to get to the host immediately.

Develop a micro-mainframe link network by watching it evolve and modifying your master plan as you proceed. Have a plan in mind, and address problems as they arise. Anticipate issues that occur as you implement the system, and know your direction. Otherwise, you end up with a mesh of products that do not permit you the luxury of developing an integrated system that also supports the services and software applications you know are to be resident on your host and available to your users.

◥ PORTABILITY, ADAPTABILITY, AND COMPATIBILITY

Figure 6-10 shows how these three factors overlap. No overlap (Figure 6-10a) can mean you have distinct problems in the future because it is difficult to build on your selected link base. The degree to which you overlap (Figure 6-10b) shows flexibility in your link selections and plan. The greater the overlap, the greater the flexibility.

Portability

Portability is being able to take a given micro-mainframe link solution and move, or port, it to link other personal computers in the same way. It means taking the same products and using them in a different department or function without having to

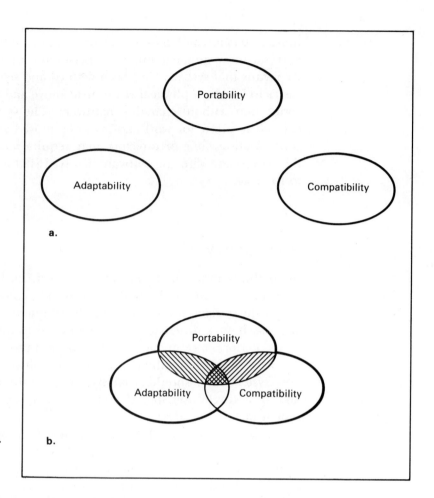

Figure 6-10. ▶

*Factors for link
planning*

modify procedures. When you plan a micro-mainframe link
network, this is the ideal situation. You have either defined all of
your requirements exactly right, or the variation in the usage of
your host systems is small: most of your users do not vary in the
types of activities they perform or the host services they expect. It
can also mean that you have standardized your approach enough
so that you can select from a list of particular types of equipment
that are interchangeable when necessary.

Portability applies to the system as well. In most large businesses, users are mobile—they move from office to office. Along with the move go the terminals or personal computers. Portability means that systems have been defined and set up so that it's easier to handle a physical equipment move and reestablish the connection without changing hardware. The system is flexible enough to allow for workstations to be moved easily. A system configuration table or directory may require modification, but the actual hardware and software involved is almost transparent to the user.

Adaptability

Adaptability means that you can use your defined hardware and software with only slight modifications to be consistent with the rest of the system. You can take a defined micro-mainframe link and use it in a different set of circumstances for a new user's needs. Performance in data transfer can be a problem, but it can be corrected by using different file transfer software or tuning the host system. You shouldn't change or tune the system for the sake of a single user, but if there are many users, tuning the system may be practical.

In some cases adaptability means modifying applications to fit network needs. However, you should not let linking requirements dictate applications and services—quite the opposite. You know what your communications requirements ought to be, and you should optimize activities to meet those goals. If you have already selected and implemented certain micro-mainframe link, LAN, or file server products into your organization, you can adapt them into areas for which they were not originally intended. Before acquiring a totally new solution that can be very costly, explore this possibility. The system and operational drawbacks of expanding link usage into other company sectors are sometimes not serious enough to demand all-new hardware and software expenditures.

Compatibility

We talk about compatibility throughout this book; if not directly, we imply it. If your company is concerned with costly expenditures, future operational performance, and consistency within the company data center, focus on compatibility. Many quality products are on the market, and you should not necessarily restrict yourself to a particular vendor. A company that uses several vendors receives better support, service, and maintenance, because its suppliers are concerned about the possibility of losing the account.

On the positive side, customer attention and support also increase if the vendor feels there is a chance to increase its business activity within the account. Vendors tend to monitor a mixed account with an eye toward the possibility of selling and installing more equipment. But when you look at the different vendor products that perform the same function, be sure that they can coexist if they must operate together.

Compatible has been defined as "capable of existing or operating together in harmony." To carry this definition a stage further, compatibility means being able to select link products that can freely work with the rest of your data processing center. It means that if you select several different link products, whether you choose to interchange them or not, they should conform to the system that you have already established.

Factors governing link functionality, features, and performance should not require you to make major adjustments to your host complex to accommodate the micro-mainframe link operation. Remember, links are used to connect personal computers to the host, not to force the host to conform to the personal computer operation.

You must make sure that products coexist with hosts as additional hosts are added and upgraded. This process can be simple if you have carefully defined what is needed and how the system complex grows. If you choose specific link products, be sure that any other vendor links conform at least closely to the characteristics of the existing links. If the basic emulation-type micro-mainframe links are to become part of a larger scheme, be sure that the more advanced system can absorb these products harmoniously.

◥ SUMMARY

This chapter covered a lot of material and made many suggestions for integrating personal computers. It discussed approaches and examples used by companies confronting questions similar to yours. While each situation is unique, every problem need not be approached differently. The same strategies will apply to a broad range of problems.

Some companies have a good grasp on what they must do and what their plans are, while others seem to flounder, feeling that it is too hard to select a group of solutions to solve their link issues. They construct barriers or pose arguments to why they can't just start to develop a plan. If you don't think about what you are doing and organize your approach accordingly, you will continue to become more confused and less in control of the personal-computer-linking situation than you are now.

Let's review what this chapter covers so you can refer to it when the need arises. This summary will refresh your memory about aspects that we discussed for planning approaches.

We discussed four approaches to personal computer integration:

- Seed
- Formal design
- Interim-to-formal design
- Interim-to-throwaway.

Each offers advantages and disadvantages as summarized in the decision process chart in Figure 6-3. The seed approach works when you want to retain control of personal computer dispersement and *observe* their usage. It's a controlled way to determine what link needs prevail for host access. More seeds can be added as needed.

Use the formal design when you want to prepare everything before linking is approached. This approach deals with defining key elements of your host access requirements and user needs before beginning the process of link selection.

The two interim approaches work in situations in which you need to resolve user host access linking problems immediately but know that the solution you choose will gravitate toward something different in the future. You are in one of two situations. Either you are buying time to establish a much more formal strategy about how your business addresses workstation integration, or you know that a completely different approach for integrating links will be defined and used, rendering the present solution obsolete.

You can confront link issues across several combinations of hosts and networks — maybe even all of them, depending upon your company. These are:

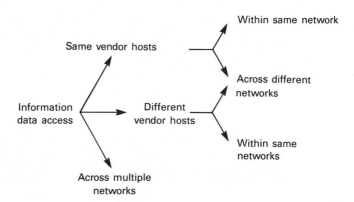

The above are the most serious considerations that demand thought. Others were identified as needing your attention. These include:

- Converting protocols across vendor products

- Detecting and isolating technical problems

- Network performance and the host
- Compatible and noncompatible workstations.

These factors demand attention when you sort out the approach you will use and decide how you cope with potentially difficult situations in your environment. When you use LANs and file servers, cross-network communications can be the norm rather than the exception. It's important to know you can gain a great deal of progress if you can eliminate several of these variables from your concerns. The process of elimination can help you arrive at a workable solution. Remember, it's how you approach the problem that is important. This process helps you identify problems and warns you when you are straying from your goal.

You can develop an initial network in two ways: bottom up and top down. If you use the bottom-up approach, you first identify specific user needs that you must address today, immediately. The top-down approach means that you assess user and business needs from the standpoint of what is good for the business. Merging the two can produce an excellent link plan.

In summarizing, we talk about portability, adaptability, and compatibility of link solutions. In a large organization with 6000 personal computers, it is impossible to promote a standard to which everyone adheres, especially with technologies and user needs as diverse as they are. With any approach you take, you must keep in mind that your information processing installation will surely change with time. All your considerations, plans, and strategies for personal computer integration must be flexible enough to grow with user needs without your having to redesign the system. Users are mobile; their needs change, and so do their opinions. Any approach you take should not lock you into a solution that is incompatible with the changing needs of your organization.

7 Developing an Implementation Plan

◥ CRUCIAL GUIDELINES
◥ DIVIDING LINK IMPLEMENTATION
◥ COSTS: REAL AND HIDDEN
◥ INTANGIBLE TRAINING AND EDUCATION COSTS
◥ HOST COSTS
◥ ESTABLISHING A PILOT
◥ INTERPRETING THE PILOT
◥ ESTABLISH THE IMPLEMENTATION PLAN

In this chapter, we'll talk about about how to develop a plan for implementing micro-mainframe link strategies. If you only have five or six personal computers in a data processing organization, then you probably do not need a formal strategy or implementation plan unless you expect to grow rapidly or want to build a base framework. If you are going to end up with 60 personal computers six months down the road, then you need a plan. If you have 8000 personal computers throughout several company divisions, then a plan is the surest way to avoid chaos.

For example, if you have a DEC MicroVAX I, with only six personal computers, your options are pretty straightforward. On the other hand, let's assume you have a DEC MicroVAX II with 10 personal computers, plans for dial-in access of another four or six PCs, and anticipate host-to-host data transfer with another MicroVAX II located elsewhere. You should sit down and decide how you are going to provide linkages for this environment. You are going to encounter issues that you must confront in establishing communications with this hardware.

Take another case of a company with 6000 personal computers dispersed across several geographical locations. Over 80 percent access the hosts via dial-in, and downloading consists of entire data files and selected information from databases. In addition, another 6000 dumb terminals access the hosts. You need a plan if you expect to address personal computer linkage in ways that allow your company to know what authorized products are used, what application data is required, and what host operations must plan for capacity and service. You will have to address the needs of individual areas because a corporate-wide plan is probably next to impossible. But you can get an understanding of your situation.

Things are different from ten years ago—even from three years ago. We are not dealing with consistent, "basic-vanilla" situations any longer. You must mix terminals and personal computers because demand and usage require you to do so. It's definitely not a game of pick-up sticks in which you throw everything out and pick up the pieces. It's also not a situation where you can nonchalantly let things happen by themselves with the hope that other people will listen to you. You can't just assemble a product matrix and say, "If your need fits the following points, buy this product." User needs are evolutionary, and product recommendations must keep this in mind.

Today's technology is still too expensive and complex for an approach that merely allows things to happen haphazardly. Every company is always watching the bottom line. Communications costs are increasing, as are the costs of servicing users, processing transactions, and transferring data.

In the "good old days," you contended only with dumb terminals whose resource drain you could calculate and predict. Today, with personal computers that you can no longer predict and calculate, you can only estimate and anticipate. Personal computers have forced a change in attitude as well as in how you cope with the expansion of user computing.

◥ CRUCIAL GUIDELINES

In developing an implementation plan, you must know your objectives: know what you want to happen, and what major stages are important.

The most important thing to remember about establishing an implementation plan is that you are working with communications products—hardware and software. These are not your usual add-on peripherals such as personal computer multifunction boards, mouse attachments, graphics cards, or additional memory. All of those products can be contained within a standalone personal computer. Literally, they have no affect on anything or anyone beyond the actual user at that particular personal computer.

A micro-mainframe link, LAN, or file server is different. Such products require hardware, software, or both to be installed in the personal computer that connects directly or remotely into the host computer. The product transfers data to or from a host or network connected to a host. The fact that it is moving and accessing data beyond its own realm makes this product a totally different entity. It is a communications device that incorporates itself into your system by the very nature of its purpose: to bring external databases and applications to the desktop.

Guideline Importance

Guidelines are as important as you wish to make them. They provide a road map of items you must consider in sizing and developing micro-mainframe link integration plans and implementing them into your installation. For some types of guidelines, such as those for education and training, cost implications are high and must be capably assessed. These are *business costs*. Organizing the approach is important, and misreading some subtle requirements can cost you a sizable amount of time and dollars. At a minimum, you must address six major guidelines in establishing a sound link implementation plan, as shown next:

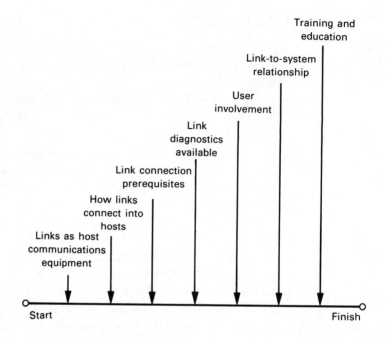

1. Treat Link Products as Any Other Major Communications Equipment That Interfaces With Your Host   Why? Because link products can create problems within your network and environment that can affect other users. They can tie up a line into the host, incapacitate an expensive controller servicing other terminals, or provide an incorrect response to host software. In a LAN, links can cause conditions that could conceivably terminate the entire network, causing all LAN users to lose their sessions. Though things are improving and LANs now offer great flexibility and usage options, caution is a prudent recommendation. Demand the same respect for links as for other expensive communications equipment.

Costs will vary with the sophistication of the product. The real effect on your budget is not only what you spend to procure the products, but what it costs you to identify problems and replace unreliable or poorly performing products. Your costs go far beyond the actual vendor purchase order. You have to hold costs of personal computer integration in very high regard because they quickly become higher than you think.

2. Know How Link Devices Connect Into the Host as Well as the Required Prerequisites   Every vendor and every manufacturer of links require certain prerequisites. They can be a specific personal computer operating system, a communications adapter card, or another vendor's link emulation card. Find out what needs to be done. You may have to establish configuration tables in more sophisticated links or assess the availability of terminal controller ports for coaxial links. It might even be a distance requirement that must be satisfied.

Other prerequisites include

- Minimum and maximum data transfer speeds
- Speed matching with controllers
- Protocol recognition
- Communications types (i.e., asynchronous, bisynchronous, SNA/SDLC, HDLC, etc.)
- Application data reformatting
  For host application access
  For personal computer use
- Data formats that they handle

Remember to consider *both* hardware and software factors, as shown in Figure 7-1.

The key question to ask your vendor is, "Once I have this product, what must I do to install, operate, maintain, and run it as you describe?" Keep in mind that you provide the vendor information about your installation. The vendor must have some idea of what you are connecting the product into and how the user is expecting to use it. If the vendor does not provide a comfortable feeling, then dig a little deeper before you acquire the product.

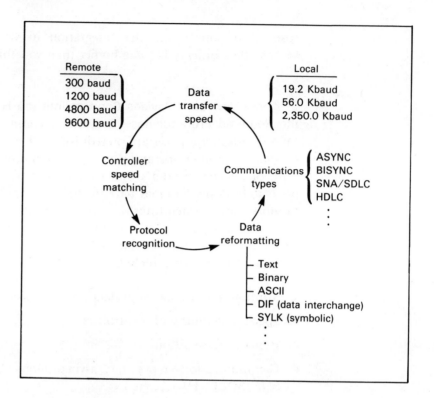

Figure 7-1. ▶

Link prerequisite factors

Here is where hidden costs begin to arise. What you see is not always what you get and need. Watch the extras that you must install or do to implement a micro-mainframe link system fully. Your costs can quickly double or triple for each user as you learn the link vendor's prerequisites.

3. Know What Diagnostics Are Available Know how comprehensive the diagnostics are, how they are executed, and what types of problems are detected and isolated. In developing a micro-mainframe link implementation plan, it is imperative to be able to locate, identify, and correct problems that arise during link phase-in. It is absolutely necessary to know whether the link product *is* the problem or *caused* the problem. Either condition must be detected during the implementation period.

Ideally, diagnostic effectiveness should be known after the prototype phase (as discussed in Chapter 9). Good diagnostics are even more critical during production implementation than in the testing phase. You are installing supposedly selected products into your normal information processing environment for everyday use. Diagnostics are absolutely essential during and after installation, in case problems went undetected or escaped the prototype test criteria.

The cost of locating and correcting problems during operation can rise dramatically. It takes time to understand and identify the possibilities of what the problem is as well as what caused it. If diagnostics are not available or if they are inadequate, this cost can manifest itself in your own people's time, lost user productivity, and corrective measures to fix the problem.

4. Maintain User Involvement   Users have gotten smarter and do not easily capitulate when confronted with a problem; they find another way. They are both resourceful and persistent. You might as well have them on your side and work together rather than try to beat them. They understand how to use the system better than you, and there are more of them than there are of MIS management.

You must include users in your implementation plan. Users can be your most valuable allies or can become totally disinterested in the project, which can kill any chances of success. Their help is often the difference between making or breaking what can be a sound and justifiable plan. Today's success depends as much on user satisfaction and productivity as on cost and network efficiency. If users are happy, they can make nearly anything happen. They can point out where the problems are and determine whether or not the problems are worth fixing. They have a clear determination of whether an implementation plan or system design can work because they are the ones who use it every day. Use them. Rely on them.

Your users can provide a full comprehensive test based on how they are actually going to use the link system. From a dollars-and-cents standpoint, it is difficult to buy that kind of integrated testing anywhere. Involve those people as early as possible.

5. Know How Link Products Work In Relation To Other Systems
Even though you anticipate and plan for link use with a specific database or application, you cannot restrict users from transferring data for other purposes. Also arising is the compatibility issue discussed earlier. Links are useful if they function consistently with the way your system moves data to its terminal devices. This is a minor problem with emulation links. However, more sophisticated links such as those from Cullinet (INFOGATE) and On-Line Software (OMNILINK) often require more attention. Why? Because they use software and hardware at your personal computer and use software on the host mainframe.

If the link offers a data reformatting capability, does it support the personal computer applications in use? Overall performance can differ from projections if link features and performance are inconsistent with the usage environment.

Here again is where you confront hidden costs that you did not anticipate. Do you have to purchase additional personal computer hardware, write conversion software, or modify existing applications? Even though you may not have to make real dollar expenditures, your people need time to address these factors, time that is lost for other business activities.

6. Provide User Training and Education   Always a sleeper, this guideline plays into the hidden and real costs of implementing a micro-mainframe link. User training and education cannot be ignored, as user manuals remain quite cryptic for the uninitiated. Vendors provide some training support, but this support is still usually supplemented by the large user's own personnel. Because these are typically technical personnel, your own technical resources are consumed and become unavailable to work on true system-related issues.

You must prepare training to explain many aspects of the system, including:

- Logon

- Entering emulation mode

- Specifying data for transfer

- Starting data transfer

- Data reformatting (if necessary)

- Swapping between host sessions

- Host and personal computer session swapping

- Interpreting error messages

- Ending host-connected sessions

- Host access limitations

- Reporting problems.

If host application interfacing is required, then you must also indoctrinate users about it. You can elect to train the trainers and have them instruct others. There are many ways to accomplish training, but it is imperative that you not overlook it. Training can mean the difference between having your MIS technical personnel bombarded with questions and having an organized plan to explain how to use the new system and products.

The costs of training are not trivial, and you can find yourself paying a lot of money for people who do nothing but teach others how to use the system. You are saddled with the cost of people, your most expensive resource. These people must be technical but also have an ability to communicate to others who are less technical. If you do not use your own personnel, then you must use a consultant or some other training organization that can address your link product needs.

◣ DIVIDING LINK IMPLEMENTATION

Divide the implementation plan into grouped phases. Each phase addresses extension to individual areas one at a time. In this way, you form an installation progression that comes more as a gradual wave than as an abrupt changeover. The illustration below defines three stages that divide an implementation plan into major tasks consisting of installation, usage, and support:

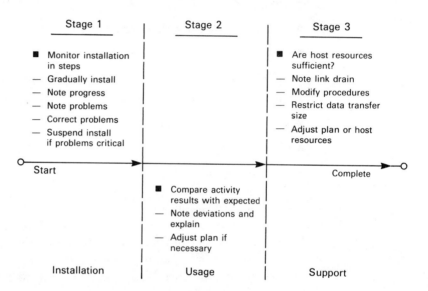

Dividing the plan in this way gives you several advantages:

- It allows you to monitor the installation in steps. Gradually putting the pieces in place a little at a time lets you monitor progress and note problems that arise. Before continuing, you define and correct the problems or decide if they are critical enough to stop installation temporarily until they are solved.

- Dividing the plan enables you to compare results of the activity with what you projected and expected. Any deviations can be caught early and explained, and adjustments to the overall plan can be made if necessary.

- You gain the confidence of the user community as the system comes on-line because the users observe its progress. This is beneficial: after a certain point users begin to handle their own questions with one another as more and more learn how to use the system. The training begins to default to users on an informal basis. You still must document and teach how to use the system, but users now have others to turn to.

- If host resource drains are more than anticipated, actions can be taken to suspend additional link installation temporarily until MIS operations management can determine a solution. Personal computer attachment can place a heavy burden on hosts if usage and transfer requirements are high. Along with other host production work, this extra burden can conceivably overrun the ability of the host to do so many things at once. Changes can require procedure modifications, data file transfer size restrictions, stipulation of certain periods for transfers to take place, and adjustment of host resources to cope with the problem.

Despite vendor proclamations of price/performance gains, a host is a very expensive investment. The less frequently you have to upgrade to a larger host, the better.

◣ COSTS: REAL AND HIDDEN

Costs for micro-mainframe links are often underestimated, which can result in an otherwise sound link strategy not being financially feasible. Costs are costs, and dollars are dollars, regardless of whether they are visible or not. It is the invisible and forgotten costs that characterize micro-mainframe links. And it is these costs that are often discovered after the decision to begin link implementation is made. Figure 7-2 shows an illustration of putting your total costs into perspective.

Do you abort the plan to link personal computers into hosts because of costs? No, because you know you still have to link them. Product selection is the key to successfully linking personal computers, but not all products give you long-term growth. Not all products offer a path for expansion without mixing vendors. Even the more software-oriented links contain

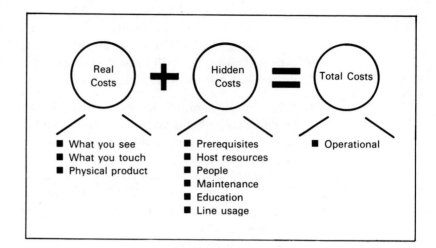

Figure 7-2. ▶

*What your total
costs are*

link emulation products from other vendors, and you have to bear the costs of this underlying requirement. You simply have to take stock of what you want to do and resolve to know where your costs are so that there are no surprises.

Costs can be *the* underlying factor that determines a product selection for you. You must know how much of your budget is reserved for after-installation activity. Too many vendors are done with the sale as soon as they deliver the product. Service and support, despite the accolades and honorable mention, is still all too frequently absent. Some companies are just not able to provide it. There are, however, many exceptions to this. Many suppliers are committed to service and support and base their business upon it as a crucial customer deliverable. Aside from large companies like IBM, DEC, and H-P, several other link companies—such as DCA, Cullinet, AST Research, Novell, and Banyon Systems, for example—understand that support is a major part of their business and marketing.

There are both real and hidden costs. Real costs include the price of the hardware, software, cables, modems, connectors, documentation, and prerequisite personal computer hardware. These are things that you can see: they are described in the vendor literature, and they are tangible. Then there are the intangibles that you cannot see and often overlook. These include installation, service, training, host resource allocation, communication line usage, terminal controller port usage, front-end communications processor storage, and so forth.

Building-Block Approach
To Costs

Approach costs in stages. Divide them into tangible and intangible items. To place link costs into proper perspective, you must group costs by types of micro-mainframe links. The price of a specific personal computer link depends on implementation support. But putting a single price on a link is difficult because user conditions vary. It is more useful to identify price ranges within which certain link products fall, giving a high and low end. This range shifts upward as link complexity increases for each group.

Emulation Costs

Often overlooked (or temporarily forgotten) is the additional support hardware required for links. This includes the cables and modems that must accompany them. Emulation links can be implemented by the vendor strictly in software, but something else is still required, if it is not already present, to make the physical connection between the personal computer and the host.

The communications mode over which emulation links operate is either asynchronous (async) or synchronous (sync), as described in Chapter 3. For async emulation mode, cabling is required with modems that operate from 300 up to 9600 baud. Techniques using data compression and packets to group data can make these speeds very efficient for achieving a high throughput of data. DCA offers a product called FASTLINK that achieves between 10,000 and 15,000 bps across a 1200 baud line, while BLAST from Communications Research Group configures data in packets or blocks to transmit across an ordinary tele-

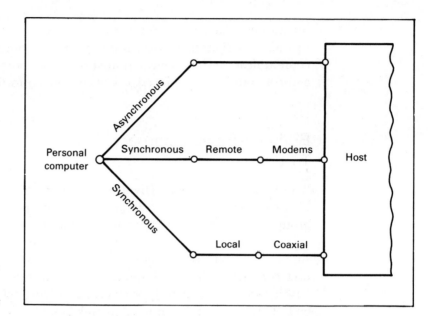

Figure 7-3. ▶

*Emulation link
connection modes*

phone line. Both products achieve their most measurable results
when transferring large volumes of data in which the blocking
begins to have a major effect. A pair of modems is always
required for host access unless a form of modem grouping at the
host called *pooling* is done. In pooling, users dial in and connect
to the first available modem not in use. If all the modems are in
use, users receive a busy signal.

The emulation link communications mode options are shown
in Figure 7-3. Note that there is a branch for each mode.

Asynchronous Emulation
Link Costs

Async modems range in price from $300 to $800, depending on
speed (300/1200 or 2400 baud). Other features affect this price
range, but for our purposes we are not evaluating modem products. All personal computers already have an RS-232 port con-

nection (an electrical interface standard) for communications, and an asynchronous adapter board is included or is optional for about $100. Simple file transfer software is available for about $100; you can expect most vendors eventually to provide this product free.

Your basic costs at the personal computer end include a modem, cable, and async adapter board. This total cost alone, in the neighborhood of $500, includes only a 300/1200-baud modem. Add the cost of the emulator ($200) and host modem ($400 minimum for 300/1200 baud). This basic emulator cost approaches $1,100, not including file transfer software at $100. For a higher performance link that includes 2400-baud modems, you can expect the total real, tangible costs of async implementation to approach $2,100 per user. This is a far cry from what many of the emulator vendors advertise as an emulation link for $195. It is only the beginning.

Figure 7-4 shows the range of emulation link costs, which include the host connection cost. Bear in mind that these costs can easily increase or decrease at least 10 percent, depending primarily on the modem's brand, quality, features, and functions. Bundling by a manufacturer can also have a major effect.

Where Your Costs Are

The intangibles of line usage costs can be significant as a percentage of the link cost on an annualized basis. What this means is that while you are connected to the host via a modem across a telephone line, you are paying for usage of the line like a regular telephone call. If your usage is high, at the end of the year you'll have a large bill—often larger than the link cost itself. Multiply this usage cost by 50, 200, or 2000 personal computer links, and you have a very sizable operation expense. Using links that provide a transfer capability whose performance is inefficient—in other words, links that transfer relatively low amounts of information or data at a given speed—means that you pay for the link every time you use it because you are connected to the line longer.

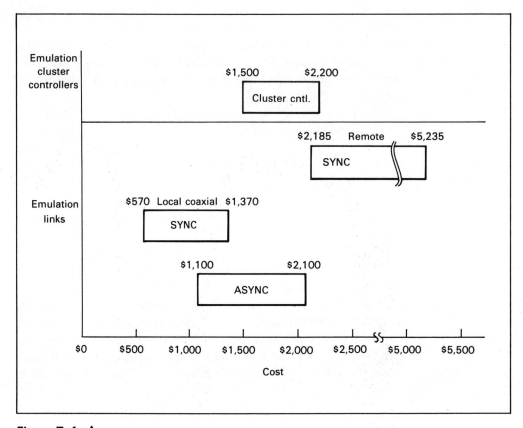

Figure 7-4. ▲

Emulation link price per personal computer (single-unit price; no discounts; fully implemented)

Line transmission time costs are a recurrent, ongoing expense that you should minimize. You cannot control what the telephone companies charge you for this service. But you can be smarter about what services you use, how you define your networks, and the link products that keep the line connection time for data transfer low. Modem costs continue to decrease as a function of competition, which affects supply and demand. Further, many hardware link manufacturers are planning to provide modems directly on link cards, while some already offer this as standard.

Asynchronous Emulation Cost Breakdown

If you reflect on the async part of Figure 7-4, over 60 percent of the link cost for low-speed linkage is in the cost of the modems. This increases to over 75 percent for higher speed transmission (1200/2400 baud), and becomes astronomical at 9600 baud. This ratio will probably continue despite continued product price reductions.

Synchronous Coaxial Emulation Link Costs

This mode is used when personal computers are local to the controller. Prices of hardware cards that insert directly into personal computers range between $495 and $1,295, depending on standard features, performance, and software. These links connect directly into a terminal controller and do not require modems. Many vendors offer software that personalizes the emulation contained on the board. A standard cable for the connection costs approximately $75. Therefore, your total host connection costs range from $570 to $1,370 (also shown in Figure 7-4).

There are no line communications costs associated with these links. Performance for data file transfer is important. If the terminal controller is not locally connected to the host, then it uses modems to communicate with the host. If the file transfer software of the coaxial card is not efficient, then time consumed during the regular data transfer can more than offset the price saving for an inexpensive link.

Synchronous Remote Emulation Link Costs

Remote synchronous emulation links require an emulation board in the personal computer, a cable, and a synchronous modem. Personal computer link boards range in price from $545 to $1,295, depending on features and data transfer speed. A cable and synchronous modems are required at both the personal computer and the host end. Because data transfer is in both directions, it is desirable to have full-duplex modems so that data can be transferred in both directions at the same time. (Half duplex enables data transfer in only one direction at a time.) The cost of a 9600-baud full-duplex modem can be as low as $1,300 to $1,900. A full-duplex modem at 1200/2400 baud can be obtained for about $800.

A fully implemented synchronous emulation link can range from $1,385 to $5,235. How can this be? Again, the majority of the cost is in the often-overlooked modems. Synchronous modems are always more expensive than asynchronous. Full-duplex operation adds an even greater cost premium.

Modems account for over 72 percent of the link cost at the low- and high-end speeds. Figure 7-4 shows the range; it can be affected as much as 10 percent with many dependencies. The cost at the personal computer end alone is approximately 63 percent of the entire cost of the link.

Emulation Cluster Link Costs

Products that provide terminal controller emulation on a personal computer connected between the host and personal computers are appearing on the market. This type of product is most prevalent in the IBM market. It acts as a controller replacing the vendor's terminal controller.

Such a cluster product requires complementary emulation boards and software in each attached personal computer. The product normally requires synchronous modems to attach to a front-end communications controller. The cost of cluster products ranges between $1,500 and $2,200 for the master. The same logic used earlier applies to figure the true total tangible cost of implementing such a link.

Factors that influence the implementation price range include how many personal computers are supported, hardware and software required, and the cost of the modems involved. Figure

7-4 displays only the price spread for such emulation cluster products themselves, not for the total link costs for implementing same. This total cost depends on how many supported personal computers are involved and the cost of the complementary hardware.

Application Interface Link Costs

These links are tied to the application involved, and they typically operate under a particular host vendor's operating system. It doesn't matter who the host vendor is; the link itself is a subset of the application it supports.

Application interface links require emulation links to physically perform the host connection, and many application interface products need a specific link product as a subset. Therefore, the user must already have this emulation link installed or obtain it before installing the application. Application links range in price from $15,000 to $35,000, not including the cost of the personal computer portion of the link itself. Examples of two such products in this area are Software International's Smartlink and McCormack and Dodge's Interactive PC Link.

One way to estimate your cost is to use Figure 7-4. Select the link mode required as a prerequisite to installing and operating the application, and overlay the costs of the two. Figure 7-5 shows the application link cost over the costs of Figure 7-4. Many application links require personal-computer-resident software to provide the handshaking to the host application. This part is more expensive than most; prices for this portion range between $1,200 and $3,000 per personal computer, depending on the nature of the vendor and the application.

Software Interface Links

These links do not qualify as application interface links because they are not tied to any one particular application. Instead, they serve as a general data transfer framework within which personal

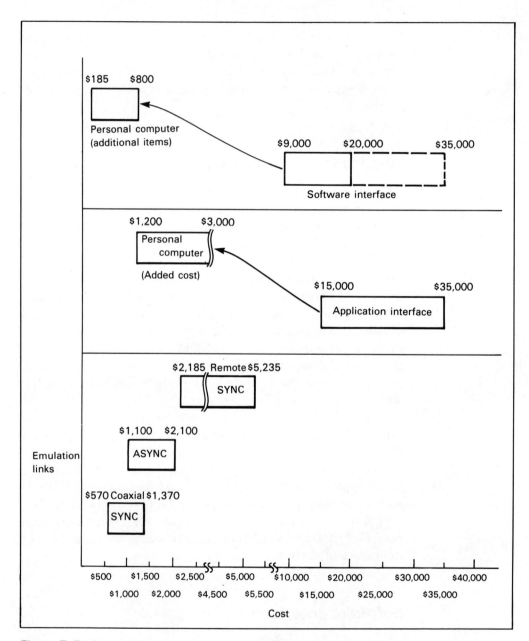

Figure 7-5. ▲

*Application and
software interface
costs*

computers can be integrated. They provide a network of high-ways that move data and database queries to and from their respective destinations. These links require software resident both at the host and at the personal computer.

Like application interface links, software interface links require emulation link support for the physical host connection and interface. They operate under control of a given host operating system and abide by any security systems that the customer uses. These products, priced from $9,000 to $20,000, can include a fixed number of personal computer connections. Other products have costs that go as high as $35,000. Examples of some products in this category include Linkware Corporation's Information Server, Simware Incorporated's SIM3278/PC, and MicroTempus Tempus-Link.

Prices for the personal computer portion range from $185 to $800 for software only. They do not reflect the cost of the asynchronous or synchronous portion described earlier. It is essential to factor in these costs because they are mandatory additions for the system operation.

Database Interface Link Costs

Two types of customers are in this category: those having an installed database system and those who do not. Database interface links are unique to a particular database system, although they support other host data file structures as well. The cost of these links is generally very high because their vendors often have a captive customer. If you do not have the database already, the cost is very high because you must purchase the database as well. If you have decided on a database system, you did so for reasons other than obtaining a micro-mainframe link. If you already own the database system, then it is only logical that you consider procuring that database's link products.

Costs of these systems range from a low of $12,500 to a high of $25,000. This price includes the attachment of a fixed number of personal computers to the host but it does not include the database price. If you must purchase a database, costs can easily rise to a range between $75,000 and $150,000, not including the additional cost of adding more personal computers. In any case, your marginal cost is generally between $300 and $1,000 for every personal computer added. However, this cost can be almost $3,000 for an additional personal computer. Three examples of products include Computer Corporation of America's PC/204, Cullinet's INFOGATE, and Software AG's Natural/Connection.

These costs typically do not include the personal computer hardware and software for the host attachment, only the facilities to provide an integrated framework into the database itself. Figure 7-6 shows the placement of costs with respect to basic emulation communications requirements.

Additive link costs can vary just like database costs. Although you can identify database vendors whose initial link cost is not as high as those discussed, these link costs are decreasing in the industry as vendors keep pace with new competition and developments.

Gateway Link Costs

As pointed out earlier, this type of link connects dissimilar networks. Gateways will grow in acceptance as local area networks (LANs) are installed. It doesn't matter who the host vendor is; gateways can be expected to enjoy a healthy growth rate as departmental LANs need to be connected into the base host network. This will be true whether the network is IBM's SNA, DEC's DECnet, Prime's PRIMENET or any other host-supported ackbone. Gateways are a solution for implementing the initial integration into the host.

Gateway costs range between $1,195 and $6,000, depending on many factors, including speed, transmission support, multisession capability, and so on. The cost of this form of connecting link is an incremental cost to your already existing personal computer situation (if your users are currently connected with a LAN, a gateway is added to give them host interfacing). Your personal computer hardware and software, for the most part, is already present. If a LAN is going to be installed, then this cost is again additive after you determine the base system cost. A

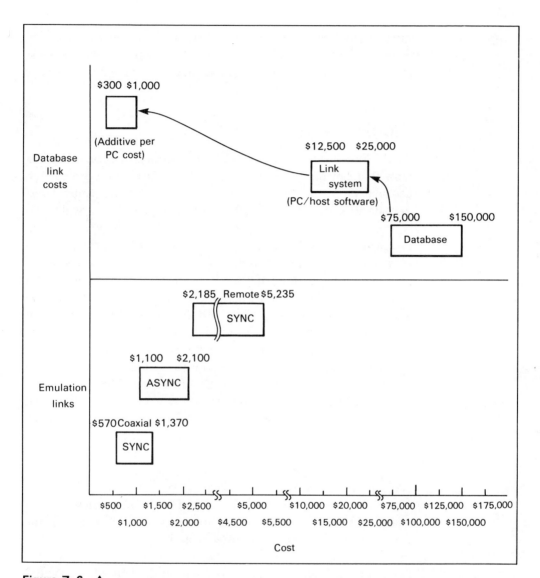

Figure 7-6. ▲

*Database interface
link costs*

number of companies are supplying gateway products, including
CXI, DCA, Pathway Design, Techland, and Trisystems, to name
just a few.

Like anything else, gateway costs are subject to decreases,

given greater shipment volumes. Price erosion can be forestalled as vendors add features and connectability options that increase the role and effect of these link products in the marketplace.

File Server Link Costs

These link products are in reality departmental processing systems that can host workload offloading. Many terms are used to describe them, but their function is basically the same. Users operate directly from the file server whether they are directly connected to it or access it via a LAN. The server in turn communicates to the host but provides capability to let the personal computer user "pass through" to the host when it is necessary.

File server implementation is primarily for companies that are concerned about departmental processing and want to isolate a part of their business while still providing the capability to interface to the host. It is an ideal approach for companies that are using the host as a database manager and traffic controller to move data and application access out to the users, instead of having the users using the host to perform all of their day-to-day activities. File servers are excellent for developing an entire network strategy that encompasses hubs throughout the company that can be tied together into a formal network environment.

The cost of file server links can vary widely because they include disk storage, local memory storage, power supplies, special emulation software, an operating system of their own, and controllers for personal computer and LAN attachment. These systems in and unto themselves are processors. In addition, the personal computer requires software and hardware to interface to the server. These are typically referred to as *interface cards*. Products offered in this arena come from vendors like Banyon Systems, Cadmus, and Nestar.

Basic systems with minimum memory (about 1 megabyte), minimum disk storage (about 24 megabytes), the operating system, several asynchronous ports, and some emulation software can be purchased for as low as $10,000. More elaborate systems with extensive memory and disk storage can cost as much as

$50,000, depending on the nature of the software, supported LAN connections, extended server-to-server interconnections, and so on. Costs of personal computer facilities to support connection to the server vary between $500 and $2,000, depending on what is required. Again, if users are remote from the server, modem support is required, and the implementation cost can quickly rise.

LAN Connection Costs

LAN costs are the most difficult to put into categories because so much depends on their particular implementation. The per-personal-computer connection cost is decreasing as more LANs are installed and as competition increases. This is, however, a two-edged sword because competition can only increase if there are more vendors. This does not make the selection possibilities any easier for customers. The best way to approach the problem is not by vendor selection, but by choosing the type of network cabling system and topology you require. Having done that, you can then sort out the vendors that offer LAN products that fit the requirement.

There are an enormous number of vendors offering LANs. These include the better-known names of 3COM, Novell, Xerox, Fox Research, Sytek, and Proteon. Others include Orchid Technology, Corvus, Concord Data, and Interlan.

LAN implementation prices can range from as low as $2,500 to as high as $35,000 for eight personal computers. This wide disparity is purely dependent on the factors cited above. Per-personal-computer connection costs for eight users range from $395 to $2,500. On average, these per-connection costs for eight users range between $500 and $900 for the more popular networks from the most established vendors, not including the cost of the personal computer.

These costs depend on your applications and what is required to interface the workstations. They depend on the access protocol, data transfer speed, cable support, cable type (baseband or broadband), and local central disk storage, among others. As the number of personal computer attachments increases, you can expect the per-connection per-user costs to decrease rapidly as you approach 16 users and then 24 users. All LAN per-user connection costs follow the same curve profile as depicted below. The curve is relative and is accurate for today's market; however, it will shift downward as technology evolves to change price characteristics.

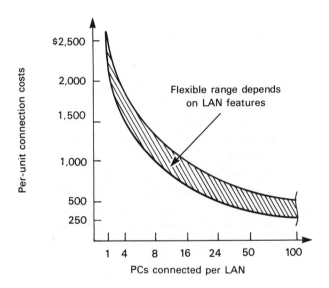

◥ INTANGIBLE TRAINING AND EDUCATION COSTS

Regardless of the type of link strategy and products selected, you must concern yourself with these expenses. No matter how simple the link, users still need some education in how to use the link system. Vendors have included menus and other forms of documentation to facilitate training, but most documentation and user manuals remain cryptic, difficult to read, and almost impossible to reference until you have become acquainted with the product. Only then do many such manuals become useful.

No matter how you cut the cake, this aspect consumes time and resources. You must consider training as a factor both in terms of costs as well as in commitment to making the system work. These are called intangible costs because you cannot put your finger on an exact number, and the costs are represented to you in terms of human resources unavailable for other system-related activities. But training is a cost that management must be made aware of from the outset.

Assume that you need a single person to learn the system and then educate users. The cost of this person varies across geographical regions, but an average salary is in the range of $35,000 to $45,000. Remember that the person must be relatively skilled and technically literate. This person can be lost to you for up to three months after the pilot is completed, just to be available to teach others how to use the system and answer questions that arise after education. Assume that your company burdens this individual at one and a half times salary on the basis of insurance, facilities, and other general administrative support, which brings the annual rate to $60,000, based on a $40,000 annual salary. Three months of lost activity then costs you $15,000.

Is this simply the cost of doing business? Maybe so, but it is a cost that must be included, especially if this period leaves you short of people and you must use external assistance on this or other projects. The vendor never sees this cost, but you do.

Link Maintenance Costs

What is your maintenance strategy? Do you do your own? Do you depend on the vendor? Or do you simply throw away the product and replace it when it fails? Whatever the approach, this is also a crucial cost.

Some vendors offer maintenance support contracts that include various levels of defined service. Normally, this amounts to 1 percent per month of the purchase price of the system. But this too varies with the type of link product. Figure 7-7 shows the options associated with each link type shown. You wouldn't necessarily abide by all of the selections in Figure 7-7; however, it is highly unlikely that you would simply throw away a LAN and gateway as a *maintenance* option. You might throw them

	Maintenance options				
	Vendor support	Third-party support	Self-maintenance (own inventory spares)	Return and replace	Throw away and replace
■ Emulation	X	X	X	X	X
■ Application interface	X				
■ Database interface	X				
■ Cluster controller	X	X			X
■ File server	X	X		X	
■ LAN/gateways	X	X			

Figure 7-7. ▶

Link maintenance options

away for other reasons, including a change in strategy. Options not checked for each link type could be viable for you, depending upon your unique situation.

Maintenance costs are a cost of doing business. If you contract with recognized third-party maintenance vendors such as TRW, CDC, Eaton, Sperry Univac, or Honeywell, then you must account for an annualized ongoing bill. This cost *can* be trivial with respect to the cost of procuring the link equipment, but much depends upon the maintenance philosophy of the company. If your philosophy is that the products are to be thrown away at the end of their useful life, then you still have a cost of doing business: replacement cost.

◥ HOST COSTS

This is an intangible of major proportions, but it is an obvious use of host resources. These resources directly affect the operation of your data center and warrant your attention. These host resources do not just pertain to the physical processor size that drives the personal computer links, but they also include controller and communications processor resources that must be allocated to support link connections. Factors include total input and output data transfer bandwidth (maximum amount of data transfer possible with a specific host processor configuration), memory storage on controllers, additional controllers, and bulk data transfer support for large data transfers.

All of these factors involve direct costs that you must address as a cost of integrating links into hosts. Links draw on all of these resources, and in some cases you can directly identify them. For example, let's take the case of a simple direct coaxial connection link in an IBM environment. If you only have one or two of these links, additional costs are minimal. The tangibles are that you have a hardware link card, its cable, and the allocation of a 3274/6 terminal controller port. The intangibles are not necessary to estimate because with so few links there is not going to be much effect on the host.

If, however, you are going to link 20 or 30 personal computers into the host, these intangibles become noteworthy. If you have 5000 personal computers, we are talking about mammoth effects on supporting resources to drive the network of links. Whether your connection is remote or local, your planning must account for the intangibles of connection.

For local link connection, these intangibles include available terminal controller ports, additional controllers if capacity is unavailable, memory storage on the controllers and host, and, if a communications processor is on the front end, its complement of storage. If dial-in links are used, are there enough ports on the front-end processor or terminal controller to service them? How much storage can be allocated and still maintain acceptable service levels to the user? At what threshold point does it become necessary to consider the addition of another host processor to handle the workload? Figure 7-8 shows the flow of host intan-

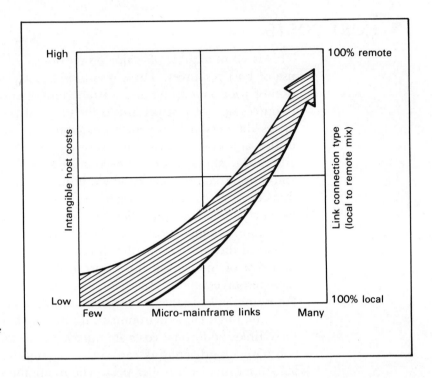

Figure 7-8. ▶

Host costs relative to workstation density

gible costs as you approach a situation in which many personal computers are almost all remotely connected.

Depending upon how you calculate costs and view your facility usage, the effect of these extra costs can be minimal or excessive. If, for example, you have facilities that are underutilized and available regardless of what you do for networking, then perhaps you view this as the cost of doing business and improving your overall operation. If you do not have excess capacity to support these links, then you clearly must acquire additional equipment and most likely increase host storage simply to support the linked personal computers.

Depending upon your own situation, various vendor host processors to support micro-mainframe links range from $10,000 to a high of $25,000 per personal computer. How is this estimated? When you start to consider all of the line costs as well as those identified above, you realize that the support infrastructure is more expensive than you thought. There is no free lunch. For

IBM systems, the costs can easily approach $25,000 per link—depending upon the links selected, the level of host support expected, and disk and memory storage needed across the system from personal computer to host. On other vendor hosts, such as DEC, DG, or H-P, the costs involved can be somewhat less but high nonetheless. These costs include the per-personal-computer cost of the link itself.

ESTABLISHING A PILOT

What is a pilot and why do you establish one? This is a major issue regardless of whether you are a small company with a few personal computers to link or a large company with many hundreds or even thousands of personal computers.

You pilot to provide preliminary testing of link hardware and software. Testing is done with applications under conditions that represent the actual environment in which those links are to be ultimately installed. There are many reasons for a pilot, and some are quite similar to those for testing a new software application or a new service for users. Shown below are key points for you to realize about what a pilot is intended to provide for links:

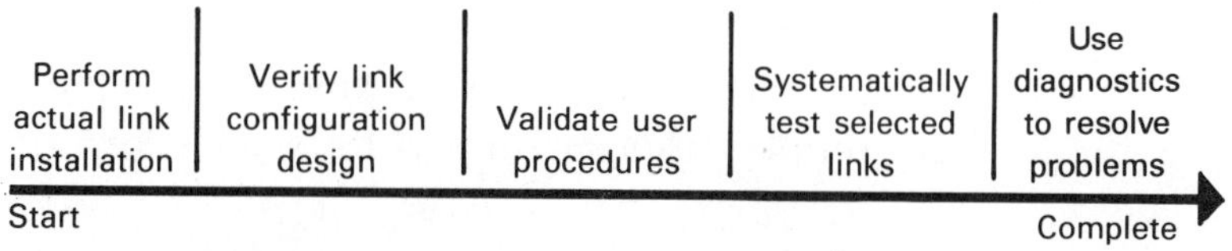
Perform actual link installation
Verify link configuration design
Validate user procedures
Systematically test selected links
Use diagnostics to resolve problems
Start
Complete

Pilot Purpose

A pilot evaluates selected link products under real-world conditions. There are at least five reasons for using link pilots.

1. A Pilot Verifies the Actual Design of the Planned Link Configuration Forgetting links for the moment, if the planned design and procedures for invoking applications and transferring data are inadequate or need to be changed, this is the place to discover it. You can make adjustments unless major issues are uncovered, not necessarily with the product, but with your intended use of the product. The link products you select for an ill-defined configuration are doomed to fail regardless of the vendor or product quality. Your pilot is a place and a means to find this out early before significant money is spent.

2. A Pilot Is Intended to Validate That Procedures to Be Established in a Production Environment Are Correct and Can Be Fully Implemented   If procedures cannot be extended beyond a few test users, you can expect to have to change something in your scheme. Procedures should be easy to use, self-explanatory, and easily understood by users. If they are not, the user cannot adequately describe any problems that arise. Lack of such problem description hinders your system maintenance people who must support the link configuration.

3. Pilots Provide a Way to Systematically Test Selected Link Products   Many times, it is not a question of whether the product works the way its documentation says it does but rather a question of whether the product satisfies the situation that you expect the link to support. If test procedures and test criteria are established correctly, the pilot becomes very useful and powerful for you and the vendors. Most vendors are more than happy to supply customer support for a pilot involving their products.

4. Pilots Permit an Opportunity to Perform Actual Product Installation Configuration and Initial Checkout   This activity gives you a chance to see just how difficult or easy it can be to bring the system up to operation and replicate it across many users. It also gives you perspective on the length of time needed to recognize and overcome installation problems. Once you have experience installing several links, you know what to look for each time.

5. Pilots Let You Use Link Diagnostics to Isolate and Resolve Problems   Maybe the product can be installed in five minutes with only a screwdriver, software can be loaded from a floppy disk in 60 seconds, and help screens be available in 3 seconds. But it is guaranteed that sometime during the pilot a problem will occur, and you will need to execute diagnostic procedures. This will tell you just how comprehensive or worthless the vendor's diagnostics really are for troubleshooting.

Pilot Approach

There are two excellent ways to establish a pilot. One is to replicate a subset of the actual environment, and the other is to define test criteria that best represent the data transfer and user conditions to be addressed. Variations of these approaches are used, but these are the two primary methods. You create real situations in which you test your premises and evaluate link products.

Pilot Environment Subset

In this approach, you provide a smaller version of the eventual operating conditions that links must satisfy. It consists of the following:

- A small core of participating users.
- Allocation of sufficient host resources for a valid pilot.
- Application selection, or facsimiles, for the final environment.
- Access to databases, files, or test beds that represent actual conditions.
- Representative data transfers across links.
- Initially, suitable insulation from normal host operations.
- Pilot expansion in concert with ongoing host activity.

A small user core is essential. Recall that we said earlier that if users are not satisfied with link performance or usability, the link system can never fully succeed, no matter what you do. Using people other than actual users is not effective.

Host Resources

Host resource allocation cannot be accomplished if the host is already at, or close to, its capacity. There is no way to partition host capacity. Special storage regions can be created within host storage, but using these regions still affects capacity for other ongoing applications. IBM offers an operating system called virtual machines (VM) that enables you to define an entire system within the VM system—in other words, to establish an entire operating system and applications within the virtual machine so that a failure does not affect other systems running under VM.

Off-hours testing can be an answer in the early pilot stages with a transition into regular hours once you know that the system is stable. With system and user personnel involved and working together, off-hours testing can be a compromise for a valid test under real conditions.

Select applications targeted for use by the installed links. If not the full applications, then use some facsimile that represents a true sample of the activity. Without this, pilots are useless because you are comparing apples to oranges. If you are not careful, you end up piloting links under one condition set only to install links in another. Figure 7-9 shows three options you have for piloting to monitor host resource usage. The user subset linked to the application subset is the most desirable, if it can be attained.

Data File Utilization

The same selection criteria apply to any files or databases to be accessed. If actual files cannot be used, then create equivalent files. The access and transfer of the data are the important factors. Links themselves, even LANs, do not have any applications on them, but they do transfer data to and from applications, as well as to the applications themselves. If several link products are being piloted, ensure that the data volume transferred is equivalent across all products for comparative evaluation.

If you can establish a pilot independent from the rest of the user operations, all the better. Often, the pilot uses the same host on which production is done. If it is not possible to get insula-

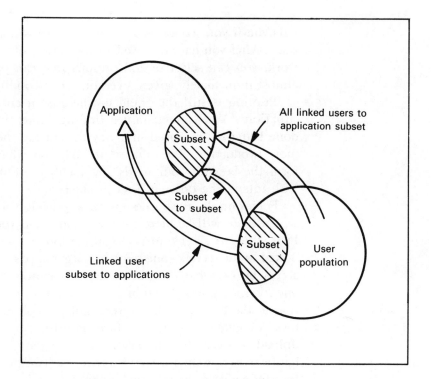

Figure 7-9. ▶

Selecting pilot applications

tion between the running pilot and effects from host activity, make note of the kind of host activity and how the pilot progresses when this host activity changes. Ideal pilot situations cannot always be obtained, so be aware of the implications of other processing on the performance of the link system.

Eventually, you expose the link pilot for operation in the regular daily environment and monitor its performance. This is the true system pilot. Common sense must prevail, and only a well-thought-out pilot process can save many problems in the future.

Pilot Expectations and Results

What you learn from a pilot is whether the link design and selected products perform as you anticipated. Although paper assessment is valuable, you need practical experience. The pilot tells you if your concepts are workable—if you are on the right track. After you have reviewed a wide variety of link designs that work, you can select several options that can perform the job almost immediately, given a certain set of conditions.

Piloting is still the grand test because it checks for unique situations. You can guarantee finding something that can be done better or improved in a way that makes the whole system more productive. The pilot results tell you what products perform the best for your needs and identify problems associated with interfacing different link products.

For example, if you design an application to run on a file server, there will be more considerations than you might think. First, there is service to personal computer users directly connected to the server—one interface. Second, pass-through to host access by personal computers requires emulation capability—one interface and emulation software. Third, file server connection to the host can use a direct cable, telephone line, or some form of gateway—one interface. Fourth, data download and upload between the file server and host requires software and hardware—one interface and software at two points. Fifth, data transfer between the personal computers and file servers require software and possibly hardware—one interface and software at two points. Figure 7-10 shows the delineation of each of these interfaces.

In this situation, there are at least five logical and two physical interfaces to check; two, possibly three, software checks for data transfer between all of the equipment; and emulation software for the pass-through host access mode. And you haven't even talked about the applications, transfer requirements, security, and backup procedures! It is not a trivial task.

◥ INTERPRETING THE PILOT

As the pilot progresses, you must evaluate partial results. Clear indications become evident. They encompass problems arising with a given product's installation, whether a link keeps its host connection or is troublesome with premature disconnects, or

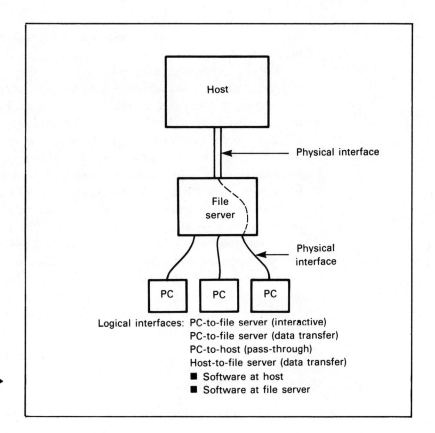

Figure 7-10. ▶

Interfaces for file server pilot

whether the link is easy to configure and use. If a LAN is in question, it soon becomes evident if another vendor's gateway is technically functional or if significant interface problems arise. The effectiveness of error recovery and isolation also becomes immediately visible.

The pilot evaluates everything from usability to problem isolation and detection. Feature regression is important, along with data transfer performance. If several link products are piloted side by side, comparing the results based upon your own ordered priority can reveal interesting information. The pilot also identifies the need for additional templates that must be written to interface data to applications. You will see this need when you try to load host data into a personal computer application, or vice versa.

There is no magic to the pilot itself, only in how it is set up, implemented, and assessed. If you do not use a methodology, you can expect results from a pilot across systems, applications, or products to be inconclusive. As noted, there are hundreds of link products on the market — ranging from simple to complex. They include hardware cards that insert into the personal computer, software-only link products, modems and multiplexers, LANs, file servers, data PBXs, and integrated voice/data PBXs.

You cannot be expected to be an expert on all of these link products, or even to be aware of them all. No matter what you select for your needs, someone will always tell you what you should have done and what products you should have purchased. Therefore, the only thing that you can do is to take advantage of specialized help when it is necessary and available, and use a pilot to validate your link plan and products before placing them in full production mode.

Pilot Summary

Rarely is a pilot perfect, and you can't expect it to be. That's not what it's for. It's a lot like writing a book. You realize how much it is that you know, how much you didn't know, and what you overlooked and had to correct on the second and third pass. Piloting is a very productive and cost-effective practice that saves time and money in the long term.

Auditing Schedule Checkpoints

Lay out an implementation plan and establish schedules. Everyone makes schedules, but everyone does not keep them. No one is perfect, and some situations can be out of your control. The most common reason for not maintaining schedules is a lack of commitment to getting the job done. Too often we hear of the project that slipped because another vendor missed delivery on key equipment. That means that either insufficient time to schedule its arrival is to blame, or communication with the vendor did not identify a slippage until too late. Either can be avoided.

The key is to account for major items that are necessary for a link system implementation. Some people use PERT charts or project management tools, while others use a blank sheet of paper with lines and entries. Use the one best for you.

◥ ESTABLISH THE IMPLEMENTATION PLAN

Develop a link implementation plan by starting with the top-level design (lines and boxes). You should subset the design into the software applications that are needed at the host and personal computer. Identify what is already available and what you need to procure. Often it helps if you can overlay an image of your host and personal computer configuration with the links as you need to connect them. This gives you a picture of what you are addressing. It is simple, and it helps you to know how your configuration is going to look.

We are not talking about the one- or two-emulation product installations. We are viewing the process as a *system* that integrates into your entire operation. We are talking about a consistent flow that lets you see how you address future needs of gateways and other link products. You do not want to redesign the link network every time a request for personal computer linking comes along.

You should apply the same principles for links as you do for software or hardware system installation and testing. These are complex products that get installed in your networks. Do not take them lightly, or you can end up with more debugging problems than you hoped for.

Link Implementation Plan Segments

The steps in the plan are as follows:

1. Installation
2. Diagnostic checkout
3. Product initialization
4. User interface testing
5. Data transfer testing
6. Checking for error handling
7. Operation with applications
8. Production operation
9. Host performance monitoring and tuning.

Not all steps require the same amount of time across different products. For an emulation product, for example, the first four steps can be very trivial for a single product checkout. The product is either going to work as specified, or it is not. If it does not, then your troubles begin. However, if you are going to install 20 to 30 of these for the first time, then items 5 through 7 become important and items 8 and 9 must be handled carefully with proper attention. Host loading is critical, and you should be prepared to make adjustments in your design, link selection, or host resource allocations if overall performance is unsatisfactory.

If more complex linking systems are installed, such as a file server or LAN with gateways, then the first three points are very critical in order to understand and stabilize the system. If you can't get past these, the others can cause even more headaches. Compound this with host-resident software for some linking products, and the implementation plan becomes even more involved.

8 Selecting Link Products

Finally, we get down to the nitty gritty. Aside from talking and developing requirements, assessing integration needs, planning link approaches, and establishing an implementation plan, there is the critical area of actually *selecting* the appropriate link products. You don't have time to review each and every link in all the categories. Therefore, you have to decide on the most logical alternatives to satisfy your defined needs. Don't confuse yourself any more than you have to. The market is already glutted with products that do that for you.

Five or six products can be of interest for emulation links. You can narrow this down to two or three, if appropriate. Software and application interface links are determined by your need to interface with specific applications. Your needs can require data file access in a more structured manner, and data reformatting can be a critical issue. Database interface links are just that: links designed to give you clean integrated access to a specific database, such as Cullinet's IDMS or Software AG's ADABAS, and gateway processor selection is governed only by your requirements. These requirements are dictated by departmental processing needs as well as the distribution of computing into geographical pockets or groups of users.

You must also consider the length of time required to prototype and pilot links. Testing plays a role in link selection. Testing on sophisticated file server products can be quite involved and extensive. Host interaction is not trivial, and resources must be allocated for the job. Host-resident software to support link attachment is also a consideration; it definitely consumes host resources. Emulation links, however, do not necessarily require elaborate testing so much as verification that they do what they should do.

◥ THE IMPORTANCE OF LINK SELECTION

Link selection is important for several reasons.

- You do not have time to test all links.
- Once you are underway in your testing, you cannot afford to introduce new products on a continuous basis, or you can never complete the job.
- You have done preliminary screening already before you introduce these links into the test environment.
- These links can do the job, if they pass the testing phase.

You have to ask yourself a series of questions, as depicted below.

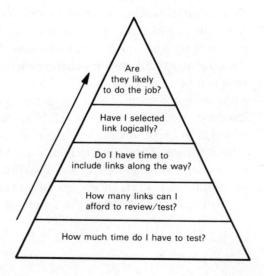

If you go through this selection process carefully, you can be sure of two things:

- Those links that do not perform as the vendor claims can be immediately identified.

- Those with serious performance flaws are easily isolated.

Admittedly, there have been too many link vendors whose products promise much but in fact deliver a minimum number of functions. Too many users expect links to solve all their personal computer connection problems even though they have not established a fundamental integration plan. Emulation links and file servers with processing capability are increasing their market share as users and MIS management become more acquainted with their capabilities. Link products that cluster personal computers in groups are evolving as an industry solution in both the IBM and non-IBM worlds.

Whatever links you ultimately select, you can be sure that you will live with them for a long time — two years at least. In most customer locations, the first six to nine months after installation are used to see if the selected products and configuration are doing what is expected. The next 12 to 24 months are spent using the system because the money is already spent. This is why it is important that you think about link selection before implementation.

Choosing Vendors

It's possible to select both a primary and a secondary link vendor, both of whom are acceptable in different areas of your business. This can be the most logical approach because you might find that emulation products are very useful in one situation, but the best selection for another business user group is to cluster personal computers using LANs and gateways, or file servers.

Link selection is where the payoff is, if you know what your short- and long-term requirements are and how you need to proceed to get them implemented. This is where you go through the process of actually sitting down and choosing the vendor and links that you think (from the literature and vendor conversations) can do the job in the best and most cost-effective manner. This chapter is devoted to helping you find out how to go about this process without making it tedious and time consuming.

Reviewing Technology

Because of the youthfulness of the micro-mainframe market, it's not an exaggeration to say that 99 percent of the link products on the market are of a new technology. At the very least, they embody the technology of the eighties. This technology is spawning an industry around the needs of users to communicate and transfer data and information. It is evolving rapidly to allow workstations to interact with each other and with hosts to an extent that was not feasible in 1982. The workstation communications issues and the sophistication of business are demanding this technology and pushing the market through stages that were impossible in the past. Users and business needs are the driving force behind this growth.

The arguments hold that this technology did not have a place in computing until the personal computer exploded on the scene. But like any other market, this too gave rise to still another market. The linking market is poised to solve today's host interconnection problems and grow through a period in which today's simple emulation link products will seem primitive by the mid-1990s.

The industry is creating building blocks from which to proceed. They are layers upon which you can plan and build your communications structures for linking existing and additional personal computers. Today's technology is not going to be so easily thrown away as people might imagine. The investment is large, and practical selection and planning can incorporate these links into extended personal computer networks. Like IBM's System/360, some of these products will be around for many years to come.

You have to review technology with an eye to how you can use it in your environment. The selection criteria discussed in this section is only a sampling of needs across different organizations. The critieria are just one starting point. Five years from now, you can expect another transition. The intent of this section is to provide you with a forum and a list of items that may trigger other needs that you have and want to resolve.

◥ SETTING LINK CRITERIA

Know what you want and set priorities. The best way to start is to list items that are specifically related to what you need the link to do, how you expect it to perform, and what the absolute necessities are that are not to be compromised. You can put this into a list that you can then use as a checklist for all products. The more complicated the link solution, the more complex the criteria.

There are various ways to view your criteria for links. We are not talking about business goals now, but rather what the link itself is expected to support. These operational characteristics include how it is to function. You can order the criteria individually by highest priority, or in groups with importance assigned within each group. You can also order the criteria in terms of relative importance from the absolute musts down to the desirables, each decreasing in relative weight. Another way is to simply list all of the factors. If you want to be sophisticated about the selection, assign an importance weight to each. If the link product in question meets the criteria, you simply designate a 1 or yes. If it does not meet the criteria, designate a 0 or no. If there is some doubt about meeting the item or there is a gray area, simply assign it 0.5.

Table 8-1 provides an extensive list of a series of criteria that you can apply to choosing a comprehensive software data transfer and control system. Depending on the compatibility of your needs and the link, these criteria will vary. For example, a 3270 emulation link cannot be expected to satisfy all the criteria listed in Table 8-1. In fact, your criteria will be substantially fewer because a link's purpose is different and very definitive. The question posed in this case will be if the emulation link is

Data Transfer and Recovery	Importance Level (Weight)	Link Product Comparison					
		Product A		Product B		Product C	
		Yes/No	Total	Yes/No	Total	Yes/No	Total
■ Full data file download ■ Selective data extraction ■ Virtual diskette capability							
■ Non-PC to host transfer DASD to DASD DASD to tape Tape to tape Standard label tape Non-label tape							
■ PC-to-PC data transfer ■ Data file transfer To existing data file To automatic new data file Between different name files							
■ Automatic data file (host) catalog ■ Transfer or move Entire generation data group (GDG) Single GDG entry Entire VSAM Cluster VSAM Cluster and index(es) ■ Automatic reformatting For PC application For host data structure							
■ Checkpoint and restart ■ Automatic Session retry upon failure Data transmission after session reestablished Restart from failure ■ On another host (remote) Schedule data transfer execution request Timer-controlled transfer Remote job entry (RJE)							
TOTALS		⊠		⊠		⊠	

Table 8-1. ▲

Link Selection Criteria

Data File Criteria	Importance Level (Weight)	Link Product Comparison					
		Product A		Product B		Product C	
		Yes/No	Total	Yes/No	Total	Yes/No	Total
■ Data set types Sequential Whole partitioned Partitioned members VSAM ISAM (indexed sequential) BDAM Multiple volume							
■ Other vendor databases IDMS ADABAS Total Other							
■ Data file formats (host) Unformatted Variable/variable block Fixed (F), fixed block (FB) FBA No record size limit ■ PC application format SYLK DIF Other							
TOTALS		⊠		⊠		⊠	
Link-to-User Interface							
■ Request/reply via batch program ■ On-line help capability ■ Interface invoked interactively ■ Notification on completed transfer ■ On-line display: error messages and codes ■ Request/reply via on-line program							
TOTALS		⊠		⊠		⊠	

Table 8-1. ▲

Link Selection
Criteria (continued)

Link System Operation	Importance Level (Weight)	Link Product Comparison					
		Product A		Product B		Product C	
		Yes/No	Total	Yes/No	Total	Yes/No	Total
■ Transfer operation Timer initiated Requires no file preallocation Standalone batch job Dynamic file allocation Dynamic file deallocation							
■ Spooling to printer capability ■ Terminate file transfer ■ Delete scheduled transfer request ■ Hold scheduled transfer request ■ Save transfer requests ■ Catalog transfer request library							
■ Transfer capability Single file per request Multiple files per request Redundant scheduling of same request ■ File transfer priority/class Ability to assign Ability to modify							
■ Requires no host system software modifications ■ "Hot" key session swapping ■ Simultaneous host sessions ■ Data compression for transfer ■ Error correction/detection							
■ SNA support ■ Transfer/display graphics ■ X.25 support							
TOTALS		✕		✕		✕	

Table 8-1. ▲

Link Selection Criteria (continued)

Security and Integrity	Importance Level (Weight)	Link Product Comparison					
		Product A		Product B		Product C	
		Yes/No	Total	Yes/No	Total	Yes/No	Total

■ Logging capability
  Sending and receiving nodes
  Data files transferred
  Volume transferred
  Transfer time
  User logon/logoff
  User ID, location
  User activity
  Error messages
  Completion codes
  Access attempts (good/bad)							

■ Security administrator support ■ On-line display/search of logs ■ Audit print journaling ■ Multi-level access authorization							

■ Operates with host security system
  Top Secret
  ACF2
  RACF
  Other
■ Upload data validation
■ User ID dial-back capability							

TOTALS							

Table 8-1. ▲

Link Selection
Criteria (continued)

Installation and Service	Importance Level (Weight)	Link Product Comparison					
		Product A		Product B		Product C	
		Yes/No	Total	Yes/No	Total	Yes/No	Total
■ System problem tract facility ■ Error message logging ■ No user programming for operation ■ No host modifications ■ Diagnostic support ■ Total-free support line							
TOTALS		✕		✕		✕	

	Link Totals Summary		
	Product A	Product B	Product C
Data transfer and recovery			
Data file criteria			
Link-to-user interface			
Link system operation			
Security and integrity			
Installation and service			
TOTALS			

Table 8-1. ▲

Link Selection Criteria (continued)

what you need. You might need something with more sophisticated capabilities, in which case you will be back to defining what those capabilities are so that you can select a link. Writing down your criteria can also lead you to realize that you only need an emulation link. However, you can find that other avenues, such as a LAN and file server, are more suited to your needs.

The list in Table 8-1 forms the basis of reviewing sophisticated links that involve data file retrieval and a level of security facilities. The criteria are in no special order. You can assign a weight or priority of your own. If you wish, you can order the criteria in a specific arrangement, or group them as shown. Depending on the complexity of the situation for which you are trying to provide links, your criteria might look totally different. They can contain more or fewer items, and you can even omit entire groups of requirements. In some cases, your criteria might not resemble Table 8-1 at all.

Comparing Link Products

If you are comparing similar links, the review process is different from comparing different vendor software application packages. Every software package, unless it is an identical clone, offers a totally different user interface. Although functions can be identical, implementing them is often quite different. You need to review software to see which is the most logical for your needs and the easiest to handle from your perspective.

Link products are different from software application packages in that they must address specific data formats and types. Host interfaces must be treated identically or the host interface cannot be recognized. Any terminal emulation that is involved must look exactly like what the users are accustomed to seeing. If there is any deviation from what is expected, either on the host end or at the user level, the product is going to find market acceptance difficult, although not necessarily impossible. In comparing links, you are comparing their basic ability to perform each function as well as the additional options they provide.

Links are used to transfer data across a wide variety of uses and needs. They cannot arbitrarily modify the required data formats or they would not work with your applications. However, they must be able to handle data reformatting, as it is often necessary for converting transferred data to work with personal-computer-based applications such as Lotus 1-2-3 and various database systems.

You compare links by reviewing the technology and evaluating how well each link addresses the issues that are important to you. This does not mean comparing what chips are used on the hardware. It does mean that you compare the products against the same set of criteria so that you know how to order and select them.

Requirements as a Guideline

It goes without saying that your requirements must serve as a guideline and not as the absolute measure of a link product's effectiveness. We can look at the concept of *effective* from two standpoints. The first is how effective the link is in meeting your technical and interface requirements. The criteria established for testing helps determine if the link does what you want it to do. You should be able to get some idea about this before you procure the link for any pilot study. The second is how the link fits your intended growth goals for the business. If the product cannot be expanded, upgraded, or integrated into an overall network scheme (and if this is important to you), then subjective criteria are important.

The key is to choose link products based on your future needs and expectations as well as on your immediate needs. For example, if you are using LANs for user interconnection, are these LANs only departmental and not connected to the host? If so, do the particular LANs used offer gateway capability for host connection? Do vendors supply gateways that can be installed to connect your LAN to the host for further database access? The market always catches up to user needs and products. LANs not currently supporting gateways might be by the time you are ready to connect to the host. This is a decision that you must make. It can also have a negative effect on future expansion if a gateway is not available by the time your host connection needs must be met.

Growth: Does It Fit?

The type of link that you select should not restrict your personal computer integration growth. Fit your link to your expected growth and the requirements that accompany that growth. If you think that your needs are going to require communications between personal computers, commonly called peer-to-peer, then begin reviewing technology that supports such implementations. Understand that technology's requirements and prerequisites, know what limitations exist today, and know whether these limitations will affect your growth if they are still limitations two years from now. This outlook and acceptance can enable you to implement the link in stages and not give up anything in the process. The main points are *structure* and *thinking ahead.*

Make sure that, whatever link you select, your needs do not outgrow its usefulness at an early stage. What can appear to be a cheap and easy solution initially can cost you more in the long term if you find that it must be replaced prematurely or supplemented with another solution. Often, you might find that the more expensive solution for personal computer linking, such as a LAN and file server (distributed or departmental processing), can prove to be the most economical if additional personal computers are to be linked with the host over a period of time.

You might also find that your data transfer requirements do not mandate high-performance, bulk data transfer links. Consequently, what you mistake as a safety margin for transfer speed can very well prove never to be used because it is far more than your requirements ever called for in the first place. When all you need is simple and straightforward host connection, a file server can be overkill and inappropriate. Read the signals and signs of the business needs and growth. Read the demands of the users and find out which demands are actually requirements. Integrate yourself with the users; they can be relied upon to tell you what you need to know.

Spending as a Requirement

Budgets are always a critical factor. You can have a very restrictive or an open-ended budget. Often, your first reaction is to think of the budget requirement as being very tight and that there is not enough money to spend to do the job right. This type of thinking drastically limits the types of links that you can consider. There are situations, however, in which the budget is very open ended for the purpose of data communications.

Spending is not always a limiting factor; it is just *a* factor. It affects how you look at solutions and how you approach personal computer linking problems. A mentor once said, "With enough time and money, you can solve any problem." This always prompts two questions. One, can the problem be solved if you invest enough money? And two, do you have the time to fix the problem if you invest the money? If the answer to both of these questions is yes, then the question becomes one of how much money and how much time. Below is an illustration of this process:

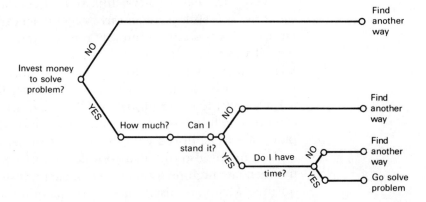

Links fall into the same situation. How much money can you invest and do you want to invest? How fast do you need to implement your system? Regardless of the budget size, budgets affect how you approach the problem. You can qualify and quantify the answers to both of these simple questions. The kinds of answers you get affect the range of links to consider, as well as the final selection.

Technical Aspects

It can't be overemphasized that you must know what the links do in order to know how they address your needs. The more sophisticated the link, the more you need to know. You must understand the concept of the link's operation, what preparation must take place, and how they integrate into your specific operations.

Often, link product data sheets do not tell the whole truth, although they do not misrepresent information intentionally. Data sheets merely tell you what that particular link product is capable of doing, not how it is going to perform for you. It is your responsibility to understand or have someone understand the nuances and operational peculiarities of the link relative to what you want it to do for you. The simpler the link, the more you can rely on the data sheets. Even so, environmental considerations, which you should discuss with the vendor, can have a bearing on the product itself.

Do the technical details of the link conform to or match the capabilities of your own data center? This may seem evident, but one particular company purchased links that offered speeds capable of 56,000 bps. It was thought that this excess capacity would be beneficial in the long term and that the company could grow with the product. However, the company's executive management did not ever intend to install lines that operated at that speed. They did not intend to acquire modem configurations that would allow taking advantage of such high performance. So the company never fully utilized the full data transfer speed of the link.

Check to ensure that links conform to the plans of the overall data center. This can seem silly, but it is crucial.

Vendors: As Important As the Product

There are many vendors of links to choose from, some larger than others. In addition, some vendors are more geographically desirable to you than others. In this market, location can be important if the customer can easily reach the vendor. This is true for companies with established branch sales offices where marketing and technical talent can be found to support the customer base in that region.

The vendor is always important. If the vendor is established, investigate their track record for customer support. Find out if their product reliability is without question. These are micro-mainframe links, and failure in operation can cost you more than just time to resolve problems. Know if the vendor's approach to linking is compatible with your outlook for your own needs and growth. Know if the vendor can be depended on to service you if problems arise, or if they defer maintenance elsewhere.

If the vendor is relatively new, small, and perhaps even a start-up company, understand what their product plans are and how the company expects to perform. This might require signing nondisclosure agreements, but if you are seriously contemplating a relationship, it can be to your benefit to do so. Sometimes, if your company is interested in early technology, these companies can provide some interesting and useful link products. If you are willing to assist the vendor in the preliminary testing stages, the results can be beneficial to both of you. Be sure you understand whether the company is financially able to stay in the market even if its products are the best. There is still the sales cycle, which is often lengthy and tedious for any product. You don't want to be left with a product that does not have a vendor in business.

Vendor Reputation

Always check out the vendor's reputation, whether the vendor is small or large. If you know the vendor's posture and history of meeting customer expectations and providing reliable products, you are in a better position to size the risks and determine what their effect could be. Investigate whether the vendors perform as they say, or if there are often initial problems in getting the products to work. For any link (or any product) that does not have a very well known, publicly visible performance record and reputation (good or bad), ask the vendor for customer references. The vendor might even keep a list of users that are available for you to talk with. Spend a little time learning how they have used the product and what their experience and satisfaction level are with the link and the vendor. In particular, try to get references from customers who are using the link in situations similar to yours.

Unfortunately, in the link industry many companies have announced links that did not perform as stated. Companies have also announced links well in advance of delivery dates, only to disappoint customers by not delivering as promised. If you are waiting for a specific link, assess the effects of long delivery delays, particularly if you were dissuaded from going with another vendor's link in anticipation of this one.

In the past, many vendors did not deliver on product claims as promised. This in itself made customers wary of readily accepting a new player. This situation is changing as customers become more aware of link capabilities and are much more astute about what they are buying. Be careful about what you are getting, and be sure that the links can be returned if they do not satisfactorily meet your requirements.

Most vendors offer a 30-day period for you to test their product. Take advantage of this and use it to its fullest. If a vendor does not want to offer this option to a prospective customer, that should trigger a signal to you. Be wary of companies that say you have to purchase the product without a trial period. Of course, some links cannot be easily installed for a 30-day test, particularly software-oriented systems such as those integrated with databases. In this case, companies often have a demonstration site or office where you can go to preview the product and perhaps even run your own data for a benchmark. Take advantage of this if it is available.

The vendor is the last resort when you have problems with a product. It is extremely important to know if the vendor is one that you can work with and feel comfortable with over the long term. You should know in depth and be comfortable with how they support their customers. Understand what their product approach is going to be, even if you have to sign nondisclosure agreements to obtain that information. Make sure that their links can at least coexist with others that you plan to use.

Maintenance, Service, and Diagnostics

Maintenance is a policy and a process. In the 1960s, maintenance meant having the vendor's highly trained specialist take your processor for four to eight hours once a month to perform general preventative maintenance. The technology, which was very expensive, constituted a major investment for your company, and it had to be properly maintained. Generally, you didn't say too much because you didn't have a choice. But today you do.

The cost of computing continues to decrease. Figures typically say what percentage of the total data processing budget is allocated to personal computers, communications, people, and so on. It is still very much a fact, however, that you spend money on computing so that you can improve your overall business operation and competitiveness.

Maintenance is a critical segment of that expenditure. Somewhere, somehow, maintenance always surfaces as a cost to you. It's like the television commercial: you can pay me now or you can pay me later. Some of you are more dependent on others for maintenance. Some of you even have a company warehouse from which to procure products and spares when you need them.

Know what your own service needs are and how they are going to change over time. It is not essential that you stock your own spare parts, but you must have some maintenance policy, just as you should for your personal computers. This should be as much a part of your plan as anything. It can simply be a single paragraph, but it should be stated and understood.

Maintenance Cost Implications

There are several service options in the linking arena. For emulation products, you can expect that over time you are not going to want to purchase maintenance on the emulation cards themselves. If the card has been installed for two or three years, it is probably more appropriate simply to throw the link hardware away and replace it with another.

For example, assume you pay $1,100 today for a personal computer emulation link board. A rule of thumb is that a maintenance contract costs you 1 percent per month of the purchase price of the card. Over a three-year period, the maintenance contract costs you $396. Not much? Assuming a 7 percent per year price erosion on an equivalent link product, you can buy a replacement card of the same function for approximately $884 sometime in the third year. This arithmetic shows that the net cost to you for the new card if you hadn't paid for maintenance on the old is in reality only $488. Although we haven't taken into account the cost of money, it is worth considering a replacement philosophy upon failure for this level of product because of improved technology reliability.

Vendor Maintenance Policy

Some vendors are not in a position to support their products and instead use a third-party maintenance company. It is sometimes good business strategy for the vendors to forge such relationships, because the cost to service and support products in the field is extremely high. Other link vendors use a "return and replace" philosophy. When the product fails, you call them, receive a replacement within 24 hours, and return the failing unit for repair. This approach is used by companies whose links tend to be hardware only, such as coaxial attached emulation cards.

Ultimately, however, vendors want to be more in control of their customers and their own sales and support staffs. This is a trend in the market, although companies in the third-party business are not in danger of becoming extinct. Third parties can certainly be relied upon to do the job, and they have offices throughout the country that can be surrogates for the actual vendor.

Understand what the vendor's policy is toward customer support and how it is going to change in the future. How, you ask? Talking with the vendor will tell you a great deal about what their attitude is toward support. You are going to have to rely on the vendor; in some cases of complex link products you have no choice. Find out how the vendor will support you in times of problems.

In some cases, vendors merely have a toll-free 800 number established for customers to call in times of trouble. This is sufficient if user problems are educational, operational, or documentation oriented. But if resolutions to technical problems are addressed this way, know what action a vendor can take if the resolution period becomes lengthy or ineffective.

Product Warranty

Warranty is another matter not to be overlooked. Warranty is different from maintenance. Warranty is how long the product is guaranteed against failure. Maintenance is what's involved in locating and fixing the problem. All products that you purchase should be warranted against failure for some period of time. Many link companies offer a one-year warranty on parts. Some still offer only 30 or 90 days with an optional service contract. One particular company, INS (Mobile, Alabama) offers a five-year warranty on its IBM 8100 link products. It is necessary to know how a vendor treats its warranty offering, what the time period is, and when the warranty starts. Some vendors start the warranty from the date of shipment, while others do not start until date of installation (within reason) after shipment.

Vendor Diagnostics

The diagnostic aspect of any hardware and software product cannot be overemphasized. It is key to isolating and resolving problems that arise. Diagnostics must be available for the particular product itself, and it is also desirable that diagnostics provide some system-level coverage.

Because links are part of your communications network, they can have problems of their own and also create problems that can affect connectivity to the host and personal computer users. For example, problems that arise on a LAN can sometimes have a catastrophic effect on other users. Certain types of problems can even cause the entire LAN to terminate operation. This doesn't happen with all LANs, and it is becoming less frequent, but when it does occur it is important to be able to diagnose what happened. LAN and associated gateway product reliability continues to improve with each passing month. But products are still not problem free, mainly because of how some users install and try to use them, not because of how the vendors have designed and implemented them. A means of diagnosing problems must be available.

Some link products now provide trace facilities that enable you to monitor a string of data or commands that can be later used to identify or recreate a problem. Information Technologies Incorporated (ITI) (Scottsdale, Arizona) provides such a capability in its Linkup series of emulation links. The information can be very helpful in identifying what went wrong. Once you know what caused the problem, you can take steps to prevent a similar problem from occurring. In addition, you have data that is useful to the vendor for correcting the situation.

Diagnostics are only as effective as they are thorough. You cannot expect to get a perfect diagnostic that can trap all problems, but you can determine whether the vendor appreciates and comprehends the effect that diagnostics have on successful link maintenance. Know how the vendor stands in this area, and certainly include diagnostic testing in your prototype. If you can't utilize the diagnostics effectively in a problem situation that you have created yourself and know the answer to, how can you rely on the diagnostics in situations in which you have no clues as to the problem?

9 Prototyping and Testing

▼ PROTOTYPES
▼ TRUSTING THE VENDOR
▼ BEGINNING LINK INTEGRATION
▼ YOU NEED A TEST PLAN AND CRITERIA
▼ ESTABLISHING A TEST METHODOLOGY

Vendors "know" that their links work because they have tested them in a multitude of environments. These links have been carefully designed to operate in installations with emulation needs, network requirements, throughput demands, and high reliability. Although there are exceptions, a vendor does not intentionally market links that do not perform. The links are unit tested, system tested, checked (generally) in customer sites (alpha test), and finally tested in customer sites (beta test), after which they are supposedly ready for the market. Links are typically not shipped with errors, although this did occur in the link industry's early days and created bad impressions.

◥ PROTOTYPES

Good vendors do not intentionally sell links that won't operate in different customer situations, although not all customer data transfer and integration situations are necessarily the same as those the vendor tests. The vendor's link product can very well be designed thoroughly, operate as specified, and provide a full range of features. Your needs and user requirements, however, pose factors that can reflect poorly on a link's performance in a particular situation. This is why you should prototype selected links in a pilot study before full installation and implementation. You need to determine if the links will perform as expected or if your environment poses requirements that make it difficult for any link to perform adequately. You could have a situation that must be redefined before any linking and connection into hosts can occur. View the prototype as a way to satisfy yourself that you have made the right link choice, but keep the opportunity to change before committing to a solution as you now pilot the application with the selected links.

How Prototypes Are Useful For Customers and Vendors

When customers prototype several link products in a pilot, some links outshine others — not because they are better designed, but because they are more adaptable to customer needs. Vendors whose links do not get selected for purchase can learn a great deal from a well-executed customer test. A link rejection does not necessarily mean that the link did not perform or cause problems, but that customer requirements imposed factors that could not be satisfied. The vendor at least gets a picture of why the link product did not ultimately get accepted. This does not make the pill easier to swallow, but it does provide the vendor with something that can be useful market input. You can benefit as well by having the vendors seek to satisfy your requirements with future product releases and enhancements.

The purpose of the prototype is to be sure that the link product does what you need it to do. Regardless of what the brochure says, it is important that you see the product in its ultimate environment before you make a commitment.

The Prototype as a Necessity

If one simple emulation link is required, then you do not need an elaborate prototype. You need only to pick an emulation link, know what it is to be used for, and purchase and install it for use. If, however, the emulation link is the first of many to be installed as part of a company program, then it is prudent to consider at least a prototype for host loading.

This means that you procure several of the selected links, install them in a controlled situation, and scale the activity to determine what host loading is probable. Impossible or useless, you say? Not true. It's useless if terminal emulation is needed only to interact with the host, if data transfer is minimal, and if application user growth is not expected. If data transfer volume of any significance is to take place, you can extrapolate this loading to determine the effect on host resources.

If the links you are procuring require host-installed software, provide additional multilevel security access capability, and use personal-computer-based hardware and software, then you want to establish a representative pilot. Why? Because you are installing a link system within your host environment. Although the link system's user interfaces and functionality may appear simple, the actual operation of the link can have a large effect on existing host system resources. Now we are talking about prototyping an application whose operational unknowns within your network can be hidden until you use the link. LANs and file server technology are the same. You know what you are getting, but you don't know how you can benefit from the technology until you apply it to your needs. These are the benefits a prototype and pilot can provide.

The Prototype as a Link Tester

If a complex application using a link is mandated (such as Cullinet's IDMS database with its proprietary link), you want to get some feel for how the application addresses your situation. This would be true for any micro-mainframe link that requires hardware in the personal computer and software resident on the host, as just described.

If very complex designs are planned, such as a file server configuration supporting one or more LANs, you clearly need to establish a prototype activity. There are just too many things that can go wrong or affect your host. These are not trivial situations. They must be addressed in a way that leaves you plenty of opportunity to understand how they operate, how they can fail, and how they must be supported.

You must also consider the factors of backup and recovery. Time to recover in a failing LAN situation must be known. Check security and data integrity exposures thoroughly in an environment that represents a subset of the final installation. If security features are available, you must know if what they provide is consistent with your host environment as well as whether they can be integrated into your procedures.

The Usefulness of a Prototype

Micro-mainframe link prototypes let you become familiar with the technology. You become aware of the nuances that accompany any new concept associated with the link technology selected. Using a prototype allows you to train a subset of the users that it will ultimately serve, acquaint users with its advantages, and demonstrate its limitations. A prototype gives you assurance about the link's applicability to your needs.

A prototype's usefulness far outweighs any time drawbacks in implementation. If done properly, the prototype can evolve into a production precursor. It can give you a look at what you are dealing with before you get committed too far down the road. If nothing else, a prototype makes you realize what you didn't know about the link, no matter how trivial, or what questions could have gone unanswered.

◥ TRUSTING THE VENDOR

Knowing a vendor and *really* knowing a vendor are two entirely different things. As a customer, you must be able to rely on a vendor and trust that the vendor can continue to provide you with the service and product upgrades that keep pace with your business. You must be able to trust a vendor and have faith in what its representatives tell you.

Implementing a prototype often gives you more information than simply whether or not the product can do the job. You see how well a vendor supports you during all phases:

- Installation
- Operation
- Problem determination
- Training.

You also see how well a vendor responds to your requests for assistance (unless those requests are simply ridiculous; it has been known for customers to beat a vendor into the ground over very small issues).

Managing the Vendor

If you are considering more than one link product, let the vendor know this. Let the vendor's representatives know that you may from time to time call on them to answer questions or render opinions about your planned configuration. It cannot be emphasized enough that a prototype is as much to let you see the vendor's attitude and approach as it is to check the performance of products under a given set of circumstances. If you are growing, you should know whether you can rely on a vendor's assistance in and tolerance of your needs.

Remember that with few exceptions, business relationships are as important as the products themselves. Witness the strength of IBM. Customers know they can rely on IBM for service and support no matter what the situation (even if they have to pay dearly for it in more ways than one). The reputation and credibility is always there. Similarly, Hewlett-Packard's (H-P) customers can rely on that company because they know that at some point (even if it is late), products are there to support their customer base. Emphasis on customer service is as much a part of the marketing process as post-sale and installation follow-up. DEC also continues to introduce products that offer existing and prospective customers a variety of options and functionality from which to choose. The customer base knows that DEC is always there and can be relied upon when absolutely necessary. Many other companies build their businesses on customer relationships as well. Smaller companies sometimes emphasize support as a key selling tool in retaining quality customers.

Trusting the vendor and its products is good business sense. A prototype is useful in measuring whether the vendor can earn it. Figure 9-1 shows what you can learn about a link and its vendor during prototyping.

◥ BEGINNING LINK INTEGRATION

There are many ways to start a link prototype and to perform personal computer integration. Because we've already talked about how to perform the personal computer integration, let's concentrate on the link prototype. It's a safe way to begin integration because it places you in a low-risk position. You can get an early look at the products before committing yourself to a specific program and vendors. The prototype allows you to define rules and guidelines by which the system is tested to determine its applicability to your needs. This puts *you* in control.

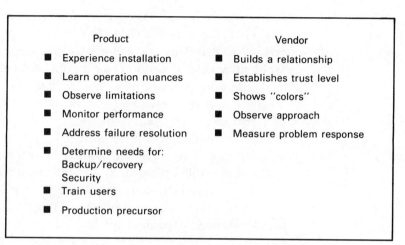

Product	Vendor
■ Experience installation	■ Builds a relationship
■ Learn operation nuances	■ Establishes trust level
■ Observe limitations	■ Shows "colors"
■ Monitor performance	■ Observe approach
■ Address failure resolution	■ Measure problem response
■ Determine needs for: Backup/recovery Security	
■ Train users	
■ Production precursor	

Figure 9-1. ▶

Benefits of using a prototype

Committing yourself to a paper plan with a specific vendor or vendors without trying the design exposes you to the possibility that there are things you overlooked. Any vendor that does not permit you at least a 30-day test of the product before purchasing should be placed on a second tier of possibilities. The industry is still young. Asking a vendor for a loan of a product for testing is not an impossibility nor an unrealistic request. There are many quality products available, and vendors standing behind their link products should be expected to assist rather than hinder you in your evaluations.

Isolating Link Integration

You should also consider how you can isolate the introduction of a particular link into the user community. This is not as difficult as it sounds. All customer installations have a particular department with host access demand, a specific individual whom they trust for product evaluations, or an individual function that requires data transfer down to the personal computer. In some cases, you have various vendor host computers. Areas using computers from DEC, IBM, H-P, or any other company can present an excellent opportunity to gain some experience.

Identify what situation is most appropriate for you, set about to decide how you can inject the link into this portion of the business, and proceed. Once you isolate *where* you perform the test, you can then address the *how*. The how entails who is involved, whether it is a meaningful evaluation, and whether management can validate or modify the original plan.

Isolating the link prototype gives you an opportunity to evaluate the product in an environment established by you with known parameters and limitations. When the test passes this hurdle, you can expand usage of the links to other areas or permit users in the same area to have host access. This is called *link phasing*.

Host Link Phasing

Phasing is the ability to take the selected products and install them for the rest of your users. It involves standards to some degree, but not in the truest sense of the word. You cannot always expect to make all information-processing host access situations comply with a particular form of link. In this case, standards are a potentially suggested list of links from which to procure for various sectors of your organization. Different sectors can require different link solutions. The point is to prevent all users from simply buying any links that they like and accessing any hosts that they choose.

Have a staged plan that operations management knows is in progress, and let operations management know that they are involved. As links are added, so must host resources be carefully apportioned to support them. For some customers, host computer power is the least of their concerns. By phasing link integration, you have a chance to institute security access procedures, determine backup policy, monitor host resource usage, measure data

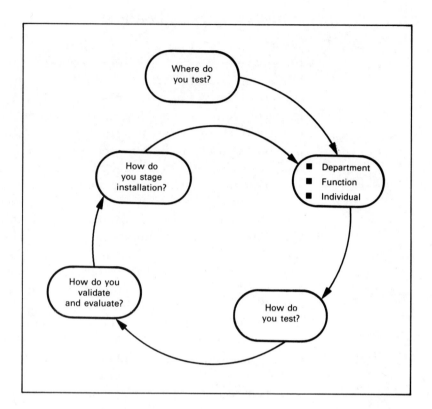

Figure 9-2. ▶

Link integration process (stages of questions)

transfer growth, and spot potential problems as the number of links increases.

With phasing, you can bring on an individual department and its users one at a time, or phase in individual functions and their users. The same principles that apply to selectively installing and making available access to host software systems apply to links. It is the process that is important, not the products. Once the link products are selected, then the process by which they are installed, tested, and maintained becomes important. This is also a process that can be a continuous loop, as shown in Figure 9-2.

Addressing Host Loading

What is host loading and how does it apply to micro-mainframe links? The host is not an infinite reservoir of resources. There can be only so many MIPS (million-instructions-per-second execution) and so many users. Links pose a different factor. Unlike interactive terminals, the load is not always predictable, because of the variable of data transfer and what users request for execution on the host. Aside from operating in terminal emulation mode (in which the personal computer operates as if it were another terminal), data transfer can impose changing rules that the host must contend with. If data can be uploaded for use by a host application, and if the application is invoked by the end user, this can pose yet another host burden. Finally, if a large number of users are linked to the host, pure database management, retrieval, and transfer queuing can become quite a load.

Figure 9-3 shows the relative order of usage priorities of host resources, starting with personal computer usage as a dumb terminal. Priority of host attention (and resources) increases with the increasing demands that users make through the personal computer. Multiply this by 50 or even 500 personal computers and you can see how the effect on the host starts to magnify. This is measurable and can be monitored during a pilot.

Peak times do exist; these tend to conform to the normal rule of early morning, pre-lunch, post-lunch, and the end of the day around 4 PM. This is because users need to transfer data down to their personal computer for the day's work and back to the host when they are done, if such uploading is allowed.

The Importance of
Host Loading

Loading is important because it tells you just how much activity and servicing your host can be expected to deliver to the linked personal computers. It tells you what percentage of the time the host must service data queries and transfer requests. If the host

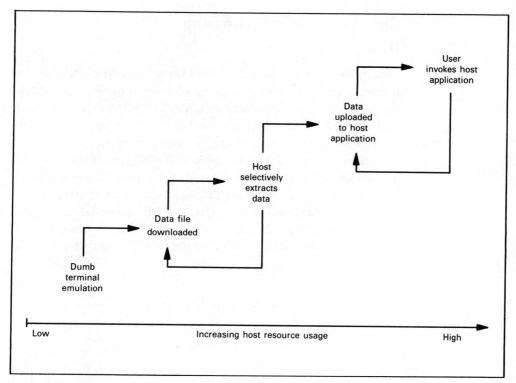

Figure 9-3. ▲

User request complexity to host drain

requires a resident software link counterpart to extract data selectively from host files, you must know how much drain such an application consumes. This is determined by the number of personal computers calling for host access and support. Loading is important because it gives you a profile of whether your resources and capacity are sufficient to support link transfer requirements.

Simulating and Estimating Host Loading

In a pilot, you can simulate loading under representative and actual conditions. You can create files for transfer that contain no pertinent data but present a sufficient load to the system with and without active job processing on the host. You can initiate progressive loads down to the personal computer and initiate simultaneous active downloads as well. You do not need to link all 100 or 200 personal computers to the host to test the load. You can estimate data, empirically measure it, and extrapolate it out to the remainder of the active on-line personal computers that are linked into the host. You can then develop a curve for data transfer that looks similar to the one shown in Figure 9-4.

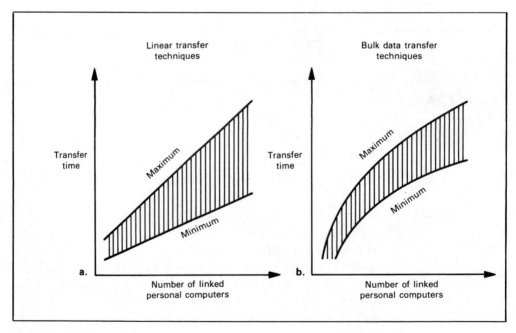

Figure 9-4. ▲

Host loading data transfer profile

Essentially, you create a minimum and maximum transfer time based on data volume transferred and frequency of transfer. Both are key ingredients of loading, which represents the total number of personal computers linked. The vertical axes in Figures 9-4a and 9-4b represent total transfer time, and the horizontal axes represent the number of personal computers.

The figures are greatly simplified, but they demonstrate the loading effects we are trying to describe. Figure 9-4a shows minimum and maximum curves that are both linear. No unusual effects change the fact that if all things are equal, each added personal computer produces a corresponding increase in transfer time. Factors that affect the slopes of these curves at a system level include

- Line transfer speeds
- Transfer efficiency (never 100 percent)
- Simultaneous transfers
- Queuing within the host
- Percentage of linked personal computers doing simultaneous data transfer.

Figure 9-5 shows curves that are not linear because some links (such as BLAST from Communications Research Group) use bulk data transfer or blocking techniques to reduce the time of transmission to a single or group of personal computers. For example, selective data extraction at the host transfers only the data needed, not the entire file. Although this typically tends to keep the curve linear and simply reduces the slope to a minimum level for any given transfer, better usage of the lines can contribute better data transfer characteristics. Data blocking into packets also affects transmission time for large blocks of data. For small data transfers, the effect of blocking into packets is not realized. As the graph shows, however, the more data that is transferred, the larger the resulting effect of transferring in blocks.

Practically speaking, an expected curve can always be created that falls somewhere in between the minimum and maximum

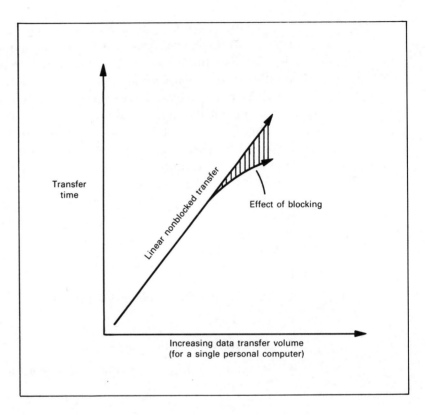

Transfer time

Linear nonblocked transfer

Effect of blocking

Increasing data transfer volume
(for a single personal computer)

Figure 9-5. ▶

*Blocking effects on
large data transfers*

shown in Figures 9-4a and 9-4b. From these curves, the important thing that you are estimating is the safety factor within
which your link products and design must operate. If your host
ports cannot support the anticipated capacity and links, or if
your line speeds are not fast enough to maintain reasonable data
transfer response times, then you probably must review your link
plans for changes.

◥ YOU NEED A TEST
PLAN AND CRITERIA

If you haven't decided to skip the prototype entirely, you and
your technical people need to have a test plan. The test plan tells

you what you are looking for, what you want to measure, what features are important to you, and what features are not relevant to your needs.

For example, you don't need to test for maximum data transfer as a stress test on the link and the host if the majority of usage is primarily data query and interactive work. You needn't load the system down if most data transfer involves entities of less than 1000 characters for each of 10 personal computers twice a day. Discretion is the better part of valor; unless you anticipate extensive growth in these cases, you probably can never expect to tax the upper limits of link transfer speed in these two situations.

You should test link features that mean something to you. Test for the capability that you plan to standardize on for the long term. Your link plan is your personal computer integration road map, so you should test features and capabilities that meet your requirements. Build your own test plan to check those items you deemed most important in your selection criteria. The plan will give you the data you need to validate your decisions and value judgments.

What Your Test Plan Means

The point is that you should order your needs and address those that are most practical for your installation. You can even have two test plans and criteria lists: one for the realities of what is today, and the other for your anticipated growth. Although you don't want to get carried away, you can also have different test plans for different departments. If you are in a large company with various functional organizations, it is highly unlikely that you can expect to standardize on a single link for all areas. Prepare yourself and your company for the possibility of different departments' requiring their own link standards. It can happen.

Your pilot prototype can perform a sequential testing of features and requirements in each case. What are you checking for in this instance? You are checking to see if the link products selected meet today's identified need and whether you can grow with them as your requirements expand. Sometimes you can find that the two are mutually exclusive for the same link product.

Management Wants to Know

If you are not management, then you report to management. Management signs the purchase authorizations and is accountable for the activities in the user base and the host installation. Management wants to know if the right decisions have been made and if a framework that can grow with the business is being built.

The test plan tells management that you understand needs and have listed the important aspects to be checked. (Maybe you don't understand the needs, but good management can ascertain this and help you make adjustments.) You don't necessarily talk to executives about test plan details, but you articulate the plan's purpose and scope, particularly about how you benefit from defining and executing a pilot against the test plan.

Like any other undertaking, a test plan must be managed. Although the outcome is important, it is the process that is critical. The outcome tells you what decisions to make. If the process is correct and the results are not what you anticipated, then the test plan is doing its job and you know where to look for improvements. The plan may be telling you that the link product selection is not correct, that the applications for the link are poor, or that your configuration and usage of links must be changed. It identifies questions that you must ask vendors or tells you to look at the link network design and determine if it is optimized for the links. If the process you defined is comprehensive and the results are as you expected, then you have validated the links, configuration, and application use (presuming that the test plan is not slanted toward a particular vendor's product regardless of the application). The process is shown in Figure 9-6 on the facing page.

Applying the Test Plan To Later Integration

Once you have a test plan, you have a guideline that can be used for complete system integration. You know what to look for, how to address problems, and how to tune the host system. You

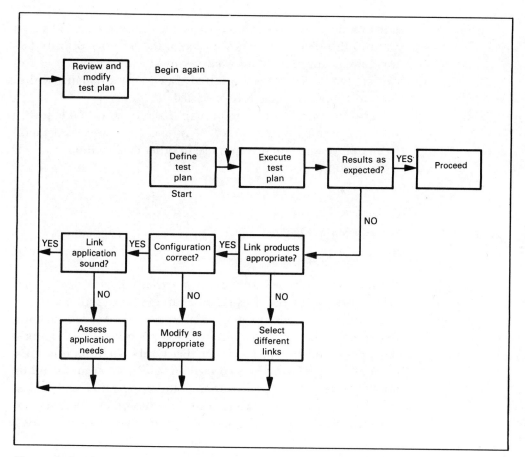

Figure 9-6. ▲

*Test plan
approach/execution*

can tell host management what criteria are important and what activity best characterizes the kinds of resources required of the host. Users and MIS operations management are your key personnel for making personal-computer-to-host integration work. You need them to have a smooth transition into the new environment.

If problems arise in the overall integration scheme, the test plan can provide clues about what is happening. For example, if a problem occurs on a capability in which the selected link did not test strongly, you can adjust to minimize the effect of that feature. In other cases, you can determine whether priority factors have changed or if users have evolved to a new link use. You can analyze to see if your original data transfer remains within the safety margins that you projected.

The test plan is like a road map that can be valuable to you over and over again. At the very least, you have developed a template that you can modify and use in other data communications linking endeavors.

What You Need To Find Out

Clearly, what you learn during the execution of a test plan is what works and what doesn't. You can expect to refine assumptions and procedures as you go. This doesn't need to be a tedious, drawn-out process. It can mean that you simply sit down for a day or two and list the key items that typify what the link must do and the performance expected. It can also mean spending another several days understanding the application or business problem that the link is to resolve. You should circulate the test plan list to others who can have insight into what is most important to know about the link products and their uses.

What You Are Going To Find Out

What you will learn is whether the link product can do what you need it to do. It will not take you long to determine if the product delivers the functionality and performance that you need. You are going to learn that products often perform as advertised but are not always suited to your particular operation. Your test plan creates an opportunity to compare and evaluate link products against each other in situations that are *uniquely tailored by you.*

◤ ESTABLISHING A TEST METHODOLOGY

A test methodology is absolutely critical to the success of the prototype and pilot. It is exactly that: a *methodology*. It is not just a series of tests in particular, but how you apply those tests, in what order, for what reasons, and with what expectations. Obviously, a test methodology must include tests that exercise the link and situation.

You should approach testing with a positive attitude. The purpose is not to see how you can make the link and the process fail. You can always find a set of conditions that, when presented in the right circumstances, can make a particular solution or design malfunction. The purpose of a test methodology is to *create situations of operation and stress that exercise the design and links in a way that permits you to observe how well they perform.* Some designs and links that do not perform well in one environment may perform exceptionally well in another.

The purpose of the methodology is to learn if the link products and your design can support your defined requirements. If you find that there are problems or deficiencies with one or the other, then you have to make changes. It is to be hoped that you have not consciously selected links that you know can't do the job. Don't look for all of the bad that can happen by defining test criteria oriented toward making the links look bad. This is not fair to you, to your organization, or to the vendors. You don't need to make links look bad; unacceptable links soon become evident and the vendor becomes aware of it quickly.

What Is Critical to Test

The methodology and tests are defined to exercise the most highly used and critical paths of the link that characterizes your proposed application. The least critical items are features that have no immediate bearing on the intended task. For example, if you have a centralized host security system for user access control, and if additional security capability accompanying a link is not a relevant factor in selection, then testing these capabilities can be irrelevant to your need.

If high-speed bulk data transfer is required, then design a set of tasks and tests to exercise the most obvious transfer situations and then some of the not-so-obvious ones. If bulk transfer is an absolute necessity, you can be sure that someone in day-to-day production will request an unusual transfer, so test for it. If your needs are for application program interfacing, then be sure that the method that vendors permit you to use is acceptable to you and your users.

Define the critical paths that your usage can take. As part of the link selection criteria, develop a list of those things that are absolutely necessary in the final environment. These criteria tell you what are the most important issues in how the system is going to be used. You can test the product for its own capabilities, but then you must test it for how it supports the role it must play in your linking network.

Comparing Multiple Links

When you construct a link test that calls for using more than one link, or if you are comparing multiple links simultaneously, you have to set up your tests to compare apples to apples. You cannot emphasize data transfer speed on one link and functionality on another. Any comparison will be inconclusive because you are not comparing like to like.

Maintain consistency of criteria throughout the testing process. Not all data is quantitative. Subjective assessment about the links that are being used is also key. In some cases, a subjective opinion about ease of use depends on the technical savvy of the individuals and how well versed they are in the use of the technology. Be sure that comments about procedures, product understanding, and error handling are applicable for the majority of users for which the system is intended. Often very technical evaluators overestimate the capabilities of the end user and forget how well they themselves are familiar with link technology and the process of using it.

In addition to recording data and observing how the tests are conducted, you must maintain consistency across link evaluations and review. You are not in a laboratory environment. If you want to obtain the best link system for the business and avoid the pitfalls of having subjective opinion guide your selections, then it is imperative that you know what you are looking for. Know how the tests and pilots are being managed, and be familiar with the skills and biases of the individuals involved in the prototype.

Some people perform a test to validate the link that they would like to have. Without a plan, it is sometimes difficult for you to accept that the link you really want is not appropriate for the particular system and task at hand. Also, the hope that a specific vendor can meet your long-term product expansion plans can place you in a precarious position if the vendor's activities do not coincide with yours.

Equivalent Tests

Remember that the prototype is merely taking the link and its associated hardware and software and executing tests to determine how it functions and if it performs as defined. A pilot actually uses the link under conditions that replicate or simulate the environment in which it will be intended to perform. There is a remarkably subtle difference. If it is possible for you to make the prototype and the pilot one and the same, all the better.

In a prototype test or pilot in which more than one link is under consideration and you are relying on the results of a set of tests for comparison purposes, the tests must be the same or equivalent. In other words, tests for a prototype do not have to be the same as for a pilot, but to ensure comparable evaluation, tests on different links within a pilot or prototype must be the same.

Equivalence is important because it is the only way you can be certain of what activity took place during the review. If you are going to go through the trouble of establishing a benchmark for product selection, then you should also take the time to establish the program of testing so that consistency is maintained across all products.

Companies exercise benchmark testing on mainframes and minicomputers if unusual software or environments are under discussion. The purpose and intent are simple: create a test that exercises the equipment to determine if it meets the needs and standards established for your requirements. You can and should do the same for micro-mainframe links.

◥ SUMMARY

As a way to consolidate this chapter, let's review the important points of why you develop and test a prototype:

1. To verify your link product selection
2. To identify important performance factors
3. To compare several different links
4. To test links as *you* want to test them
5. To familiarize yourself with the technology
6. To see the extent and nature of vendor support
7. To prepare for a comprehensive pilot application
8. To estimate host resource requirements
9. To identify issues of further link integration
10. To evolve toward an installation process.

If you are integrating a number of personal computers, do not treat this area lightly. The prototype is a test of the link itself in an isolated or predetermined situation. It differs from the pilot in that the pilot simulates or represents an actual environment using the link. Use the prototype to the best of your advantage and understand how the link functions. At the very least, the prototype provides a way for you and your users to educate yourselves about links and the power they can offer to facilitate improved data movement.

10

Evaluating Results
Of Link Selection
And Piloting

◥ WHAT TO DO WITH THE DATA
◥ QUESTIONS FOR LINK REVIEW
◥ MAKE A LINK SELECTION

One of the most important parts of reviewing any new product or service is the part *after* completing the prototype and pilot. Now that you have your implementation plan and have completed (at least partially) your prototype, you have information in hand and are ready to evaluate. The post-project review provides the most insight into what actually got accomplished and gives perspective on whether it fits the originally designed plan. This is time to take stock before making a commitment to acquiring links that are to have a lengthy life span in your communications plans.

A post-project review should be handled like any debriefing. You look at the information, note any extenuating circumstances that occurred during the evaluation period, and ensure that the data you have collected is sufficient to make decisions. If something went wrong, or if selected links did not meet criteria and expectations, you should find out why. It doesn't matter if something is not quite right, so long as you know why. You should also determine whether the pilot process itself could have been the reason for any errors. Get subjective comments from those who participated in or executed the pilot process and digest those comments into something that makes sense. The post-project review doesn't have to be lengthy unless there are abnormalities in the results or unless the link comparisons are far apart. The latter suggests that the test did not get performed consistently.

What to Do With The Data

If you established the test criteria correctly, you have an important list (or matrix) of information on each link product under examination. Start with the list as the beginning of your review. Give each item a quick glance and review how each link performed and met your prioritized criteria. If you note significant differences between any links, this is a good place at which to begin your review.

Look at differences in data and ask why they exist. It is not necessarily bad if two links do not test exactly alike, but it *is* bad if the difference cannot be explained. If two equivalent link products from different vendors differ drastically on the same test point, then there must be a reason. It is in your best interests to know why this difference occurred. You may be confronted with pilot test data that is suspect for all the links tested. If this is the case, then you should quickly review your entire test plan and interview the people conducting the test.

If there are differences in link results, another possibility is that two different vendor links of reputed equivalence are equal only under certain circumstances. That does not make the vendor wrong or untrustworthy; it means that the environment in which the vendor performed measurements is not the same as the environment in which you are operating. That is the reason for the pilot study: to identify factors that affect your overall system.

Results and Requirements

With the data in hand, you can quickly go down your test criteria and decide if you have enough assurance at this time to proceed with the decision to procure. It is also possible that if you cannot get this far with the data at hand, you must reassess the requirements that you gave priority. The data can indicate that changes are required in your original requirements. The data can also mean that, all things being equal, equivalent positive results tell you that you have more than one choice to meet your needs.

Your requirements can change because one factor can affect another. There can be any number of possibilities. For example, you can find that the requirement for bulk data transfer for binary data overshadows your need for interactive retrieval of text data files. This calls for a link that handles binary as well as text data and offers fast transfer speed. For more complex needs, you may find that it is necessary to initiate multiple file transfer with a single request or dynamically allocate and deallocate data sets at the host on user demand. These are just some of the things that a good user test can uncover. It can influence you to go back and adjust priorities and perhaps modify your initial selection criteria. If you are focused on a comprehensive link system using sophisticated host software, you may choose to work around any test deficiencies to achieve other link capabilities.

Remember, now is the time to make adjustments to your link selection or application needs and consider carefully before you commit yourself to what is an expensive link proposition. You can make a decision now to proceed and buy, or you can select other products for testing. Your review and decision, as shown below, is really quite simple.

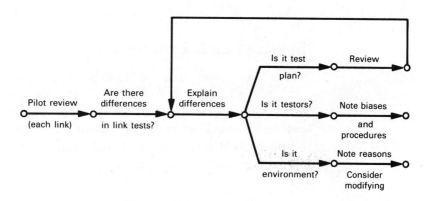

Does the Link Do What You Wanted?

The link must perform to your satisfaction. If you are using a terminal emulation link, satisfaction is limited to specifics of usability and performance. There is only so much an emulation link can do and deliver. Its basics are already defined, and you will notice if they do not perform. However, as you progress to more complicated designs that we have discussed (such as file servers, LANs, and database integrated links), the spectrum of what you want links to do gets wider.

Considering how much you pay for these products, users of more elaborate link systems expect more and deserve more. A more elaborate system can provide better long-term growth, but you always confront the short-term users as well, no matter where you are in the installation cycle. People always want results now, and they must be satisfied with progress toward that end. You have to know if the link system that you are installing is meeting the needs of today's users. At the same time, you must make a determination about how the links meet your long-term company goals. Some of the basics never change, no matter what the product.

The important point is to ascertain that the links under test have met all your high-priority criteria and have met most of the lesser criteria on your list as well. Those items that you currently deem not to be as important as others can some day become very important as the nature of your user activity changes. You should leave yourself enough flexibility to achieve enhancement and upgrade to your link network in the future.

Selected Link Elimination

If you have more than two link products under test, you can probably eliminate a few immediately after your prototype. Selecting products and choosing the right link approach for you can be as much a matter of product elimination as choice. Immediately disregard all potential products that have not met the preliminary or initial screen in the prototype and pilot.

Don't waste time continuing their review if you can see that they already do not measure up to what you need or want.

Evaluating emulation capability is relatively straightforward. The product either emulates the terminal device or it doesn't. Other characteristics such as file transfer speed, coprocessing, multisessions, and multihost attachment are features of the link hardware and software, not the emulator portion. There are certain fixed functions that emulator links for a given host vendor's equipment must all possess. You can quickly see whether they offer the same speed characteristics and data support. Emulation links, however, do differ in how their user interfaces are established and how they treat session setup. DCA's IRMA board is so dominant in the IBM market that any emulation link products that are not compatible are quickly at a disadvantage and should be suspect to the buyer. Let's face it: no one wants to end up with a product that can't be interchanged if it becomes necessary.

Evaluating Prototype Results

During a prototype, you pay attention to results as they arise instead of waiting until all the data is completed and you see it for the first time. This kind of testing is not a laboratory experiment in which you run a test, collect the data, and plot it for an analysis report. You constantly have to know what the progress is, what the problems encountered were, and if you had to circumvent any operational aspects for your needs. Aside from simply checking off the test criteria as they are addressed, you must also note subjective issues and observations made during the pilot. These issues are indeed important in clarifying your decisions about the results.

When testing large, sophisticated personal computer linking systems, a management report that identifies key points that influence final purchase decisions is generally delivered. Technical aspects need to be put in context with the business use and usability factors. Finally, remember that you need to have the technical evaluators put the results in language that tells you what it all means. You have to be able to know what the evaluators are telling you in terms that make sense for you to understand.

What the Post-Evaluation Tells You

Long before the prototype or pilot is complete, you often get indications of how much difficulty your people had in installing, using, and maintaining the system. Normally, you can expect to know beforehand what link products offer the most promise for you. You can even expect to be surprised about some things that you thought would occur and didn't. You may have to make some hard decisions: it's possible that you won't select products that you were sure would be right until you placed them in your own situation. This can be eye-opening, surprising, and difficult.

After all is said and done, any preconceived notions that you had about links can be drastically altered as a result of your testing—not because your link preferences were changed, but because your opinions about them were changed. The results of your testing can lower your expectations about all the problems that links are purported to solve and don't. Yet you can better understand just how much proper link selection and design can contribute to improved productivity of your people and overall network operation. You will find yourself thinking much more realistically about the application of this technology in a practical sense to resolve problems, issues, and connectivity (which is what you were after).

The results can alter your perspective and outlook on links and give you more experience about what you can do later as well as help you understand the degree to which links can affect your business. The test results add flavor to your understanding about the categories of products and where the complexities lie, especially if your business is large and you are installing emulation links, file servers, and LANs. Making these products talk to one another is still another challenge, but prototyping products can lend credence to what you can and cannot do. This is true whether you are dealing with systems from IBM, Burroughs, Sperry, DEC, H-P, DG, or any other minicomputer or mainframe manufacturer.

Pros and Cons of Assessment

The pros and cons of testing and installing any link product can leave much to interpretation. There is no correct or incorrect way to proceed at this stage. To begin with, you must review the key issues that surrounded the prototype and pilot. As a reminder, a prototype tests the viability of a product specifically, while the pilot places the link in a subset of an actual environment for use with real applications and transfer requirements. The difference is a lot like saying, "Let's buy this link and see if it works. Now let's use it the way that we intend to and see if it does the job." Pros and cons cannot be overlooked because they never go away.

◥ QUESTIONS FOR LINK REVIEW

Does the product give you flexibility to use it in other information processing and transfer situations? Can you extend support into other applications? Can you integrate what you already have into a more extensive system based on this new design? Can you intermix different vendors' links that perform equivalent functions? Do you want to? Is it possible that you can have a longer product usage span than you anticipated? If so, do you need to consider other alternatives? Do the links in question permit or limit your expansion in the future? Do you care?

These are all part of the pros and cons. You can find that the simple emulation links work fine, but overcoming the problems and complexities of selecting and installing a more complex LAN system gives you more flexible options in the long term. These options can prove the most economical over time. There are cons in selecting an emulation link, also. You may have those links longer than you might expect, and yet you must still graduate to other personal computer integration techniques simply to maintain growth with your own user needs. The trade-offs are there for you to see.

Perhaps you find that another approach is necessary even after you have implemented a given scheme. The plot thickens as you progress into another realm of managing the integration process. Emulation links are good now and are going to be around for a long time. They are quick to use and relatively easy to install. Once in, they stay a long time.

What about LANs and gateways? Your growing need and dependency on distributed systems and processing are compelling you to use these products in departments and user groups with specific needs. They permit levels of information management and movement that are becoming more accepted as users find benefits can often outweigh limitations and drawbacks. There are areas in which using LANs and gateways is both practical and logical. You must ask yourself not why these products won't work but how you can have them work more effectively for your own environment.

The pros of such products are that they can provide incremental information movement capability that is independent from your host except when data access is needed or host application access is required. Costs per connection decrease as you increase the number of user connections. You may find that isolating such products within departments is an ideal situation until you need to connect to the host. On the downside, there are still issues of global data security and integrity. These are all things that come into play as you review whether the products are applicable to your needs.

A systems approach is still a key item for any well-run data center. Don't close out solutions because they are too simple or appear too complex. View your needs from the top down to know how long you can expect to stay with a system that is dynamic. Understand from the bottom up what basic access facilities your users need. Look down the road at your changing environment and anticipate new link technologies.

◣ MAKE A LINK SELECTION

By now you already know what it is you want to do, and you are waiting patiently for prototype or pilot results to validate the links. Many companies select a single vendor supplier with a qualified backup just in case. This is true for emulation products. For more complex systems, you make a commitment to the vendor and hope the vendor makes a commitment to you.

Make your selection, place your order, and begin the process of installation. It's time, as they say, to "cut and run." Link the personal computers into the system in a systematic way and let users have what they wanted with the many precautions described throughout this book. Well-laid plans can be aborted and circumvented. Standalone personal computers do not do you much good if they cannot merge with the rest of your system to act as another powerful resource for which you have already spent millions of dollars.

A Micro to Mainframe Link Vendors

Listed in this appendix are the names, headquarter addresses, and telephone numbers of many micro-to-mainframe/mini-computer link vendors.

Applied Data Research, Route 206 and Orchard Road, CN-8, Princeton, NJ 08540. Telephone (201) 874-9000.

Applied Information Systems, Inc., 500 Eastowne Drive, Suite 207, Chapel Hill, NC 27514. Telephone (919) 942-7801 or (800) 334-5510.

Applied MicroSystems, Inc., P.O. Box 832, Roswell, GA 30077. Telephone (404) 475-0832.

Artificial Intelligence Corporation, 100 Fifth Avenue, Waltham, MA 02254. Telephone (617) 890-8400.

Ashton-Tate, 10150 West Jefferson Boulevard, Culver City, CA 90230. Telephone (213) 204-5570.

AST Research Inc., 2121 Alton Avenue, Irvine, CA 92714. Telephone (714) 863-1333.

Attachmate Corporation, 3241 118th South East, Bellevue, WA 98005. Telephone (206) 644-4010.

Burroughs Corporation, 1 Burroughs Place, Detroit, MI 48232. Telephone (313) 972-7000.

CAP Gemini Software Products, Inc., 2350 Valley View Lane, Dallas, TX 75234. Telephone (214) 247-5454.

Chi Corporation, 26055 Emery Road, Cleveland, OH 44128. Telephone (216) 831-2622.

Cincom Systems, Inc., 2300 Montana Avenue, Cincinnati, OH 45211. Telephone (513) 662-2300.

Cipherlink Corporation, 3807 Wilshire Boulevard, Suite 700, Los Angeles, CA 90010. Telephone (213) 387-5371.

CLEO Software, (a division of Phone 1, Inc.), 1639 North Alpine Road, Rockford, IL 61107. Telephone (815) 397-8110.

Communications Research Group, 8939 Jefferson Highway, Baton Rouge, LA 70809. Telephone (504) 923-0888.

Communications Solutions, Inc., 992 S. Saratoga-Sunnyvale Road, San Jose, CA 95129. Telephone (408) 725-1568.

Computer Associates International, Inc., 125 Jericho Turnpike, Jericho, NY 11753. Telephone (516) 333-6700.

Computer Corporation of America (CCA), Four Cambridge Center, Cambridge, MA 02142. Telephone (617) 492-8860.

CompuView Products, Inc., 1955 Pauline Boulevard, Ann Arbor, MI 48103. Telephone (313) 996-1299.

Comshare, Inc., 3001 South State Street, Ann Arbor, MI 48104. Telephone (313) 994-4800.

Condor Computer Corporation, 2051 South State Street, Ann Arbor, MI 48104. Telephone (313) 769-3988.

Context Management Systems Corporation (Lemain, Inc., exclusive distributor), P.O. Box 3010, Agoura, CA 91301. Telephone (818) 706-3141.

Cullinet Software, Inc., 400 Blue Hill Drive, Westwood, MA 02090. Telephone (617) 329-7700.

CXI, Inc., 3606 West Bayshore Road, Palo Alto, CA 94303-4229. Telephone (415) 424-0700.

The Datalex Company, 650 Fifth Street, San Francisco, CA 94107. Telephone (415) 541-0780.

Datastream Communications, Inc., 2520 Mission College Boulevard, Santa Clara, CA 95050. Telephone (408) 986-8022.

Decision Link (a division of Lagunal Laboratories), 1300 East Normandy Place, Santa Ana, CA 92705. Telephone (714) 835-9100.

Digital Communications Associates, Inc. (DCA), 1000 Alderman Drive, Alpharetta, GA 30201. Telephone (404) 442-4000.

Diversified Data Resources, Inc., 25 Mitchell Boulevard, Suite 7, San Rafael, CA 94903. Telephone (415) 499-8870.

Forte Communications, Inc., 2205 Fortune Drive, San Jose, CA 95131. Telephone (408) 945-9111.

Frontier Technologies Corporation, 3510 North Oakland Avenue, P.O. Box 11238, Milwaukee, WI 53211. Telephone (414) 964-8689.

Gateway Microsystems Incorporated, 9501 Capital of Texas Highway, Suite 105, Austin, TX 78759. Telephone (512) 345-7791.

Hawkeye Grafix, Inc., 23914 Mobile Street, Canoga Park, CA 91307. Telephone (818) 716-5220.

Hewlett-Packard Company, 1820 Embarcadero Road, Palo Alto, CA 94303. Contact your local sales office.

Honeywell Information Systems, 200 Smith Street, Waltham, MA 02154. Telephone (617) 890-8400 or (800) 328-5111.

ICOT Corporation, 830 Maude Avenue, Mountain View, CA 94039. Telephone (415) 964-4635.

IDE Associates, 35 Dunham Road, Billerica, MA 01821. Telephone (617) 663-6878 or (800) 257-5025.

IE Systems, Inc., 112 Main Street, P.O. Box 359, Newmarket, NH 03857. Telephone (603) 659-5891.

InfoCenter Software, Inc., 171 Main Street, New Paltz, NY 12561. Telephone (914) 255-8925.

Information Builders, Inc., 1250 Broadway, New York, NY 10001. Telephone (212) 736-4433.

Information Processing, Inc., 401 Whooping Loop, Altamonte Springs, FL 32701. Telephone (305) 331-5200.

Information Resources, Inc., 200 Fifth Avenue, Waltham, MA 02154. Telephone (617) 890-1100.

Information Technologies, Inc., 7850 East Evans Road, Scottsdale, AZ 85260. Telephone (602) 998-1033.

Intel Corporation, 12675 Research Boulevard, P.O. Box 9968, Austin, TX 78766. Telephone (512) 258-5171.

Intelligent Technologies International Corporation, 151 University Avenue, Palo Alto, CA 94301. Telephone (415) 328-2411.

InterChart Software, Inc., 104 Carnegie Center, Princeton, NJ 08540. Telephone (609) 987-1590.

Intercomputer Communications Corporation, 3195 Linwood Avenue, Cincinnati, OH 45208. Telephone (513) 321-3199.

International Business Machines Corporation (IBM), Old Orchard Road, Armonk, NY 10504. Contact your local IBM representative.

Linkware Corporation, 77 Rumford Avenue, Waltham, MA 02154. Telephone (617) 894-9330.

Local Data, Inc., 2701 Toledo Street, Torrance, CA 90503. Telephone (213) 320-7126.

Mackensen Corporation, 3323 Pearl Street, Santa Monica, CA 90405. Telephone (213) 452-5520.

Management Decision Systems, Inc., (see Information Resources, Inc.).

Management Science America, Inc., 3445 Peachtree Road North East, Atlanta, GA 30326. Telephone (404) 239-2000.

Martin Marietta (Information Technology Division), P.O. Box 2392, Princeton, NJ 08540. Telephone (609) 799-2600.

MasterLink, Inc., 82 Mitchell Boulevard, San Rafael, CA 94303. Telephone (415) 499-8466.

Mathematica Products Group, Inc., (see Martin Marietta).

McCormack & Dodge Corporation, 1225 Worcester Road, Natick, MA 01701. Telephone (617) 655-8200.

The Mega Group, 17701 Mitchell Avenue North, Irvine, CA 92714. Telephone (714) 474-0800.

Micro Decision Systems, P.O. Box 1392, Pittsburgh, PA 15230. Telephone (412) 854-4070.

Micro Tempus Inc., 440 Dorchester Boulevard West, Suite 300, Montreal, Quebec, H2Z 1V7 Canada. Telephone (514) 397-9512.

Microlog, Inc., 222 Route 59, Suffern, NY 10901. Telephone (914) 357-8086.

Midwest Data Source, Inc., 1010 Nimitz Road, Cincinnati, OH 45230. Telephone (513) 231-2023.

The MOM Corporation, (a division of National Product Marketing, Inc.), Two Northside 75, Atlanta, GA 30318. Telephone (404) 351-2902.

NCR Corporation, 1700 South Patterson Boulevard, Dayton, OH 45479. Telephone (513) 445-5000.

Network Research Corporation, 2380 North Rox Avenue, Oxnard, CA 93030. Telephone (805) 485-2700.

Network Software Associates, Inc., 19491 Sierra Soto, Irvine, CA 92715. Telephone (714) 768-4013.

OBS Software, (a division of On-Line Business Systems, Inc.), 115 Sansome Street, San Francisco, CA 94104. Telephone (415) 391-9555.

On-Line Software International Inc., Fort Lee Executive Park, Two Executive Drive, Fort Lee, NJ 07024. Telephone (201) 592-0009.

Oracle Corporation, 2710 Sand Hill Road, Menlo Park, CA 94025. Telephone (415) 854-7350.

Orcima Corporation, 6095 East River Road, Minneapolis, MN 55432. Telephone (612) 572-1000.

Package Solutions, Inc., One Huntington Quadrangle, Suite 2C10, Melville, NY 11747. Telephone (516) 752-1640.

Pansophic Systems, Inc., 709 Enterprise Drive, Oak Brook, IL 60521. Telephone (312) 986-2263.

Pathway Design, Inc., 177 Worcester Street, Wellesley, MA 02181. Telephone (617) 237-7722 or (800) 343-0515.

Performance Software, Inc., 452 Southlake Boulevard, Richmond, VA 23113. Telephone (804) 794-1012.

Persoft, Inc., 2740 Ski Lane, Madison, WI 53713. Telephone (608) 273-6000.

Polygon Associates, Inc., 1024 Executive Parkway, St. Louis, MO 63141. Telephone (314) 576-7709.

Quadram Corporation, 4355 International Boulevard, Norcross, GA 30093. Telephone (404) 923-6666.

Ryan-McFarland Corporation, 609 Deep Valley Drive, Rolling Hills Estate, CA 90274. Telephone (213) 541-4828.

SAS Institute, Inc., P.O. Box 8000, SAS Circle, Cary, NC 27511-8000. Telephone (919) 467-8000.

Simware Inc., 14 Concourse Gate, Suite 100, Nepean, Ontario, K2E 7S6 Canada. Telephone (613) 727-1779.

SIS/SunData, 1285 Drummer Lane, Wayne, PA 19087. Telephone (215) 341-8700.

Softronics, Inc., 3639 New Getwell, Suite 10, Memphis, TN 38118. Telephone (901) 683-6850.

Software AG of North America, 11800 Sunrise Valley Drive, Reston, VA 22091. Telephone (703) 860-5050.

Software Dynamics, Inc., P.O. Box 247, Dunedin, FL 34296-0247. Telephone (813) 733-8784.

Software International Corporation (subsidiary of General Electric Software Products Company), One Tech Drive, Andover, MA 01810. Telephone (617) 685-1400.

Solaris Computer Corporation, 1994 Tarob Court, Milpitas, CA 95035. Telephone (408) 943-1818.

Sterling Software Marketing, Inc., 11050 White Rock Road, Suite 100, Rancho Cordova, CA 95670-6095. Telephone (916) 635-5535 or (800) 824-8512.

The Systems Center, Inc., 1320 Greenway Drive, Suite 300, Irving, TX 75038. Telephone (214) 659-9318.

Techland Systems Inc., 25 Waterside Plaza, New York, NY 10010. Telephone (212) 684-7788.

Tecmar, Inc., 6225 Cochran Road, Solon, OH 44139. Telephone (216) 349-0600.

Tesseract Corporation, 101 Howard Street, San Francisco, CA 94105. Telephone (415) 543-7320.

Thomas Engineering Company, 2440 Stanwell Drive, Concord, CA 94520. Telephone (415) 680-8640 or (800) 832-8649.

Thorn EMI Computer Software Inc., One Industrial Drive, Windham, NH 03079. Telephone (603) 898-1800.

3Com Corporation, 1365 Shorebird Way, P.O. Box 7390, Mountain View, CA 94039. Telephone (415) 961-9602.

Tominy, Inc., 4221 Malsbary Road, Building #1, Cincinnati, OH 45242. Telephone (513) 984-6605.

UCCEL Corporation, UCCEL Tower, Exchange Park, Dallas, TX 75235. Telephone (214) 353-7100.

Urgeo Software, Inc., P.O. Box 305, Cheney, WA 99004. Telephone (509) 455-6058.

VM Personal Computing, Inc., 6 Germantown Road, Danbury, CT 06810. Telephone (203) 798-6755.

Wall Data Incorporated, 17769 North East 78th Place, Redmond, WA 98052-4992. Telephone (206) 883-4777 or (800) 433-3388.

Winterhalter, Inc., 3853 Research Park Drive, Ann Arbor, MI 48106. Telephone (313) 662-2002 or (800) 321-7785.

Xerox Computer Services, 5310 Beethoven Street, Los Angeles, CA 90066. Telephone (213) 306-4000.

Tangram Systems Corp., P.O. Box 5069, Cary, NC 27511-1999. Telephone (919) 828-7411.

ABM Computer Systems, 3 Whatney, Irvine, CA 92714. Telephone (714) 859-6531.

Avatar Technologies Inc., 99 South Street, Hopkinton, MA 01748. Telephone (617) 435-6872.

Emulex/Persyst, 3545 Harbor Blvd., Costa Mesa, CA 92626. Telephone (714) 662-5600.

IBM, Entry Systems Division, P.O. Box 1328, Boca Raton, FL 33432. Telephone (800) 447-4700.

Inc Corporation, P.O. Box 91395, 70 Blackburn Drive, Mobile, AL 36691. Telephone (205) 633-3270.

Micro Plus, 3200 N. Federal Highway, Boca Raton, FL 33431. Telephone (800) 992-2209.

Phaze Information Machines, 7650 Redfield Road, Scottsdale, AZ 85260. Telephone (602) 991-6855.

Protocol Computers, 6150 Canoga Ave. #100, Woodland Hills, CA 91367. Telephone (818) 716-5500.

Software Synergy Inc., 466 Main St., New Rochelle, NY 10801. Telephone (914) 633-0400.

Software Research Corp., 1 Natick Executive Park, Natick, MA 01760. Telephone (617) 655-1133.

Tangent Technologies, 5720 Peachtree Parkway, Suite 100, Norcross, GA 30092.

The Software Link, 8601 Dunwoody Place, Suite 336, Atlanta, GA 30338.

Woolf Software Systems, 6754 Eton Avenue, Canoga Park, CA 91303. Telephone (213) 703-8112.

Adminet Inc., 12 York Street, Ottawa, Can. K1N 556. Telephone (613) 230-7027.

Advanced Computer Communications, 720 Santa Barbara Street, Santa Barbara, CA 93101. Telephone (805) 963-9431.

Protocol Computers Inc., 2925 Briarpark, Suite 420, Houston, TX 77042. Telephone (818) 716-5500.

XICOM Technologies Corp., 130 Slater Street, Suite 1015, Ottawa, Ontario, Can. K1P 6E2. Telephone (613) 238-4744.

Communications Machinery Corporation, 1421 State Street, Santa Barbara, CA 93101. Telephone (805) 963-9471.

TeleVideo Systems Inc., Systems Division, 550 E. Brokaw Road, San Jose, CA 95112. Telephone (408) 971-0255.

Trisystems Corporation, 74 Northeastern Blvd., Nashua, NH 03062. Telephone (603) 883-0558.

Xyplex Inc., 100 Domino Drive, Concord, MA 01742. Telephone (617) 371-1400.

American International Communications, 4745 Walnut St., Boulder, CO 80301. Telephone (303) 444-6675.

Baseline Inc., 6649 Peachtree Industrial, Suite A, Norcross GA 30092. Telephone (404) 263-9587.

FEL Computing, P.O. Box 200, East Dover, VT 05341. Telephone (802) 348-7171.

Micro Decision Ware Inc., 2995 Wilderness, Boulder, CO 80301. Telephone (303) 443-2706.

Microstuf, Inc., 1845 The Exchange, Suite 140, Atlanta, GA 30339. Telephone (404) 952-0267.

Banyon Systems Inc., 135 Flanders Road, Westboro, MA 01581. Telephone (617) 366-6681.

Blaise Computing Inc., 2034 Blake Street, Berkeley, CA 94704. Telephone (415) 540-5441.

Carleton Corporation, 245 First Street, Cambridge, MA 02142. Telephone (617) 494-1232.

Compunix Corporation, 17955-B Skypark Circle, Irvine, CA 92714. Telephone (714) 261-6175.

Consolink Corporation, 1275 Sherman Drive, Longmont, CO 80501. Telephone (303) 651-2014.

Dilithium Press, 8285 S.W. Nimbus, Suite 151, Beaverton, OR 97005. Telephone (800) 547-1842.

Hayes Microcomputer Products, 5923 Peachtree Industrial Boulevard, Norcross, GA 30092. Telephone (404) 441-1617.

Cognos, Inc., 275 Slater Street, Ottawa, Can. K1P 5H9.

ICC, 3195 Linwood Ave., Suite 2A, Cincinnati, OH 45208. Telephone (513) 321-3199.

B Local Area Network Vendors

Listed in this appendix are the names, headquarter addresses, and telephone numbers of many LAN vendors.

Advanced Computer Communications 720 Santa Barbara Street, Santa Barbara, CA 93101. Telephone (805) 963-9431.

Alspa Computer, Inc. 477 Division Street, Campbell, CA 95008. Telephone (408) 370-3000.

Altos Computer Systems 2641 Orchard Parkway, San Jose, CA 95134. Telephone (408) 946-6700.

Apple Computer 20525 Mariana Avenue C/R, Cupertino, CA 95014. Telephone (408) 996-1010.

Applitek Corporation 107 Audubon Road, Wakefield, MA 01880. Telephone (617) 246-4500.

AST Research, Inc. 2121 Alton Avenue, Irvine, CA 92714. Telephone (714) 863-1333.

AT&T Information Systems 100 Southgate Parkway, Morristown, NJ 07960. Telephone (201) 898-8000.

The Braegen Corporation 525 Los Coches, Milpitas, CA 95035. Telephone (408) 945-1900.

Bridge Communications, Inc. 1345 Shorebird Way, Mountain View, CA 94043. Telephone (415) 969-4400.

Calma/General Electric 1282 Hammerwood Avenue, Sunnyvale, CA 94089. Telephone (408) 743-4606.

Codex Corporation 20 Cabot Boulevard Mansfield, MA 02048. Telephone (617) 364-2000.

Complexx Systems, Inc. 4930 Research Drive, N.W. Huntsville, AL 35805. Telephone (205) 830-4310.

Compucorp 2211 Michigan Avenue, Santa Monica, CA 90404. Telephone (213) 829-7453.

Concord Data Systems 303 Bearhill Road, Waltham, MA 02154. Telephone (617) 890-1394.

Contel Information Systems, Inc. 130 Steamboat Road, Great Neck, NY 11024. Telephone (516) 829-5900.

Control Data Corporation 8100 34th Avenue South, Minneapolis, MN 55420. Telephone (612) 853-8100.

Corvus Systems 2029 O'Toole Avenue, San Jose, CA 95131. Telephone (408) 946-7700.

CR Computer Systems, Inc. 5456 McConnell Avenue, # 182, Los Angeles, CA 90066. Telephone (213) 822-5112.

Data General 4400 Computer Drive, Westboro, MA 01580. Telephone (617) 366-8911.

Datapoint Corporation 9725 Datapoint Drive, San Antonio, TX 78284. Telephone (512) 699-7151.

The Destek Group 830 E. Evelyn Avenue, Sunnyvale, CA 94086. Telephone (408) 737-7211.

Digilog Business Systems Welsh Road & Park Drive, P.O. Box 425 Montgomeryville, PA 18936. Telephone 628-4810.

Digital Equipment Corporation 146 Main Street, Maynard MA 01754. Telephone (617) 897-5111.

Digital Microsystems, Inc. 1840 Embarcadero, P.O. Box 2040, Oakland, CA 94606. Telephone (415) 261-1034.

Excelan, Inc. 2180 Fortune Drive, San Jose, CA 95131. Telephone (408) 945-9526.

Gateway Communications, Inc. 16782 Redhill Avenue, Irvine, CA 92714. Telephone (714) 261-0762.

Honeywell Information Systems 200 Smith Street, Waltham, MA 02154. Telephone (617) 895-6768.

Inforex 186 Middlesex Turnpike, Burlington, MA 01803. Telephone (617) 272-6470.

Interactive Systems/3M 225-3 3M Center St. Paul, MN 55144. Telephone (612) 736-2701.

Interlan, Inc. 3 Lyberty Way, Westford, MA 01886. Telephone (617) 692-3900.

International Business Machines Corporation Old Orchard Road, Armonk, NY 10504. Contact your local IBM representative.

Kantek, Inc. 13730 N.E. 20th Street, Suite J, Bellevue, WA 98005. Telephone (206) 644-2970.

Lanier Business Products, Inc. 1700 Chantilly Drive, N.E., Atlanta, GA 30324. Telephone (404) 329-8132.

Link Telecommunications, Inc. 2400 Computer Drive, Westborough, MA 01851. Telephone (617) 366-7400.

Logical Business Machines 1294 Hammerwood Avenue, Sunnyvale, CA 94089. Telephone (408) 744-1290.

Magnolia Microsystems, Inc. 2264 15th Avenue West, Seattle, WA 98119. Telephone (206) 285-7266.

Microdata Corporation 17481 Red Hill Avenue, Irvine, CA 92713. Telephone (714) 250-1000.

NCR Corporation 7700 S. Patterson Boulevard, Dayton, OH 45479. Telephone (513) 445-2075.

Nestar Systems Corp. 2585 E. Bayshore Road, Palo Alto, CA 94303. Telephone (415) 493-2202.

Network Systems Corp. 7600 Boone Avenue North, Brooklyn Park, MN 55428. Telephone (612) 425-2202.

North Star Computers, Inc. 14440 Catalina Street, San Leandro, CA 94577. Telephone (415) 357-8500.

Prime Computer, Inc. Prime Park, Natick, MA 01760. Telephone (617) 655-8000.

Proteon, Inc. 4 Tech Circle, Natick, MA 01760. Telephone (617) 655-3340.

Racal-Milgo Information Systems, Inc. 6950 Cypress Road, P.O. Box 15662, Plantation, FL 33318. Telephone (305) 584-4242.

Siderial 9600 S.W. Barnes Road, Portland, OR 97225. Telephone (503) 297-5531.

Syntrex, Inc. 246 Industrial Way West, Eatontown, NJ 07724. Telephone (201) 542-1500.

Sytek, Inc. 1225 Charleston Road, Mountain View, CA 94043. Telephone (415) 966-7300.

Tele-Engineering Corporation 2 Central Street, Framingham, MA 01701. Telephone (617) 877-6494.

3-Com Corporation P.O. Box 7390, 1390 Shorebird Way, Mountain View, CA 94039. Telephone (415) 961-9602.

Ungermann-Bass, Inc. 2560 Mission College Road, Santa Clara, CA 95050. Telephone (408) 496-0111.

Vector Graphic, Inc. 500 N. Ventu Park Road, Thousand Oaks, CA 91320. Telephone (805) 499-5831.

Wang Laboratories, Inc. One Industrial Avenue, Lowell, MA 01851. Telephone (617) 459-5000.

Xerox Corporation 1341 W. Mockingbird Lane, Dallas, TX 75247. Telephone (214) 689-6000.

Xyplex, Inc. 100 Domino Drive, Concord, MA 01742. Telephone (617) 371-1400.

Trademarks

The following names are trademarked products of the corresponding companies.

3270-PLUS™	Information Technologies
ADABAS™	Software AG
ADP™	Automatic Data Processing
Answer/DB™	Informatics General
Apple™	Apple Computer, Inc.
Application/Link™	Hewlett-Packard
BLAST™	Communication Research Group
ConnectWare™	Information Technologies
DBase/Answer™	Information General
DEC®	Digital Equipment Corporation
DECnet™	Digital Equipment Corporation
Ethernet®	Xerox Corporation
FASTLINK™	DCA
Forte™	Forte Corporation
GoldenGate™	Cullinet
IBM®	International Business Machines Corporation
IDMS™	Cullinet
IMAGE™	Hewlett-Packard
INFOGATE™	Cullinet
Interactive PC Link™	McCormack and Dodge
IRMA®	Digital Communication Associates

IRMALine™	DCA
LinkUp™	Information Technologies
Lotus®	Lotus Development Corporation
Lotus 1-2-3®	Lotus Development Corporation
Lotus/Answer™	Information General
Macintosh™	Apple Computer, Inc.
MicroVAX I™	Digital Equipment Corporation
MicroVAX II VMS®	Digital Equipment Corporation
MSA™	McCormack and Dodge
Multiplan®	Microsoft Corporation
MVS™	International Business Machines
Natural/Connection™	Software AG
Natural/Link™	Software AG
OMNILINK™	On-Line Software
OmniNet™	Corvus Systems, Inc.
PCLink™	McCormack and Dodge
PeachLink™	McCormack and Dodge
PRIMENET™	Prime Computer
Smartlink™	Software International
SNA/SDLC Synchronous Data Link Control™	International Business Machines Corporation
SNE™	Software Research Corporation
Symphony®	Lotus Development Corporation
System/360™	International Business Machines Corporation
Tempus-Link™	Micro Tempus
Tempus Library™	Micro Tempus
The Source™	Source Telecomputing Company
UNIX™	American Telephone and Telegraph (AT&T)
VisiCalc®	VisiCorp Corporation
VM™	International Business Machines Corporation
VMS™	Digital Equipment Corporation

INDEX